THE
SEVENTY FACES
OF TORAH

Also by Stephen M. Wylen
Published by Paulist Press

The Jews in the Time of Jesus
Settings of Silver: An Introduction to Judaism

THE
SEVENTY FACES
OF TORAH

*The Jewish Way of Reading
the Sacred Scriptures*

Stephen M. Wylen

Paulist Press
New York/Mahwah, N.J.

Scriptural quotations in English, though often retranslated by the author, are taken from or based on the TANAKH: The Holy Scriptures © 1988 by the Jewish Publication Society, Philadelphia.

Etz Hayim: Torah and Commentary, general editor David L. Lieber, produced by the Jewish Publication Society for The Rabbinical Assembly and The United Synagogue of Conservative Judaism, Philadelphia, 2001.

The Humash: The Stone Edition, ed. Rabbi Nosson Scherman, contributing editors Rabbi Hersh Goldwurm, Rabbi Avie Gold, Rabbi Meir Zlotowitz, The ArtScroll Series, Mesorah Publications, Ltd., New York, 1993.

The JPS Torah Commentary, 5 vols., Jewish Publication Society, Philadelphia, 1989.

The Pentateuch and Haftorahs: Hebrew Text, English Translation, and Commentary, ed. Dr. J.H. Hertz, Soncino Press, London, 1936, second expanded edition, 1960.

The Torah, A Modern Commentary, eds. W. Gunther Plaut, Bernard Bamberger, William W. Hallo, Union of American Hebrew Congregations (Reform Movement of Judaism in America), New York, 1981.

Cover design by Cynthia Dunne
Book design by Lynn Else

Library of Congress Cataloging-in-Publication Data

Wylen, Stephen M., 1952-
    The seventy faces of Torah : the Jewish way of reading the Sacred Scriptures / Stephen M. Wylen.
        p. cm.
    Includes bibliographical references and index.
    ISBN 0-8091-4179-5 (alk. paper)
    1. Bible. O.T. Pentateuch—Criticism, interpretation, etc., Jewish—History. 2. Bible. O.T. Pentateuch—Hermeneutics—History. 3. Judaism—Sacred books. 4. Rabbinical literature—History and criticism. I. Title.

BS1225.52.W95 2005
296.1—dc22

                                                                    2005000451

Published by Paulist Press
997 Macarthur Boulevard
Mahwah, New Jersey, 07430

www.paulistpress.com

Printed and bound in the United States of America

*To the students at the Hebrew Union College–Jewish Institute of
Religion and to seminarians of every faith tradition:*

May you grow in knowledge every day.
May you demonstrate wisdom beyond your years of service.
May you always feel in your heart the spirit and dedication
that filled your soul when you first began
your studies toward ordination.

Acknowledgments

I am grateful to Fr. Lawrence Boadt for conceiving this book and for asking me to write it. Thanks to Devorah Weissberg, professor of Talmud at Hebrew Union College in Los Angeles, for reading some of the early chapters of this book and making many valuable suggestions for improvement. Thanks to Rabbi Ben Hollander for advising me on the dimensions of Torah study in Israel today and for being my first teacher and guide in the study of the *parashat hashavua'*, the weekly Torah portion. Thanks to Talmud teachers Noam Zion, of the Shalom Hartman Institute in Jerusalem, and Devorah Weissberg for their insights into the Talmud, which I have incorporated into this book to the best of my ability. Thanks also to Professor Alyssa Gray of Hebrew Union College for helpful suggestions about the history of the Talmud. Thanks to my midrash teacher Norman Cohen for introducing me to the joy and the wisdom of midrash, and to teachers Yigal Yannai and Stanley Dreyfus for introducing me to the commentators. Thank you to Dr. Steven C. Michael for helpful suggestions. Special thanks to Len Alper, whose careful reading and innumerable invaluable suggestions helped to shape this work much for the better. Thanks to all the members of Temple Beth Tikvah in Wayne, New Jersey, for their support. And I owe eternal thanks to my wife, Cheryl, and my children, Jeremy, Elisheva, Shoshana, and Golda, for always being there for me in so many important ways.

Contents

Chronology:
Time Line of Biblical History

1700 BCE[1]	Historical era of the patriarchs (Abraham, Isaac, and Jacob). The Middle Bronze Age
1250 BCE	Historical era of the exodus story
1200–1000 BCE	Period of Israelite tribal settlement in Canaan. Early Iron Age.
1000–900 BCE	United Kingdom of Israel and Judah under Saul, David, Solomon
900 BCE	Civil war: Israel (Samaria, Ephraim) in the north; Judah in the south
800 BCE onward	Era of successive empires: Assyria, Babylon, Persia, Greece, Rome
722 BCE	Assyrians conquer kingdom of Israel, exile and scatter the inhabitants
586 BCE	King Nebukadnezzer of Babylon conquers rebellious Judah, burns the Temple of King Solomon, destroys Jerusalem, exiles much of the population to Babylon
536 BCE	Cyrus the Great of Persia conquers Babylon, permits the Jewish return to Judah
516 BCE	Rebuilding of the Temple. End of prophecy. Biblical times come to an end shortly thereafter, in the perspective of the Hebrew Bible
450 BCE	Ezra the Scribe brings the Torah of Moses from Babylon to Jerusalem

---

1. Dates are approximate in this time line. When Jews use the Christian system of numbering years from the birth of Jesus, they use BCE (before the Common Era) in place of BC, and CE (Common Era, the era to which we are common) in place of AD.

330 BCE	Alexander the Great conquers the Persian Empire. His generals create Greek kingdoms in the Middle East. By this time the various books of the Prophets have been added to the Scriptures
270 BCE	According to legend, Ptolemy II of Egypt commissions the Septuagint, the Greek translation of the Bible, for his library at Alexandria
170 BCE	Composition of the book of Daniel, the last book of the Hebrew Bible to be written.
168–165 BCE	Revolt of the Maccabees. An era of semi-independence for Judah. No book written after this point accepted into the Hebrew Bible.
63 BCE	Roman general Pompey conquers Jerusalem and adds Judah, now called Judea, to the Roman Empire
10 BCE	Approximate era of Hillel and Shammai, known in Jewish tradition as "the Fathers of the World," the chief transmitters of the oral Torah of Judaism.
33 CE	Crucifixion of Jesus in Jerusalem
70 CE	Destruction of the Second Temple at the conclusion of the Jewish revolt against Rome
80 CE	Rabbinic Sanhedrin at Yavneh
ca. 100 CE	Sanhedrin votes on which books to include in the Writings, closes the Hebrew Bible
132–135 CE	Bar Kochba revolt (second Judean revolt against Rome), death of Rabbi Akiva
140 CE	Sanhedrin reconvenes in Galilee
200 CE	Sanhedrin at Sepphoris, Rabbi Judah HaNasi; publication of the Mishnah
425 CE	End of the Sanhedrin; authority shifts to academies in Babylon
634–638 CE	Arab conquest of Mesopotamia, of Palestine; the Muslim era in the Middle East begins
ca. 500–700 CE	Publication of the Babylonian Talmud
1280	Publication of the *Zohar* by Moses deLeon
1475	First press-printed Hebrew book, the Torah with Rashi's commentary

Introduction

Judaism Becomes a Scriptural Religion

"And the Lord said to Moses: Write down these commandments, for according to the speech of these words I make a covenant with you and Israel" (Exod 34:27). *When the Scriptures were read in the synagogue, the translator stood beside the reader and rendered the Hebrew into the vernacular. The reader is forbidden to take his eyes off the scroll, for the Torah was given in writing, as it says, "Write down these commandments." The translator is forbidden to look into the scroll, since the Targum (translation, interpretation) was given orally, as it says, "according to the speech of these words."*

(Pesikta Rabbati 14b)[2]

Ezra Brings the Torah to Jerusalem

Ezra the Scribe traveled from Babylon to Jerusalem around the year 450 BCE at the head of a group of Jews returning from exile to the Judean homeland of their grandparents. Ezra brought with him two important documents. He carried a letter from Artaxerxes, the Persian emperor, granting him absolute authority over all the Jews in the Persian province of Judah. Ezra also brought with him a longer document, a scroll containing the Torah of Moses. Ezra would use the teachings in this scroll, the earliest Jewish Scriptures, to guide him in the reestablishment of Jewish life in the province of Judah.

---

2. Adapted from C. G. Montefiore and H. Loewe, eds. and trans., *A Rabbinical Anthology* (New York: Schocken Books, 1974), p. 161.

1

Historical Background

Back in Babylon the prophet deutero-Isaiah was proclaiming, "A voice cries, in the wilderness make straight the way" (Isa 40:3). This is how it came about that bands of Jews were traveling the long and difficult passage from the great city of Babylon, on the Euphrates River, to the remote town of Jerusalem, which had seen better days:

The Israelites were divided into two kingdoms, Israel in the north—also called Ephraim or Samaria—and Judah in the south. In 722 BCE the Assyrian Empire conquered and destroyed the northern kingdom, but Judah survived the Assyrian onslaught. A generation later King Nebukadnezzer of Babylon extended his empire to include the kingdom of Judah. The Jews rebelled, and in 586 BCE Nebukadnezzer's army ravaged the land, destroyed Jerusalem, and burned the Temple of Solomon to the ground. The Babylonians carried off the Judean leaders into exile and resettled them in Babylon. The Judean people, who formerly called themselves the children of Israel, came to be known throughout the empire as "Jews"—that is, people from Judah. There remained in the land of Judah only illiterate farmers, the *am ha'aretz,* or "ordinary folk."

Babylonian rule lasted for fifty years after the destruction of Jerusalem. Then Cyrus the Great of Persia conquered Babylon. Cyrus looked kindly upon the Jews. The Persian emperors permitted Jews to return voluntarily to their homeland and restore their former worship and way of life. The kingdom of Judah was reconstituted as a province of the Persian Empire. Included among the exiles were the literate classes of the people—the Temple priests, the nobles, the professional scribes. Resettled in Babylon, these Judeans had preserved what they could of the literary classics of Judah and Israel in their native language, which we call Hebrew, and the traditions that were written in the Torah of Moses, which Ezra brought with him back to the land of Judah.

The Jews Return to Their Homeland

While the exile community in Babylon became prosperous, increased, and flourished, the folk who remained behind in Judah struggled just to get by. They might have disappeared from history, just as their northern neighbors the Israelites had been displaced by the Samaritans after the Assyrian conquest of Israel. But the Babylonians never got around to bringing new settlers into Judah, and the Persians allowed the Jews to return to their homeland. Most of the exiles remained in Babylon, where they had put down roots, but many of the Jewish nobles and priests returned to Jerusalem to restore the fortunes of their country. Among these were two heroes who eventually had biblical books named after them. Nehemiah, a Jew with high office in the Persian court, returned to rebuild the walls of Jerusalem. Ezra the Scribe came back to restore the nation's forgotten way of life in service to God. The final prophets, Haggai and Zechariah, supervised the reconstruction of the Temple of God in Jerusalem, replacing King Solomon's Temple, which Nebukadnezzer had burned to the ground. Some of the long-lived residents in Judah who remembered the First Temple from their childhood saw the rebuilt Temple in their old age. Malachi, the last of the biblical prophets, urged the Temple priests to be faithful and industrious in their service to God.

The Public Reading of the Torah

On the first day of the seventh month in the Jewish calendar—the day that Jews now call Rosh Hashanah, the new-year festival—Ezra stood on a platform in one of the city gates of Jerusalem to read to the people from the Torah of Moses, which he had brought with him from Babylon. The scene is described in chapter 8 of the book of Nehemiah. The people of the province of Judah all gathered in the city gate plaza for the occasion. The borders of Judah at that time contained only Jerusalem and her surrounding villages, so it was possible for most of the population to gather in one place. Ezra read to the people from the Torah from morning until midday.

As Ezra read aloud, people called meturgemanim translated and explained the words to the people. This was necessary for two reasons. First, the Torah was written in Hebrew, the spoken language of ancient Judah and Israel. When the Babylonians conquered their empire, three generations before the time of Ezra, the Babylonian language, Aramaic, became the lingua franca of the entire Middle

East.[3] The meturgemanim had to translate from Hebrew into Aramaic so that the people would understand.[4] Second, the people needed an explanation because even in translation the words of the Torah were not directly understood. There was discontinuity between the cultural, social, and scientific assumptions contained in the Torah and the culture and worldview of the Judean populace who now listened to these words from the mouth of Ezra the Scribe. The Torah presumes a world in which Jews live independently in small agricultural villages. But the Jews who gathered in Jerusalem to listen to Ezra lived in an extensive empire, and many Jews were now engaged in urban commercial activity. Even the conditions of farm life were quite different from what they had been in ancient Israel. Furthermore, the worldview of the Jews had been transformed by intimate contact with the cultures of Babylon and Persia. The translators had to explain the Torah of Moses to the people, translating ideas into terms to which they could relate in their current life.

The book of Nehemiah tells us that when Ezra read to the people, they were dismayed to discover that this day was a holiday and they knew nothing about it. The people of Judah did not know of the existence of Rosh Hashanah until they heard about it in the Torah. At the next public gathering, Ezra read to the people again. This time they learned about the harvest festival of Sukkot, again apparently for the first time. The people obeyed the instructions they heard in the Torah of Moses. They gathered citrons, palm branches, willows, and myrtles, built themselves harvest booths, and observed the festival. It is clear in the book of Nehemiah that the people were not following an inherited custom; they were trying to live "by the book." This was something new, indicative that Judaism was now a scriptural religion as it had not been before. The people were sad that they did not know their own laws and traditions, but Ezra told the people not to mourn their ignorance. He encouraged the people to do what the Torah commands and to celebrate their festival with good cheer.

---

3. Aramaic remained the common language from Egypt to the borders of India for the next twelve hundred years. Aramaic was displaced by Arabic after the Arab conquest of the seventh century CE.

4. Although the Torah is written in Hebrew, it uses the Aramaic alphabet rather than the old Hebrew alphabet. The alphabet that Jews today call Hebrew is actually Aramaic, just as English readers use the Latin alphabet.

Ezra established the custom of reading the Torah in the public squares of Jerusalem every Sabbath and every Monday and Thursday morning. These were the days on which the villagers came into Jerusalem. On the Sabbath they came because it was a day of rest from work, and on Monday and Thursday because these were market days, when the farmers brought their produce to sell in town. The custom established by Ezra has endured among the Jews. Even today, in synagogues throughout the world, Jews read from the Torah every Sabbath morning and afternoon and every Monday and Thursday morning. The custom has continued unbroken since Ezra the Scribe first read to the people at the Water Gate in Jerusalem.

The Torah Is Published

When Ezra read the Torah in the city gate, the people responded enthusiastically. They accepted the Torah. Ezra blessed God when he began and when he concluded the reading, and the people all responded, "Amen," which means "Accepted." By means of this public reading and acclamation, the Torah was officially published. From that moment on, Judaism was a religion with a Scripture. Over the next five centuries, the Jews added other holy books to the Holy Scriptures. The Torah of Moses was finalized in the time of Ezra, perhaps with a bit of further editing in the ensuing decades. It consists of five books: Genesis, Exodus, Leviticus, Numbers, and Deuteronomy. Later the Jews included the books of the Prophets in the sacred library. In the time of Jesus the Jewish Scriptures consisted of the Torah and the Prophets, which is the New Testament term for the Jewish Scriptures of Jesus.[5] Early in the second century, a third section of sacred literature, the Writings, was added to the Jewish Scriptures. With this the Jewish Bible was completed and closed, twenty-four books by the traditional count.[6]

---

5. The New Testament, which was written in Greek, calls the Torah *nomos*, meaning "law," and so English translations of the New Testament call the Scriptures "the law and the prophets." A more accurate translation of the word *Torah* is "teaching" rather than "law."

6. The church called the Jewish Bible the Old Testament. It added to the Old Testament a fourth section, the Apocrypha, which consists of ancient Jewish holy books that the final Jewish Bible editors did not consider scriptural but that other groups of Jews did.

Since the invention of the printing press, a book is considered published when a printer makes a press run of the book. In the days of laborious mechanical typesetting, which lasted until the recent development of computer typesetting, people would not publish books unless they thought they could sell at least a few thousand copies. A book would be published if the publisher thought it possible to print and sell enough copies to make a profit after the cost of manufacturing the book or if someone with wealth was willing to pay the costs of printing.

In ancient times the process of publication was quite different. Books could only be produced by laborious and expensive hand-copying, one copy at a time. Undoubtedly, many books existed in a single copy, of interest only to their author and his or her circle. For a book to be published in the sense that we understand publication—to be circulated, widely read, and talked about—a book required an enthusiastic audience and a group of literate people willing to copy it again and again. For a book to survive more than a single generation, it had to be adopted by an institution that outlasts human lifetimes—a government, an organized religion, a society of powerful leaders with a program for the world, or some other such institution.

The Torah of Moses that Ezra the Scribe read to the Jewish public in Jerusalem around 450 BCE was endorsed by the hereditary Jewish priests, who ruled over the Jewish community in both Babylon and Judah. The Torah also enjoyed the support of the Persian government. The Persians had a policy of supporting all forms of traditional piety and letting all of their subject peoples rule themselves according to their ancient sacred norms and customs. The Persian emperors fancied themselves the champions of all the gods in their realm. Thus, the empire supported the Jewish priests in their project of promoting the Torah, and the Persian rulers backed the Torah with the power and authority of their government. As we have seen, the people themselves gave their enthusiastic support to the Torah.

With the combined support of the people, their leaders, and the Persian government, the Torah of Moses became the "Constitution" of the restored nation of Judah. This assured that many copies of the Torah would be written and distributed. Within a short time after Ezra the Scribe, Jews everywhere were living faithfully according to the laws of the Torah, as interpreted to them by the priests and scribes of their day. There were significant Jewish communities at that time in Egypt, Syria, Babylon, and Persia as well as in the province of Judah.

The Persians experimented with Jewish self-government. They restored the preexilic Judean government, establishing the high priest Joshua and a king of the Davidic dynasty, Zerubbabel. Nehemiah served as governor and absolute ruler of the land at one point. Ezra in his time was appointed absolute ruler. He was of priestly family, and his designation as "Scribe" indicates not a job description but a high office of some type. Also among the returned exiles were the last persons to claim the authority of prophets: Haggai, Zechariah, and Malachi. We do not know the chronological order of these various leaders. But after a short period all kings, prophets, and secular governors disappeared from Judah, and the Jewish province was ruled by a high priest. The priesthood was hereditary, and the high priest was a descendant of Zadok, who had served as high priest in the time of King David. The high priests continued to rule over the Jews in Judah throughout the Persian, Greek, and Roman periods, until the Romans destroyed the Temple in 70 CE. The priests ruled according to their understanding of the Torah of Moses, the Jewish Sacred Scriptures. The Torah was not just a religious book; it was the law of the land for Jews in Judah, as the Constitution is for Americans today.

A few points about the publication of the Torah in the time of Ezra the Scribe are especially significant for our purposes:

- The Torah was given to the people aurally, through public reading. The Torah that the people knew was not the written book but what they heard when the book was recited in public.

- The Torah never existed apart from its interpretation. Beginning with the first time the Torah was read in public, the written text was accompanied by the translation and explanation of authorized interpreters.

- The Scriptures are difficult for us to comprehend at times because they assume a culture, a scientific understanding, and a worldview very different from our own. This was just as true for the people who first heard the Torah recited in public. The Torah as Sacred Scripture always required people to consider one worldview from the platform of another. Cultural interplay has always been essential to our sense of what constitutes Scripture.

The Origins of the Torah: Traditional View

The Torah often claims that a particular set of words were spoken by God to Moses. In the first Torah book, Genesis, God is quoted as speaking to Adam, Noah, and Abraham and communicating indirectly to Isaac, Jacob, and Joseph. The Torah states that God spoke in the hearing of all the Israelites at Mount Sinai. The book of Deuteronomy indicates that this communication consisted of the Ten Commandments. The book of Exodus tells how Moses brought two tablets, the Book of the Covenant, down from Mount Sinai. The book of Deuteronomy (ch. 31) claims that Moses placed a book with revelations from God in the hands of the hereditary priests.

Not long after Ezra the Scribe published the Torah, it became a standard belief among Jews that God dictated these five books in their entirety to Moses on Mount Sinai. Most Jews believed that when Moses came down after forty days on top of Mount Sinai, after Israel's exodus from slavery in Egypt, he brought with him the whole Torah. God spoke the words and Moses wrote them down, acting as secretary for the divine dictation. Even the unusual spellings and occasional enlarged or small superscript letters that we find in the handwritten scrolls of the Torah were determined and dictated by God. Even the decorations that sit atop certain letters, the decorations that are called "crowns," were dictated by God as Moses wrote them down. The Torah describes the forty years of wandering in the desert and Moses' final speech to the Israelites in the days just before his death, while Israel was encamped on the plains of Moab across the Jordan River from Jericho. All of these events occurred after the revelation at Mount Sinai, yet according to tradition, even these words about subsequent events were given by God to Moses at Mount Sinai. Moses faithfully recorded the events of the next forty years before their occurrence.

The final twelve verses of the Torah describe the death of Moses across the Jordan and how God buried him in an unknown grave on

Mount Nebo. Some Jews believed that these final twelve verses were added by Joshua, Moses' aide-de-camp and successor, after his death. Others insisted that even these twelve verses were dictated by God to Moses at Mount Sinai, with Moses weeping over his own death and failure to enter the promised land while God commanded him to write.

The Torah never claims for itself that it is all the spoken word of God, but this became a standard Jewish belief. Judaism's evolution was based upon the presumption that with the Torah the Jewish people were in earthly possession of the word of God, expressing God's eternal will for all time.

To this day Jews read from the Torah in public worship, just as Ezra read from the Torah in the public square in ancient Jerusalem. After the reading, the Torah scroll is held up and displayed to the people so that they can see for themselves that it is the actual Torah, and no fake or substitute, that is being read. As the Torah is displayed, the traditional liturgy provides the following song to be sung in Hebrew: *This is the Torah which Moses placed before the Children of Israel. From the mouth of God to the hand of Moses.* This verse summarizes the traditional Jewish view of God's revelation of Scripture.

The Origins of the Torah: Historical View

Modern historical scholars do not accept the view that the entire Torah was given in one time and place, from God to Moses, by divine word with no human intervention beyond the writing down of the letters. Catholics, liberal Protestants, and liberal Jews accept the historians' view that the Torah was written down over a period of time, displaying the work of different human hands and various time-bound human ideas of what God says.[7] Historians reconstruct the history of the biblical text on the basis of internal evidence within the Bible itself, comparative studies with other ancient Near Eastern literature, and the evidence of archeology. Historians differ on many of

---

7. The Catholic Church formally endorsed the historical method of scriptural interpretation in 1960.

the details, but what follows is a general summary of the historical view on how the Torah came to be.

From the time period attributed to Moses (ca. 1250 BCE) to the time of Ezra the Scribe (ca. 450 BCE), the Torah did not exist in the form in which we now have it, though many of the textual materials that eventually entered the Torah may have existed in oral traditions, in other books, or in earlier forms. The Jews in this era, the era of earliest Israel and of the kingdoms of Israel and Judah, must have had various writings in which they recorded their sacred traditions, but they did not have any formal Sacred Scripture. When people needed a message from God, they consulted a prophet, or they asked questions of the oracular Urim and Tummim, which the high priest carried on his person.[8] They did not consult a book.

The Babylonians conquered the kingdom of Judah and added the land to their expanding empire. Babylonian policy was to mix up their subject people by moving them around. They exiled the Judean leaders to Babylon in two groups. The first group, which included the prophet Ezekiel and the Judean king Jehoichin, were marched to Babylon and resettled there around 600 BCE. Some years later the Judeans rebelled under King Zedekiah. The Babylonian army conquered Jerusalem and destroyed the city. In 586 BCE it burned down the Temple of Solomon and took the rest of the priesthood and nobility and many of the surviving people into exile in Babylon.

The leaders of the Judean exile community included great prophets such as Ezekiel and Second Isaiah (the author of Isa 40–66). These leaders were determined that the Judeans would not lose their identity like their brothers from the kingdom of Israel, who were scattered and disappeared after they were conquered by the Assyrian Empire in 722 BCE. We have no written record of what was done in Babylon to preserve Jews and Judaism, but we can reconstruct the process from various sources, including the later work of Ezra. The Jews in Babylon continued to worship their God even though they were denied the opportunity to offer the animal sacrifices that had been at the center of biblical religion. The Jews served God by strictly

---

8. The Urim and Tummim were dice or colored sticks that the high priest carried in a pouch hanging from his neck. He cast them to receive a yes-or-no answer to questions that were addressed to God.

observing the Sabbath as a day of rest, by avoiding biblically prohibited foods, by circumcising their male children on the eighth day after birth, and by marrying only among themselves to keep from assimilating into the Babylonian world. They may have initiated prayers, though the synagogue and regular liturgical worship were still far in the future.

The learned, literate class of Judean exiles, consisting mostly of priests, gathered and preserved what they could of the literary heritage of the Jews. They had access to, or recent memories of, many books that had been in the library of the Jerusalem Temple and the king's palace. When times are good, people treat their heritage casually. Times of destruction and persecution are times of collation and preservation, when societies try to save what they think they can from the vast heritage of the past. They try to preserve a few precious coals from the great hearth fires that burned in the good times.

The Bible mentions numerous books of ancient Israel that are now lost to us, including the book of Yashar, the book of the Wars of the Lord, the annals of the kings of Israel, and the annals of the kings of Judah. Copies of some of these books might have been preserved in Babylon. Other traditions were preserved in the memories of the priests who had served in the Temple and among the palace scribes. These traditions, texts, and memories were sifted and collated by the school of scribes that arose in Babylon. These sacred memories from ancient Israel and Judah were written down in a scroll. Ezra brought a copy of this scroll with him from Babylon when he returned to Judah. This was the Torah of Moses, which became the Jewish Torah.

The book of Deuteronomy had already been published in the kingdom of Judah in the time of King Hezekiah, then was lost and rediscovered in the time of King Josiah, one of the last kings of Judah. The other four books may have already existed in earlier forms, or they may have been composed and edited from various sources.

Historical scholars differ over how historically accurate the memories of the Babylonian Jews really were. Some very skeptical historians believe that the entire story of Israelite history is an invention of the late monarchs of the kingdom of Judah. They do not believe that there ever were patriarchs, nor an Egyptian slavery, nor an exodus, nor an event at Mount Sinai, nor do they believe that the Israelites were desert wanderers who conquered the land of Canaan from an earlier population. Many doubt the existence of the early kings of Israel—Saul, David, and Solomon. These skeptical historians believe that the Israelites were an indigenous group of people in the land of Canaan who developed a unique religious culture and later invented a story to explain their distinction from other peoples of the land.

Other, less skeptical historical scholars believe that the historical materials in the Torah were reworked by later editors but contain many accurate historical memories. These scholars believe that as the Israelites emerged, with their two kingdoms of Israel and Judah, various tribal groups contributed their own ancient memories. Some recalled an exodus from Egypt and a meeting with God at Mount Sinai or Horeb, and others remembered a righteous ancestor named Abraham. Some recalled years of desert life before entering the land and displacing its earlier inhabitants. As the people of Israel emerged around their worship of a unitary God, the various tribal traditions were unified into a national history. Thus a kernel of historical truth may lie behind many mythical traditions. No events recorded in the Bible are corroborated by any outside Near Eastern literary sources until the invasion of Judah by Pharaoh Shishonk, which is mentioned in Egyptian military records and also in the Bible as taking place toward the end of the reign of King Solomon.

Even if the Torah contains fairly accurate historical memories, it is likely that these memories were reworked and retold to fit the needs of later times. This should not surprise us. The history of the American Civil War, for example, needs to be retold in every American generation as our understanding of race relations, the relationships between the various regions of our country, and our sense of the meaning of the American Constitution and American history evolve with the times.

It is my belief that the Egyptian slavery and exodus, an event at Mount Sinai, and an infiltration of the land of Canaan by desert-dwelling Israelites are all based on historical events, even if these events have been retold according to a later understanding of their content and meaning.

The Torah, as we have it, was distilled to meet the needs of an embattled Judean state during its last decades. In its final form it was designed to meet the needs of the Judean exiles in Babylon and of those who came back to restore the Judean nation in the early Persian period. The Torah is called the Torah of Moses. It speaks about the time and the life of Moses and the laws that God gave through Moses. But according to historians, the Torah speaks directly to the Jewish people in the time of Ezra.

Chapter One

One Bible—Two Different Books: Jewish Torah and Christian Old Testament

A king gave to his two servants a gift of wheat and flax. The first servant set aside the wheat and the flax, and he did nothing with them. The second servant ground the wheat into flour and made a loaf of bread. He beat the flax into linen and made a cloth to cover it. After a while the king came back and said to his two servants: "Show me the gift that I have given you." The first servant, to his shame and disgrace, displayed the wheat and the flax. The second servant displayed a loaf of bread covered with a linen cloth. So, too, when the Holy One gave the Torah to Israel, He gave it as wheat to be turned into fine flour and as flax to be turned into cloth for garments.

(*Tanna deBe Eliezer 2*)

A Parable

Imagine that you and a friend are invited to a demonstration of the welding of a sculpture. You are both given goggles to wear on your face, since, as is well known, the light from welding is so bright that no one can look directly at it without going blind. As it happens, one pair of goggles is tinted blue and the other is tinted red.

After the demonstration the two observers discuss what they saw. They agree that there was a flame and a bright light, and their description of this light is similar except for one thing: one observer claims that the light cast a blue glow upon everything, but the other observer claims that the light cast a red glow. The two observers can

15

debate endlessly over the true color of the light, or they can agree that their different observations were a result of the difference between the goggles they were wearing, with the result that their descriptions of the demonstration will be harmonious and they will be at peace with one another.

In this parable the bright light is the word of God. The welding demonstration is the act of divine revelation, and the sculpture that results from the demonstration is the twenty-four books of the Hebrew Bible. Jews and Christians can agree with everything in the parable up to this point, as they all agree that the Hebrew Bible is a revelation from God. The different-colored goggles represent the different religious perspectives of the two religions. The blue goggles represent the way Jews read the Bible, and the red goggles represent the way Christians read the Bible. The Jewish reading results in Jews' seeing the Bible as "Torah," the teachings of Judaism, whereas the Christian way of reading the Hebrew Bible makes it the "Old Testament" of Christianity.

We can name what causes the coloration of the Jewish and Christian readings of the Hebrew Bible. The Christian reading is colored red by the New Testament and the teachings of the Church Fathers. Mainline denominations follow church tradition. Pentecostal Christians read the word according to the guidance of the Holy Spirit, which is individualistic but not by any means random. Christians read the Old Testament through the goggles of these writings and traditions. The Jewish reading is colored blue by the Mishnah, the Talmud, and the books of midrash—the sacred literature of the Rabbis, the Jewish Fathers. In the course of this book, we will learn about these rabbinic writings and how they color the Jewish way of reading Scripture.

When Jews and Christians are able to acknowledge that as we read the Hebrew Bible, we are both reading the same Sacred Scriptures but we are reading them in a different way, then we can be agreeable and discover a great realm of mutual understanding. We will also have a deeper understanding of divine revelation, and this will make our own religious response to God more profound and true. These are the goals of this book.

The Act of Reading

Jacques Derrida (b. 1930) is a French Jewish philosopher who founded the school of thought known as deconstruction. Modern philosophy is much taken with the question of how the experience of reality is received in the human mind and shared through communication. The meaning of words, speech, and writing is essential to this inquiry. Derrida's central point is that *the meaning of a written communication is given by the reader, not the writer.* Applied to the Bible, this means that the message of the Bible is not determined by the author (God, a prophet) but by the reader (humankind, transmitters of religious traditions).

It is not surprising that deconstruction is so relevant to our study of how Jews and Christians read the Bible. Derrida bases his philosophy on how the ancient rabbis read the Bible, through the process that the rabbis called midrash. Derrida claims that all reading is a process of midrash—of taking the meaning that the reader finds in his own psyche and applying or discovering that meaning within the written text.

Deconstruction is the most significant school of literary criticism in the early twenty-first century, but the insights of deconstruction are ancient. The Greek philosopher Aristotle taught long ago that there are three sources of a play—the playwright, who writes the words; the actors, who speak them; and the audience, which listens. The role of the audience is as creative as the role of the playwright and the actors. The play becomes a play only as the audience participates.

Public preachers, like congregational clergy, know exactly what Aristotle was speaking about. The preacher works very hard on a sermon but cannot know in advance whether the sermon is good or bad, whether it will captivate the congregation or put it to sleep. It is the congregation, the audience, that determines the value and message of the sermon, not the preacher.

William Faulkner, the great southern novelist, was often asked by interviewers what this or that novel means. Faulkner always refused to answer such questions. He understood that his novels would lose their greatness if their meaning were limited to what he intended when he wrote the words. Faulkner wanted the reader to supply the meaning, because this process was what made his books popular and worth reading. Similarly, Herman Melville always denied that there was any higher meaning to his magnum opus, *Moby Dick*. He insisted that it is merely a whaling story, though clearly *Moby Dick* is much more than this. Melville left it to the reader to decide the true meaning of his great novel.

The same process of reading for meaning that functions with great literature functions even more so in relation to the greatest literature, the record of divine revelation. What does the Bible mean? Well, what does it mean to *you*? The answer to this question is determined, first and foremost, by one's religious tradition. Jews will always read the Bible one way, Christians a different way. Various sects of Jews and of Christians will have their own subset ways of reading, but these readings will usually be within the boundaries of the broader tradition of the religion.

Translating into Greek

Emmanuel Levinas (1906–2000) was another French Jew who achieved world fame as a philosopher. In his boyhood Levinas was a brilliant talmudic scholar in Kovno, Lithuania, which in those days was the world center of traditional Jewish scholarship. Levinas earned his doctorate at the Sorbonne in Paris. After the Second World War, he renewed his Talmud studies under the tutelage of Chouchani, the mysterious teacher who also instructed Elie Wiesel in those years. Beginning in 1957, Levinas, as a leader in the Alliance Israelite Universelle, gave an annual Talmud lecture to the leading Jewish intellectuals of France. These worldly, assimilated Jews were astounded by the relevance of Jewish Scriptures to contemporary issues, as expounded by the great teacher Levinas.[9]

As we have noted, the first time the Torah was read in public, it required the meturgemanim, the translators, to explain the text to the public. Levinas believed that the Scriptures always have to be reexplained in the language and cultural idiom of the time and place of

---

9. A number of Levinas's annual lectures have been translated into English and published in Emmanuel Levinas, *Nine Talmudic Lectures*, trans. Annette Aronowicz (Bloomington: Indiana University Press, 1990).

the student. Once we verbalize what the Scriptures are talking about in our own contemporary terms, we will discover the divine voice speaking through the written word.

Levinas called this act of cultural restatement *translating into Greek*. He took the terminology from the fact that the first published translation of the Hebrew Bible was the Septuagint, the Greek translation used by the Jews of Alexandria in the time of the Ptolemys, the Greek rulers of Egypt. Levinas believed that the cultural distance between the Scriptures and the reader is an integral part of what makes the Scriptures holy. It is as if the Holy Spirit were asleep in the text, and nothing can wake it up but the need to translate the words into another cultural idiom. Returning to the parable with which we began this chapter, one cannot see the bright light except through the colored glasses.

Some Jewish Ways of Reading the Bible

The word *Torah* defines the first five books of the Hebrew Bible, the Five Books of Moses. For Jews, it also signifies a way of reading all sacred literature. Jews read the Bible in such a way that it reveals Torah, God's will for the Jewish people. Here are some Jewish ways of reading the Bible as Torah that might be of special interest to the Christian reader.

When Jews read the Bible, the God whom we Jews meet there is in the image of a father who loves his children with an overwhelming passion. This father has very high expectations of his children, but he also indulges them. He loves to treat them well and make them happy. Some Christians believe that the God of the Old Testament is a stern God of strict judgment without mercy, but a religious Jew would not be able to discover such a deity in the Hebrew Bible.

> Exod 34:6–7: *The Lord passed before [Moses] and proclaimed: the Lord, the Lord, a God compassionate and gracious, slow to anger, abounding in kindness and faithfulness, extending kindness to a thousand generations, forgiving iniquity, transgression and sin; yet God does not remit all punishment, but visits the*

*iniquity of parents upon children and children's children, upon
the third and fourth generation.*

According to Abraham Ibn Ezra, the great Spanish Torah scholar
of the Middle Ages, the two mentions of "generation" in this passage
suggest a ratio. It is not that God punishes great-grandchildren for the
deeds of their ancestors; it is that God's mercy exceeds God's judgment by 1,000 to 4, a ratio of 250 to 1.

> Exod 21:23b: *The penalty shall be life for life, eye for eye,
> tooth for tooth, hand for hand, foot for foot, burn for burn,
> wound for wound, bruise for bruise* (similar in Lev
> 24:19–22).

In the Christian understanding, this verse is the basis for the
idiom "an eye for an eye," which means to demand vengeance for
wrongs suffered. It contrasts with "turning the other cheek," which
Christian ethics demands. It would come as a surprise to any Jew that
this verse was a demand for vengeance. The Jewish Sages long ago
asked, "Could this verse possibly be intended literally? But what if a
one-eyed man poked out the eye of a two-eyed man? Surely it would
not be justice to take out his eye and blind him! What, then, if a man
with blue eyes poked out the eye of a man with brown eyes?" We can
see that no two human beings can ever be compared. In Judaism, the
biblical passage known as the *lex talionis* is proof of the unique value
of each individual. The *lex talionis* also teaches the equality of all
human beings before the law. Any person must receive the same justice for the same wrong, regardless of social status. Legally, this passage is understood to require monetary compensation to a person one
has injured. The assailant must pay the injured party for the value of
his limb, for his lost time, for his pain and suffering, and for the costs
of his medical care. To a Jew it is obvious that this, and not a demand
for vengeance, is the meaning of the *lex talionis*.

The Torah says *Lo tiv`ar aish b'yom HaShabbat—You shall not burn
any fire throughout your settlements on the Sabbath day* (Exod 35:3).
Jewish tradition understands this verse to mean that one should not
kindle a new fire on the Sabbath. The Jewish reading of the Torah
permits a fire lit before the initiation of the Sabbath, on Friday

evening, to burn into the Sabbath night. Jewish tradition goes beyond this. It is a sacred obligation for every Jew to light Sabbath lights at the family dining table on the eve of the Sabbath, shortly before sundown. It would be a transgression of the divine will to fail to light the Sabbath lights. The Sabbath lights are the most celebrated ritual of Judaism. They provide joy in Jewish homes for the celebration of the Sabbath, and romance for the sacred bond of husband and wife, which is renewed on the Sabbath.

The Torah tells us that when God rebuked Cain for murdering his brother Abel, Cain was crestfallen. God then said to Cain, *Why are you so distressed, and why is your face fallen? Surely if you do right there is uplift. But if you do not do right sin crouches by the door; its urge is towards you, yet you can be its master* (Gen 4:6–7). This passage is the basis of the Jewish view that human beings are capable of doing good if they so choose, despite the fact that human beings have an obvious tendency to do evil. The belief that human beings are capable of choosing goodness is essential to the Jewish view that human beings may achieve personal salvation through obedience to the commandments of the Torah. Jews focus on the promise in Deuteronomy that says of God's commandments, *"The thing is very close to you, in your mouth and in your heart, to observe it"* (Deut 30:14).

The Torah states three times, *You shall not boil a kid in its mother's milk* (Exod 23:19; 34:26; Deut 14:21). In the Talmud the ancient rabbis discuss the meaning of this passage. They were aware that this command could be applied literally, to prohibit a cruel Canaanite religious rite in which a newborn kid was cooked in its own mother's milk and then eaten by the celebrants. Even though they knew of this possibility, the Sages insisted that the true application of this commandment is that Jews must separate meat from dairy foods. The threefold repetition means that meat and dairy must be separated for cooking, for serving, and for dining. In practice this means that Jews must have two sets of dishes, flatware, and pots and pans—one for meat meals and one for dairy meals. This rule reinforces the rabbinic teaching that the family dinner table is the sacrificial altar of God. A sacrificial ritual is a sacrament that requires rules, just as in Christianity the rite of Holy Communion is conducted according to proper form.

As we have seen from these examples, one could never guess just from reading the written Scriptures what Jews hear them saying.

It is even more difficult to understand the Jewish way of reading the Bible if one is used to reading Scripture with Christian eyes. To understand the Hebrew Scriptures as Jews understand them, one must read them with Jewish eyes, as interpreted in the Mishnah, Talmud, and midrash.

TaNaKh versus Old Testament

The twenty-four books of the Hebrew Bible were recognized as Sacred Scripture in three batches. In the time of Ezra, the Jews sanctified the first portion of the Bible, the five books of the Torah. In the succeeding few centuries, they sanctified the books of the Prophets. As mentioned earlier, in the time of Jesus, the Bible consisted of the Torah and the Prophets. In the late first century CE, the high court of the Rabbis closed the final section of the Hebrew Bible, the Writings.

One way that Jews and Christians read the Hebrew Bible differently is the different emphasis they place on different books and sections of the Bible. Neither Jews nor Christians pay equal attention to all passages in the Bible. We craft our religious message by focusing on some passages and ignoring, even suppressing, others. All Jews and Christians quote from Isaiah, *You shall beat your swords into plowshares* (Isa 2:4), but we ignore the prophet Joel when he reverses Isaiah's prescription and says, *You shall beat your plowshares into swords* (Joel 3:10).

In Christianity the entire Hebrew Bible (as well as the Apocrypha, for some Christians) is equally revered as the Old Testament. Christians tend to place their greatest focus on the Prophets and on the book of Daniel. These books are the most quoted in the New Testament and in early Christianity as support texts for the doctrine of the Christ.

In Judaism, the division of the Hebrew Bible into three sections remains of major significance. The Prophets and the Writings are considered to be inspirational only. Religious doctrine and religious practice may be based only on the five books of the Torah, which function as the Constitution of the Jewish people. In the traditional Jewish understanding, the Torah alone is the direct word of God. The books of the Prophets were composed at a lower level of divine revelation, which Jews call the Spirit of Prophecy. The message of the Prophets is from God, but the words are the words of the prophet himself. Jewish tradition says, "Moses saw as through a bright mirror, and the other prophets saw as through a dark mirror." The books of the Writings are composed at a lower level yet of divine inspiration, which Jews call the Holy Spirit. The words of the Writings have definite human authorship and may even be fictional, but the author is inspired by God. The Psalms, for example, were ascribed to King David under the inspiration of God's Holy Spirit.

Jews have a tendency to use the word *Torah* to describe the entire Bible, even though, properly speaking, the Torah is just the first five books. Because these five books are the most important, the others are subsumed under their title. To many English-speaking Jews, the word *Bible* sounds vaguely Christian, but the term *Torah* sounds comfortably Jewish.

Two Religions, One Bible

Jews and Christians can debate each other in a way that no other two religions can. This is because they share a common Scripture, the Hebrew Bible. Although Muslims also revere the Jewish and Christian Scriptures as divine revelations, Muslims do not refer to these sacred texts in the way that Christians refer to the Hebrew Bible for inspiration and teaching. Muslims refer to the Koran as the ultimate source of religious truth. The New Testament, by contrast, is so closely associated with the Hebrew Bible that the message of the New Testament can only be fully comprehended by one who is conversant with the Hebrew Bible.

It is often stated that the Americans and the English are two nations united by a common language. The English playwright George Bernard Shaw, however, joked that the Americans and the English are two nations "divided by a common language." Shaw's joke is funny because it reflects a certain truth that functions on two levels. First, because we share a common language, we are better able to disagree with one another and engage in invidious or angry debate. Second, our language is common only up to a point. A word or phrase that has one meaning to the English resonates differently in

the ear of an American. We humbly recognize that we do not understand the French, but because of our common language, we English
and Americans are apt to misunderstand one another without even
realizing it. This can lead to anger and hurt feelings.

Shaw's joke applies well to Jews and Christians. They are two
religions united, and divided, by a common Scripture. For Jews, sharing our Scriptures with the world's most numerous and powerful religious people has been a mixed blessing. On the negative side,
judgmental Christian responses to the different way that Jews read
the Hebrew Bible, together with some of the anti-Jewish readings
given to those Scriptures in Christian tradition, have been a cause of
anti-Semitism. On the positive side, the fact that Christianity adopted
the Jewish Scriptures as its own has made this tiny Jewish people into
an enormously significant factor in the history of the Western world
and the evolution of its culture. From antiquity to the present, the
Jews have never numbered even twenty million, yet they play a central role in the consciousness of the entire world. Jews realize that all
of this attention often hurts us more than it helps us, when it plays
out as anti-Semitism or anti-Zionism. At the same time, Jews are
enormously proud and pleased about their significant role in the
world. Few Jews realize the extent to which their importance depends
upon the acceptance of the Jewish Scriptures as true revelation by the
Christian and Muslim worlds. Although anti-Judaism and anti-
Semitism have always been a problem for the Jews, could such a tiny
people have survived from antiquity into modernity without all the
attention that has been focused on them as the subjects and recipi-
ents of divine revelation? Perhaps not. It must surely, on balance, be
very much in the Jews' favor that Christians and Muslims validate the
Hebrew Bible as the word of God.

Returning to Shaw's joke, we affirm that Jews and Christians are
both united and divided by their shared Scripture. If Jews and
Christians read the Hebrew Bible completely differently, then they
would have nothing to debate with one another. They would be like
any two religions with no common ground for discussion. If Jews and
Christians read the Hebrew Bible exactly the same way, they would be
one religion, not the two different and self-contained religious systems that they are. The confusing fact of the matter is that Judaism
and Christianity are neither the same nor opposite to one another.

Their disagreements are nuances on a shared understanding of the Hebrew Scriptures.

This shared understanding has two causes. First, when Christianity came into being, it inherited not only a written Scripture but also six hundred years' worth of interpretation from the public reading and explanation of the Bible in the weekly Sabbath gatherings of the Jews. Second, Jews and Christians have lived in close proximity since the rise of Christianity. They have learned from one another, shared ideas, and been influenced by a common culture.

As an example of the first reason for our shared understanding, we may take the Jewish and Christian debate over the meaning of the Messiah. From the rise of Christianity to world prominence until the dawn of the modern age, this was the central point of debate between Jews and Christians. Christians claim that the messianic passages in the Hebrew Bible point to Jesus Christ. Jews claim that these passages point to the future Jewish king who will restore them to their homeland. This debate was only possible because Jews and Christians were in complete agreement about which biblical passages were to be read as messianic predictions.

How did this come about? Historians have demonstrated that the prophets of Israel were not consciously predicting a Messiah. The idea of the Messiah first makes its appearance in Jewish religious literature in the second century BCE, in the apocryphal *Psalms of Solomon*. During the two centuries from then until the rise of Christianity, the set of biblical verses to be read messianically had become a common heritage of all Jewish sects. By the time Christianity split from Judaism and became a separate religion, the "messianic verses" were part of their shared way of reading the Hebrew Bible.

As an example of the ongoing mutual influence of the two religions, we may take the Christian and Jewish allegorical readings of the Song of Songs, the book of biblical love poetry. This book was included in the Writings only at the twelfth hour, on the word of Rabbi Akiva, who insisted on an allegorical reading of the book. This took place about a century after the birth of Christianity. The Jewish allegory and the Christian allegory agree with each other nearly verse by verse, except that the Jews apply the allegory to the love between God and Israel, whereas, to the Christians, the Song of Songs is an allegory of the love between Christ and his church. Can the similarity of these allegorical readings not be linked to the fact that the Christian school of Eusebius was right down the street from the Jewish school of Rabbi Abbahu in the city of Caesarea? Eusebius, the third-century church father, was responsible for the transmission of the Christian reading of the Song of Songs, and Abbahu was the leading Jewish teacher of the time. Surely the Jews and Christians compared notes to create a parallel allegory.

Chapter Two

The Ever-Expanding Torah

Moses received the Torah at Mount Sinai and handed it to Joshua. Joshua gave it to the Elders, and the Elders to the Prophets, and the Prophets delivered it to the men of the Great Assembly. They said three things: Be deliberate in judgment, raise up many disciples, and make a fence for the Torah.
(*Pirke Avot* 1:1)

Closure of the Hebrew Bible

In 66 CE the Jews of Judea rebelled against the Roman Empire. At the end of the war in 70, the victorious Romans destroyed the Second Temple. With the destruction of the Temple, the Jewish service of God through animal sacrifices came to an end, never to be reinstituted. The primary focus of the written Torah is on animal sacrifice and its related topics of hereditary priesthood and ritual purity. The entire book of Leviticus, the second half of Exodus, and major portions of Numbers and Deuteronomy give details of the sacrificial system. What would become of the Torah without sacrifices?

In the first century there were many sects of Jews. Some of these sects based their religious visions on the proper conduct of the sacrifices (the Sadducees, for example) or around a revised, idealized version of the sacrificial system (for example, the Essenes). For these sacrifice-oriented Jewish sects, Judaism had all but come to an end with the elimination of sacrifice. Judaism might have died out—and perhaps the Romans thought it would without the Temple—but for other sects of Jews, the elimination of animal sacrifice was liberating, however much they may have shared the grief of the national disaster.

As we have already learned, the written scroll of the Torah always existed alongside an oral tradition of interpretation, beginning with the very first public reading of the Torah. One group of Jewish leaders, the Pharisees, had such a symbolic interpretation of the sacrificial portions of the Torah that their form of Judaism indeed functioned better without the reality of sacrifice. The successors to the Pharisees came to be called Rabbis. The Romans granted some of these Rabbis authority to rule the Jews after the disaster of 70. The Rabbis gathered in the town of Yavneh, west of Jerusalem near the Mediterranean coast. The rabbinic Sanhedrin, the high court of Rabbis in Yavneh, reinterpreted the Torah according to their own vision of Judaism. The Torah of the Rabbis is the Judaism that a modern-day Jew would begin to recognize. It is a Judaism based not on animal sacrifice but on observance of the mitzvot, the commandments of the Torah, as interpreted in rabbinic tradition.

While the title "rabbi" persists in Judaism to the present day, when Jews speak of "the Rabbis" they mean the Rabbis who sat in the Sanhedrin at Yavneh and, in the next few centuries, in Galilee and in the academies of Palestine and Babylon—the Rabbis whose reinterpretation of Judaism became the standard religion of the Jews.

The Rabbis granted themselves great authority in order to resuscitate Judaism after the disaster of the Roman war. They eliminated the priestly dues and offerings, forcing the priesthood to become workers and farmers like other Jews and functionally eliminating the caste system of ancient Judaism. The Rabbis devised new rituals and meanings for all the festivals, which had formerly been distinguished primarily by the extra sacrifices of each holiday. Among the daring deeds of the Rabbis, they completed and closed the Jewish Bible once and for all.

Two sections of the Bible, the Torah and the Prophets, were already fixed and established. Many other Jewish books were vying for sacred status. Different sects and factions of Jews undoubtedly had their own favorites, and some books were more universally accepted among all factions of Jews. The Rabbis had their own criteria to determine which books were canonical—Holy Scripture—and which were not.

Around 100 CE the rabbinical court at Yavneh voted on which books would finally be included in the Bible and which would be excluded (Mishnah *Yadaim* 3:5). Two books squeaked in despite the reservations of many of the Rabbis. Ecclesiastes was accepted on the premise of its authorship by King Solomon, despite its many heretical passages. Song of Songs is a book of ancient love poems, of a type probably recited by the master of ceremonies at weddings. As mentioned, it was included in the Bible on the authority of Rabbi Akiva, the most learned of the Yavneh Sages, who read this book as an allegory for the love between God and Israel. Our sources are silent about the book of Esther, but it is possible that it slipped into the biblical canon of accepted books last of all, because of its popularity and its association with the beloved festival of Purim, and despite the opposition of the Rabbis to its inclusion.

Some very lovely books that the church included in the Old Testament Apocrypha were dismissed by the Rabbis. We cannot always be sure why, but some of the Rabbis' criteria seem clear to us. No book that spoke about historical events after the early days of the Persian Empire was accepted. The Rabbis thought of the time of Ezra and Nehemiah as the end of the biblical era. No book written after the Maccabees took over the Jewish revolt against the Greeks in 168 BCE was accepted into the biblical canon. Apparently the Rabbis' sense of history told them that biblical writing was no longer possible after this era. Perhaps they thought that the Holy Spirit that inspired the biblical Writings was no longer active after this time, or perhaps they were aware of some transformation in the Jewish consciousness that took place at that time. The Rabbis also rejected some books on a technicality, because details in these books disagreed with the Rabbis on various aspects of Jewish law and practice.

Mishnah: The Writing of Scriptures Continues

The Rabbis believed that their oral tradition of interpreting the Bible was an integral part of the Holy Scriptures. They believed that God gave the Torah in two parts. One part was the Written Torah, which God dictated to Moses on Mount Sinai. The other part was the oral tradition, the tradition of interpretation that told Jews how to live by the Torah laws. Such customs as lighting Sabbath candles and separating meat from milk, mentioned in the previous chapter, derive from the oral Torah. The opening verse of *Pirke Avot,* the *Sayings of the*

Fathers, details the chain of tradition by which the Rabbis believed the oral Torah was transmitted. Jews learn that the oral tradition is as much a part of Torah as are the written books of the Bible.

The Rabbis believed that their oral Torah goes back in a continuous chain of tradition all the way to Moses, and from Moses to God. Moses taught his oral teachings to his disciple, Joshua. Joshua taught the tribal elders, who taught the prophets. (Note that the rivals of the Rabbis, the hereditary priests, are bypassed in the chain of transmission.) The prophets taught the early Sages, who taught the great Pharisees who were known by name. The Pharisees taught their successors, the Rabbis.

Shortly after the close of the Bible, the leaders of the Rabbis began to put the oral Torah into writing. Thus the composition of written Scriptures continued in Judaism, even though technically the era of divine revelation was considered to be at an end.

Rabbi Akiva was one of those who voted on closing the Bible. Acknowledged as the greatest Torah teacher of his time, Akiva had a set of written notes that he used to organize the lectures in his academy for training rabbinic scholars.

The Rabbis had a prohibition against writing down the oral Torah. The written Torah and the oral Torah had to be preserved in their respective media. It was against the rules to recite the written Torah from memory or to recite the oral Torah from notes. Akiva kept his notes private, for his personal use only, and he spoke from memory in his lectures. His notes were passed to his student Meir, and from the hands of Meir they passed in the next generation to Rabbi Judah the Prince. Rabbi Judah is also called Rabbi Judah the Patriarch, depending upon the translation of his formal title, Nasi. In Jewish tradition he is known simply as "Rabbi"—the Rabbi par excellence.

Rabbi Judah Hanasi

Rabbi Judah was absolute ruler over all the Jews of Judea and perhaps the entire Roman Empire. He was what the Romans called an ethnarch—a king who ruled over a people rather than a territory. The Romans gave Rabbi Judah complete authority over the internal affairs of the Jews. He was immensely popular with his Jewish subjects, and he had a large personal fortune. Here was a person who could do as he wished!

Rabbi Judah strove to fulfil a Jewish version of Plato's idealized philosopher-king. He honored the rabbinic Sages and became a highly learned rabbi himself. He was renowned for knowledge and wisdom. Rabbi Judah took two major steps to ensure the future of Judaism. He sent two of his finest disciples to the Jewish community of Babylon, in the Neo-Persian Empire. He commissioned them to establish two schools of rabbinic scholarship there, beyond the reach of the Roman Empire. Second, Rabbi Judah wrote down and published a book of the oral Torah. This book is entitled the Mishnah, which translates roughly as "oral teaching," "that which is repeated until learned." The Mishnah is an encyclopedia of rabbinic legal opinions, organized by subject matter. In a later chapter we will study the Mishnah and other rabbinic writings in greater detail.

Rabbi Judah the Prince and his fellow rabbis published the Mishnah around 200 CE. This was not long after the time when the early Christian church was making its own addition to the Bible, the New Testament. The New Testament and the Mishnah differ from one another in style and content, but they are parallel texts in the role they play in Christianity and Judaism, respectively. The New Testament is the Christian continuation of the Hebrew Bible. The Mishnah is the Jewish continuation of the Hebrew Bible.

New Testament and Mishnah

The New Testament rereads the Hebrew Bible in a way that yields the Christian message, so much so that Christians who are familiar with the New Testament discover Christ in every verse of the Hebrew Bible. The Mishnah rereads the Hebrew Bible in a way that yields the message of Judaism. Mishnah study has always been reserved for Jewish scholars. Jews do not sit and read the Mishnah the way Christians read the New Testament. Even so, thanks to the teaching and preaching of Torah in the synagogue, Jews became familiar with the Mishnah's sense of the meaning of Torah and they incorporated this into their belief system.

Virtually all Jews know that Christians interpret the Hebrew Bible through the New Testament, but because of the greater numbers and worldly power of Christendom, Christians are generally less aware of the Mishnah. Many Christians wonder why Jews do not find Christ in the Hebrew Bible as they do. The answer is that Jews read the Hebrew Bible through the lens of the Mishnah, not through the lens of the New Testament.

Jewish tradition posits the following conversation between Moses and God at Mount Sinai (*Tanhuma, Ki Tissa* 60): Moses spends forty days and nights on top of Mount Sinai memorizing the oral Torah after he has written down the five books of the written Torah at God's dictation. Moses finds it difficult to learn the oral Torah, like any good rabbinical disciple who struggles with his studies. Moses says to God, "God, why don't you just write down this part of the Torah as you wrote down the other part?"

God replies to Moses, "In the future other people will come along claiming to have the true interpretation of the Torah. When they make this claim, you will be able to show them the oral Torah and say to them, 'Do you have this? Do you possess the Mishnah? If you don't, then you don't really have the whole Torah, so you cannot interpret the Torah correctly.'"

The rival claimant to the Torah is not named in the passage, probably for fear of reprisal, but it is clear enough that in this passage the Rabbis are responding to the claims of the church.

The church said to the Jews, "You should join us because with the New Testament we have the completion and fulfillment of God's word, as predicted in your own Scriptures." The Rabbis replied, "We have in our possession the completion and fulfillment of our Scriptures. You do not know about it because we did not commit it to writing until after you came along." This response was not intended to impress the church but to encourage Jews to remain true to the Jewish way of reading the Torah.

The Mishnah and the New Testament are, respectively, the Jewish and Christian continuations of the writing of Scripture. It is interesting that for centuries Jews bemoaned the end of prophecy. Then, when both Jews and Christians undertook to write additional Scriptures, neither religion claimed for their authors the status of prophet. Christians do not call Paul or the Gospel writers prophets, nor do Jews assign the title of prophet to the Rabbis quoted in the Mishnah. Yet both religions granted full scriptural authority to these new writings. Both religions saw their new Scriptures as the completion and only proper explanation of the earlier Hebrew Scriptures.

It is not useful, accurate, or meaningful to compare Judaism with Christianity by comparing the Old Testament with the New Testament. A proper comparison results only from comparing the Mishnah with the New Testament. It is difficult for one person to master both of these texts, but this is what is needed for any meaningful comparison of the two separate faiths.

It is false and misleading to suggest that Judaism is the religion of the Old Testament whereas Christianity is the religion of the New Testament. Judaism and Christianity represent two different ways of reading the Hebrew Bible. The Mishnah reflects the Jewish reading of the Hebrew Bible, and the New Testament reflects the Christian reading.

Let us repeat what we have just said, because this is the central lesson of this book: *One cannot compare Christianity with Judaism by comparing the New Testament with the Old Testament. A proper comparison of Christianity and Judaism compares the New Testament with the Mishnah. These two works were written at about the same time, reflecting the Christian and Jewish ways of reading their common heritage, the Hebrew Bible. Judaism is not the Old Testament religion. Judaism and Christianity result from two different ways of reading the Hebrew Bible.*

The Expanding Oral Torah

The Mishnah contains only a portion of the oral Torah of the Rabbis. The oral Torah continued to grow in every generation as the Rabbis confronted new legal and social issues and applied the Torah to them. Over the centuries Jews continued to write books that attained scriptural status in the sense that they gave the authorized way of interpreting and living by the Hebrew Bible. We will have the opportunity to study in detail the various genres of Jewish scriptural literature. For now, let us briefly review the major works:

Tosefta: Organized according to the subject matter of the Mishnah, the Tosefta contains many rabbinic opinions that Rabbi

Judah did not record in the Mishnah. The Tosefta is, in a sense, a comment upon, and adjustment to, the Mishnah. The Tosefta never achieved the same sacred status as the Mishnah. Whenever the two books disagree on a point of law, Judaism follows the Mishnah.

Jerusalem Talmud: This is also called the Palestinian Talmud or the Talmud of the Land of Israel. In the early fifth century, the great rabbinic academies of the land of Israel in Tiberias and Caesarea were closed. The scholars of the age wrote down a compilation of their oral Torah teachings. They organized these teachings around the Mishnah. The collection of continued teachings of the oral Torah that the Sages of the academies wrote down is called the Gemara, which, like the word *mishnah,* is another word for "teaching." The Mishnah and the Gemara together are called the Talmud, also "teaching." Each discussion in the Gemara begins with the topic of the relevant Mishnah, but it may then drift to any other topic. Following the oral nature of the material, like a conversation between a group of friends, the Gemara leaps unpredictably from topic to topic. Because of the hurried nature of the writing process, the Jerusalem Talmud is rather disordered and difficult to follow. Also, following the originally oral nature of the material, the Gemara is not written down in complete sentences. Its style is elliptical—that is, with clipped and enigmatic phrases, like reminder notes that contain just enough information to jog the memory of a person who has all the rest of the necessary information in his head.

Babylonian Talmud: With the academies of the land of Israel closed, the two Babylonian academies founded by Rabbi Judah the Prince took over the lead in the ever-unfolding Jewish interpretation of Scripture. In Sura and Nehardea, later in Sura and Pumbeditha, the Rabbis of Babylon continued to study and interpret the written and oral Torahs that were handed down to them by previous generations of Rabbis. Eventually the Rabbis of Babylon composed their own Gemara and published their own Talmud.

The Rabbis of Babylon had time to polish and edit their Talmud. The Babylonian Talmud is much longer than the Jerusalem Talmud. In print, the Babylonian Talmud fills three thousand two-sided folio sheets. The Mishnah is about the same size as the Hebrew Bible, but the Talmud is many times larger, large enough to fill a three-foot shelf in its many volumes. Like the Talmud of the land of Israel, the

Babylonian Talmud disorganizes what the Mishnah organizes. Any subject may arise on any page. The Gemara is a literary creation, but it is written in the form of minutes to a conversation between friends. Possibly this style recreates the pattern of discussion between the scholars that took place in the classes at the Babylonian academies.

The Babylonian Talmud was published between the fifth and seventh centuries. The Gaonim, the heads of the Babylonian academies, promoted their Talmud to other Jewish communities. By the ninth century, Jews throughout the world recognized the Babylonian Talmud as the ultimate authority on questions of Torah. If one wants to know what the Torah teaches on any given subject, one discovers this by reading not the Hebrew Bible but the Talmud. The Talmud, in rabbinic Judaism, is the ultimate word of the Torah. This remained true for nearly all Jews for a millennium, from the ninth to the nineteenth century. For Orthodox Jews today, the Talmud remains the final word on Jewish law, belief, and practice.

The Babylonian Talmud, containing the Mishnah and expanding on it, holds a place in Judaism parallel to that which the New Testament holds in Christianity. Just as Christians read the Hebrew Bible through the lens of the New Testament, so Jews read the Torah through the lens of the Talmud.

Translations of the Bible: Ancient translations of the Bible are important tools for interpretation. Where a translation attempts to be literal, it shows us how ancient Jews understood the words and phrases of the Bible. These ancient translators may have had sources, now lost to us, on the meaning of old Hebrew words. Where a translation attempts to be interpretive, it shows us how ancient Jews were interpreting and preaching the Bible when it was read aloud in the synagogue.

The first published translation of the Bible was the Greek Septuagint. The Greek-speaking Jews of Alexandria, the great city of Hellenistic Egypt, used the Septuagint as their official Scriptures. Its large Jewish population made Alexandria comparable to the New York metropolitan area in our times as the most important Jewish center outside the land of Israel. The Jews of Alexandria adapted to the Greek language and culture of their city. Since they did not know the Hebrew language, they developed an accepted Greek translation of the Bible.

The name Septuagint—"seventy"—derives from a legend about the origins of the Septuagint. The Jews told the story that Ptolemy II, founder of the great library at Alexandria, wanted a copy of the Bible for his library (Talmud *Megillah* 9). He asked the high priest in Jerusalem to send him seventy Jewish scholars learned in Hebrew and Greek. Ptolemy locked each of the scholars into an isolated cell for a period of seventy days. Each scholar had paper and pens and a copy of the Hebrew Bible. Each was instructed to write a translation of the Bible. When the seventy days were over, lo and behold!—each of the seventy Greek manuscripts agreed with the others, word for word.

The legend suggests that God's Holy Spirit guided the translation of the Bible into Greek. In the eyes of the Alexandrian Jews, they had in their hands not a mere translation of the Bible but the Bible itself. Similarly, biblical literalists in America today claim that the King James translation of the Bible is absolutely literal.[10]

The Aramaic Targum: The Jews of Israel and Mesopotamia spoke Aramaic, not Greek. In later antiquity a number of translations of the Bible into Aramaic were published. Unlike the Greek-speaking Jews, the Jews of Israel and Mesopotamia preserved the Hebrew Bible. It was not too difficult for an Aramaic speaker to learn the

---

10. I once had cause to use the Septuagint in a way that shows how useful ancient translations can be in demonstrating the meaning of the Bible. Leviticus 11:6 incorrectly claims that the rabbit chews a cud. We must presume that God knows which animals chew a cud and which do not. This incorrect information about rabbits suggests a level of fallible human involvement in the writing of Scripture. Some of those who claim that the Bible is eternally valid and correct in all matters claim that *arnevet* in the Torah is not a rabbit but a creature of similar appearance that did chew a cud. We can test this claim by seeing how *arnevet* is understood in ancient translations.

This word plays a famous role in an old Jewish legend about the Septuagint. The legend reports that the Jewish Sages purposely mistranslated the Torah in nine places in order to avoid offending King Ptolemy II. The Sages changed the word for "rabbit" because Ptolemy's wife was named Bunny, and the Sages did not want Ptolemy to say, "The Jews put my wife's name into their book as a joke."

As it happens, the Septuagint word for "rabbit" is indeed the standard Greek name for that creature. This fact undermines the Jewish legend. More significantly, it supports the view that the Bible contains information which is factually incorrect. The rabbit of the Torah is indeed a rabbit, though it does not chew a cud. It also happens that Ptolemy II's wife was not named Bunny, but King Ptolemy I was nicknamed Bunny, and he disliked the nickname intensely. The Jewish legend preserves a transformed version of this true historical memory.

closely related language of Hebrew. As we have seen, however, whenever the Bible was read aloud in the synagogue to the people, it was always accompanied by a translation into Aramaic. This translation was not literal but interpretive. The translation was itself a sort of sermon. Over time, certain ways of translating became standardized in the oral tradition. These oral traditions are preserved in the Targum (pl. Targumim), the Aramaic biblical translations.

The most renowned and accepted Targum is Targum *Onkelos.* Onkelos is the Aramaic translation of the name Aquila, Rabbi Akiva's disciple. Onkelos wrote a new Greek translation, now lost, but his name somehow became attached to the Aramaic translation of the Bible. It became a custom among Jews to read the weekly lectionary portion of the Torah three times through, once in Hebrew and twice in Aramaic. This custom was retained even into the Middle Ages, when Jews no longer spoke Aramaic. There are Jews even today who read the weekly Torah portion in Aramaic. The Talmud is written primarily in Aramaic, so it is a simple step for Talmud scholars to study also the Targum. Targum *Onkelos* shows us how Jews preached the Torah in the ancient synagogue.

Rabbinic Judaism retained Hebrew for the public reading of Scripture. The Rabbis insisted that Jews learn Hebrew to study the Bible. But they retained, for Bible study, the Targumim, especially Targum *Onkelos,* as tools that were also canonical in themselves.

Midrash: Midrash is the nonliteral reading of the Scriptures. Midrash is the interpretive, homiletic, sermonic way of reading. Midrash is the deconstruction of the Bible. In midrash, context no longer matters. Every verse, phrase, even word, can be isolated and given its own interpretation. The word *midrash* describes a process of biblical interpretation and a genre of literature. Midrash derives from oral tradition, from the public preaching of the Scriptures in the synagogue. Over the centuries a large body of standardized midrashic interpretations developed. These were further embellished by creative preachers and writers. From the third century to the tenth century, the Jews published many different volumes of midrash. Although the Jews of Babylon created the greatest Talmud, our published works of midrash all come from the Jewish community of the land of Israel. Despite the political devastation of the land and the persecution of Jews in the eastern Roman Empire, creative

Jewish life continued to thrive in the promised land, as represented by the great body of midrash books. Some of the greatest works of midrash are described here.

Halakic (Legal) Midrash: The *Mekilta* to Exodus, the *Sifra* to Leviticus, and the *Sifre* to Numbers and Deuteronomy are the major works expounding rabbinic Jewish law through the process of midrash. The halakic midrash is, in essence, the Mishnah written backward. We have noted that the Mishnah is organized by subject matter. The Mishnah seldom quotes the Torah, since the Mishnah has its own authority within the oral tradition of the Sages. In the halakic midrash, the legal opinions of the Mishnah are derived from their biblical sources by logical exposition—to show that if we had to justify the oral Torah by the written Torah, we could do so. The works of halakic midrash may have been composed in response to challenges against the authority of the oral Torah of the Rabbis.

Homiletic Midrash: The works of homiletic midrash teach the nonlegal aspects of Judaism—Jewish faith and hope, doctrines and ethics. The first published work of homiletic midrash is the fourth-century *Bereshit Rabba (Genesis Rabba)* to the book of Genesis. This book gives verse-by-verse interpretations of Genesis, with emphasis on certain key verses. *Bereshit Rabba* defends the doctrines of rabbinic Judaism against its main rivals in Byzantine times—Gnosticism, Christianity, and perhaps other unknown faiths and Jewish sects. *Bereshit Rabba* encourages Jews to remain faithful to Judaism, promotes the central doctrines of Jewish monotheism, and holds out the promise of future messianic redemption for Jews who remain faithful in difficult times of persecution and external challenge.

Leviticus Rabba contains midrashic homilies that have been cleverly strung together by a literary editor. The editor created megasermons made up of multiple midrashic texts. *Pesikta Rabbati* and other works contain sermons built around the Jewish holiday lectionary. Various works entitled *Tanhuma* present Jewish lessons in midrashic form. All of these books of midrash are literary creations based on centuries of oral preaching tradition.

The Topical Focus of the Midrash:
Rereading the Torah

Not all verses in Scripture receive equal attention in the midrash, as the opening verses of the weekly scriptural readings are the focus of much midrash. In the ancient synagogue, the sermon preceded the public reading of the Torah. The preacher would often craft his homily to make it conclude with the opening verse of the weekly Torah reading.

Over time, certain verses became the focus for discussion on certain topics. For example, "After the death of the sons of Aaron" (Lev 16:1) became the place to discuss the injustice of the death of the righteous before their time. The opening verse of the Torah, "In the beginning," became the place to discuss God's intention in creating the universe, the topic of causality, which was of such interest to the Greek philosophers. The great Jewish teaching on repentance is based on a phrase in Numbers 5:7, "He shall confess the wrong that he has done."

To a Jew, the written Torah is like an entry hall full of doors. Every separate verse in the Torah is a doorway into a room. The teachings of Judaism that have been attached to a verse through the midrash are the lovely furnishings which fill each room. When a Jew sees an interesting verse in the Torah, he or she wants to run to the midrash and the later commentaries to see what beautiful teachings are attached to that verse. Many a Torah verse has become what midrash scholars call a locus classicus, a traditional location, for the teaching of a major topic in Judaism.

Although the books of the library of midrash are not included in the Jewish Bible, the content of these books is regarded as scriptural. Jews consider the biblical stories that are retold in the midrash, and the interpretations found there, to be part and parcel of the Bible itself, as if they were written in the scriptural text.

For example, in the written Torah we first meet Abraham, father of the Jewish nation, at the age of seventy-five. God tells Abraham to leave his father's house and his homeland and go to the land of Canaan. The written Torah says nothing about the life of Abraham up to this point. It is common knowledge among Jews, on the basis of this midrash, that when Abraham was born, Nimrod, the king of

Babylon, saw by a great star in the sky that a true prophet was born. Abraham's father, Terah, hid the baby boy from Nimrod in a cave. There God miraculously fed him and educated him until he crawled out at the age of three. Jews retell the story of how young Abraham kept watch one day in his father's idol shop. He took a hammer and smashed all of his father's idols. How do Jews know all of these details of Abraham's early years? They are found in the midrash. To Jews, these stories are not extrabiblical; they are as much a part of the biblical story of Abraham as the divine promise in Genesis 15 or the binding of his son Isaac on the altar in Genesis 22. The midrashic exposition of the Bible is part of the Bible itself.

Commentaries: In the High Middle Ages, the Jews experienced a cultural shift. Their world was divided between the Christians and the Muslims. The Babylonian academies lost their luster. The centers of Jewish life shifted to the Rhineland (Ashkenaz) in Christendom and to Baghdad, then Spain (Sepharad), in the Islamic world.

In this new cultural climate, Jews developed different methods of interpreting Scripture. The midrashic process came to an end. The body of midrash was preserved as a classic from the past. Two great anthologies were the last great products of midrash to be produced—*Midrash Hagadol* in the Sefardic world and·*Yalkut Shimeoni* among the Ashkenazim. The great Jewish scholars of the Middle Ages composed commentaries on the Torah, a new genre of biblical literature. These commentators used methods of scriptural analysis that were current in their own times, to shine a new light upon God's word. The greatest are Rashi (Rabbi Shlomo Yitzhaki, France, 1040–1105), Abraham Ibn Ezra (Spain, 1092–1167), and Nahmanides (Spain, 1194–1270). The words of the commentators are not considered scriptural in themselves. They are, however, considered the necessary key to the Jewish understanding of Scripture. This is especially true of Rashi, who commented on the entire Bible and Talmud. From the High Middle Ages on, Jews understood these sacred texts according to Rashi's explanation.[11] If Jews read the Scriptures with Jewish eyes, then Rashi provides the spectacles.

---

11. A Jewish joke: Rashi says to his wife, "I like you in that blue dress, but I like the red one better." She replies, "Rashi, do you have to comment on *everything*?"

Zohar: As late as the High Middle Ages, Jews were still granting scriptural status to additional books. Around 1280, Rabbi Moses deLeone published the *Holy Zohar*. The *Zohar* is a mystical commentary on the Torah. It gives a rationale to the commandments according to the doctrines of the Kabbalah, the Jewish mystical system that arose in Provence and Catalonia in the twelfth century. The *Zohar* claims to record conversations between rabbinic disciples and their master, Rabbi Simeon bar Yohai, who lived in Galilee in the second century. Jewish mystics believe that Simeon bar Yohai is the author of the *Zohar*. Historians find it more likely that Moses deLeone, who published the *Zohar,* was also its author. The book is written in an artificial version of ancient Aramaic. It expounds the doctrine of the *sefirot,* the ten emanations of God. The *Zohar* interprets many biblical stories as symbolic of the interaction between the *sefirot* within the being of God. In the *Zohar,* the Torah is not merely a revelation from God; it is the self-revelation of God.

As the Kabbalah spread among the Jews of many lands, the *Zohar* grew in popularity. Many communities of Jews came to see the *Zohar* as not just a commentary on the Scripture but as Scripture itself. Their view was that the Bible is the written Torah, the Talmud is the oral Torah, and the *Zohar* is the secret or esoteric Torah. Bible, Talmud, and *Zohar* together constitute the complete word of God.

When the Jews of Yemen were evacuated to Israel during Operation Magic Carpet in 1952, many Yemenite Jews brought nothing with them from their old homes except their copy of the *Zohar.* As the ultimate revelation of God, this book was all they felt that they needed to live religiously.[12]

Torah as Dialogue

Jews keep on adding new books to the sacred bookshelf even though they closed the Bible nineteen hundred years ago. They are

---

12. A few years ago a friend of mine, an Israeli of Iraqi origin, gave me a tour of his home near the Israeli town of Kfar Saba. He claimed to be entirely secular in outlook, but in his daughters' bedroom was a beautifully bound multivolume copy of the *Zohar* on a special shelf. "Just to be on the safe side," my friend said with a smile.

able to do this because they consider Torah to be a process. Torah in the narrowest sense is the word that Moses brought down from God at Mount Sinai at the beginning of Jewish history. Torah in the broadest sense is what happens whenever two or more Jews get together to discuss sacred matters. When Jews join in dialogue to discuss a matter that is raised in the Jewish holy books, God joins the discussion as another party. In this way the Torah constantly grows and evolves. As God was revealed at Mount Sinai when God gave the Torah, so God continues to be revealed whenever Jews expound the Torah.

Rabbi Abraham Joshua Heschel reports (*The Earth Is the Lord's*) that in Eastern Europe, when one Jew greeted another, even an ordinary Jew, he would often say to his fellow, *Sog mir a shtickl Torah*— "Say me a little Torah." This was an invitation to a dialogue, usually about a difficult passage of the Talmud. These Jews believed the saying in *Pirke Avot* that "when two Jews get together and words of Torah pass between them, the *Shekinah,* the Divine Presence, makes a third among them" (*Pirke Avot* 3:3).

Let us see briefly how this works: In a passage in the halakic midrash *Sifra*, Rabbi Akiva and Ben Peturah discuss the following partial verse from Leviticus, *that thy brother may live with thee* (Lev 25:36). What does it mean to act so that your fellow may live with you? They discuss the case of two travelers in the desert. One of them owns a skin of water; the other is without water. If the owner of the water drinks it all, he will live. If he shares the water, they will both die. Ben Peturah says they drink together, live together, and die together. Rabbi Akiva says that the owner of the water drinks and lives; the obligation to preserve the life of your fellow does not extend to suicide. With whom do you agree? When you debate this question with a friend, you are engaging in a discussion between five parties: Rabbi Akiva, Ben Peturah, you, your friend—and God!

Listening to the Voice of God

People ask, "Why did God speak to people in the old days, but God no longer speaks to anyone today? Why did prophecy cease?" The answer of the Jewish Sages is that God is speaking today. God is speaking to us more clearly than to any of the prophets except perhaps Moses. God's voice is available today not just to special people but to everyone. All you have to do to hear God speaking is engage in Scripture study. Divine revelation—Torah—continues in an ongoing process from Mount Sinai to the present moment.

Chapter Three

The Seventy Faces of Torah

Rabbi Shimeon said: "Woe to the human being who says that Torah presents mere stories and ordinary words! If so, we could compose a better Torah right now with ordinary words and better than all of them!

Is it to present matters of the world (that the Torah exists)? Even rulers of the world possess words more sublime. If so, let us follow them and make a Torah out of them!

Ah, but all the words of Torah are sublime words, sublime secrets!...

This story of Torah is the garment of Torah. Whoever thinks that the garment is the real Torah and not something else—may his spirit deflate! He will have no portion in the world that is coming....

But the essence of the garment is the body; the essence of the body is the soul!

So it is with Torah. She has a body: the commandments of Torah....

Those who know more do not look at the garment but rather at the body under that garment.

The wise ones, servants of the King on high...look only at the soul, root of all, the real Torah!

...The soul we have mentioned is the Beauty of Israel.... The soul of the soul is the Holy Ancient One....

As wine must sit in a jar, so Torah must sit in this garment. So look only at what is under the garment! So all those words and all those stories—they are garments!"

(*Zohar* 3:152a)[13]

---

13. *Zohar: The Book of Enlightenment*, trans. Daniel C. Matt (Mahwah, NJ: Paulist Press, 1983) pp. 43–45.

All Wisdom in One Book

If you go to any bookstore, you will generally be able to purchase a thin book with a title like *Everything You Need to Know to Be
Happy in Life*. The genre is so popular that a new specimen arises in
print every few years and enjoys a huge if brief run of popularity.
Between the covers you will find a concise collection of pithy sayings
and perhaps some humorous or heartwarming stories that show how
to apply the wisdom.

Best-selling authors are not the only ones to try their hand at
this genre. Egomaniacal world leaders from Mao Tse-Tung to
Mu'ammar Gadhafi have published their collected wisdom for living
in little books of sayings by which all their loyal subjects may emu-
late the perfected life of the ruler. Simple books of popular psychology and business advice also attempt to summarize in a few simple
rules all that one needs to know to succeed in life.

Considering how easy it is to give advice for good living and
how readable and entertaining such literary fare can be, it is amazing
how difficult and distant the Bible can be. And yet somehow the Bible
has remained for centuries and millennia the Western world's
acknowledged source of morality and guidance while best-sellers
come and go. What is it about the Bible that succeeds where the simple guides fail to impress? Or to look at it from the other direction,
why is it that the Bible does not resemble the simple guidebooks for
living?

Modern-day people may think it is only our modern cynicism
and skepticism or our modernistic literary taste that makes the Bible
difficult to access. Not so! Even in the Middle Ages, pious Jewish
scholars were openly speculating on the question why the Bible often
raises matters whose relevance to us is difficult to discern. Even in the
rabbinic era in antiquity, when the Scriptures were only a few centuries old, the Sages often had a hard time explaining to themselves
why certain passages would be in the Bible.

To Rashi, the great medieval commentator, the Torah exists primarily for the sake of the commandments within it. But the very first
commandment directed toward the Jewish people is not to be found
until chapter 12 of the second book, Exodus. Commenting on this
chapter, Rashi asks, "Why did the Torah not begin here?" Of course

he has an answer, but still he could speculate openly on the seeming irrelevance of the first third of the Torah. The ancient Rabbis had a saying, "Blessed is he who spends a whole day speculating about the list of the five kings who ruled in Edom before Israel entered the promised land" (Gen 36:31). The Rabbis thereby affirmed the importance of every word of Scripture, but they also showed that they were able to identify the most seemingly irrelevant passage in the entire Torah. In reading the rabbinic literature, one can see that many topics in the Torah troubled the ancient Rabbis, as they trouble us:

- The book of Genesis focuses on the life stories of a group of seminomadic shepherds. What relevance can the details of their existence have for us?

- The book of Exodus begins with the stirring tale of slavery and exodus, the revelation at Mount Sinai, the Ten Commandments, and the covenant code of laws. But the final half of the book gives excruciating details about the construction of a long-gone desert sanctuary for offering sacrifices to God. An accounting is given, and repeated, of all the materials used in the construction of the tabernacle.

- The book of Leviticus includes a lengthy excursus on skin diseases and on mold outbreaks in houses.

- We are taught in Leviticus 19: "You shall love your neighbor as yourself." The very next verse gives the inexplicable laws of forbidden mixtures, prohibiting the wearing of linen with wool and the sowing of two types of seed in the same farm field.

- The book of Numbers, embarrassingly, commands the Israelites to fight a war of extermination against the Midianites and against the seven indigenous peoples of Canaan. Considering the later rabbinic emphasis on the community of humankind and the sanctity of every human life, how are we to deal with these texts?

Despite all of these textual difficulties, we continue to study the Torah and to find within it all of the teaching and inspiration for the virtues of compassion, charity, and kindness that form what we have come to call the Judeo-Christian ethic. Such is the power of interpretation! A simple list of the necessary religious virtues would not have the didactic effect that comes from discovering these virtues in the text through a process of interpretation handed down through tradition over countless generations.

The *Holy Zohar* acknowledges that if the Torah were really saying what it appears to be saying, "we could write a better Torah ourselves, using our own words." Our religious faith obligates us to acknowledge that the Torah must exist for the sake of its interpretation, not for the stories, laws, and rules that make up its apparent content.

Borrowing a symbol from medieval romantic folklore, the *Zohar* compares the Torah and its interpretation to a beautiful princess in disguise. One who sees only the externals of the Torah, the stories and rules, is fooled by the disguise. He does not know that he is standing before a princess. One who lives by the commandments enjoys the physical beauty of the princess. The one who recognizes the hidden aspect of Torah that makes its message eternally relevant takes the princess as his beloved. This person knows the princess, the Torah, not just by her appearance but also in her soul.

The soul of the soul of the Torah, the innermost level of Torah, is the actual being of God. The one who penetrates the Torah on this level has become the husband and soul mate of the beautiful princess. His life is nobility, joy, and fulfillment. The person who plumbs the Torah to its greatest depth finds himself standing in the very presence of God.

Reading in Depth

Consider, if you will, three quotes, one each from three different genres of literature:

- During the fast times at Wall Street High, investors paid little notice to a company's balance sheets and capital structures. Since the world would be ever awash in capital, why worry whether your company had plans for a drought? (*New York Times,* Money&Business, June 16, 2002)

- Call me Ishmael. Some years ago—never mind how long precisely—having little or no money in my purse, and nothing particular to interest me on shore, I thought I would sail about a little and see the watery part of the world. (Herman Melville, *Moby Dick*)

- When God began to create the heaven and the earth, the earth was unformed and void, with darkness covering the surface of the deep and a wind from God sweeping over the water—God said, "Let there be light!" and there was light. (Gen 1:1)

The first quote is from the business section of the newspaper. When we read these words, we understand that their purpose is merely to convey some information of current and passing interest. We note that the writer uses a cultural reference to the film *Fast Times at Ridgemont High,* but we do not rush to rewatch the film to understand better the cultural reference. We understand that the passage was written hurriedly, against a deadline, and the reference is merely cute. We also note that the writer uses a metaphor of water supply, but we do not examine the metaphor beyond the information it is intended to convey. This is just a newspaper article.

The second quote is from one of the greatest American novels. Herman Melville is a great author, and we respond to his authorial skill with reverence. When the narrator begins by asking the reader to call him by the name Ishmael, we understand that this request is pregnant with meaning. The author is conveying much more than the name of the fictional narrator. We go to our Bible and study the story of Ishmael, comparing it to the plot of *Moby Dick,* seeking clues. We wonder why the narrator chooses to be *called* Ishmael, as opposed to some other appellation. Is Ishmael his real name? If not, why has he chosen to be called by this name? In college classrooms throughout the country, students who have meditated on this famous opening line debate its meaning with their classmates and their professors. We understand that great authors choose their words carefully and pack them with multiple meanings. There is something here that will reward study and interpretation.

Now let us consider the third text, the opening verse of the Torah. We presume divine authorship, or at least divine inspiration, for these words. If the greatest novel of Herman Melville has more levels of meaning than the hurriedly scribbled words of a newspaper reporter, then we should expect that the words composed over eternity by the Author of everything would be infinitely more profound and full of hidden meaning. As *Moby Dick* rises above the daily paper in terms of carefully chosen and meaningful words and phrases, many times more so does the Bible rise above any other work of literature in the meaning of its diction and syntax, its choices of topic and mode of presentation. College scholars who would give only a glance to the morning paper spend a lifetime analyzing the works of a single author. We examine the Bible endlessly in the confidence that a close examination will always yield new lessons and insights. Ben Bag Bag, a second-century Jewish scholar, said of the Bible, "Turn it over and turn it over again, for everything is in it" (*Pirke Avot* 5:25). No other book is worthier of a close and careful reading.

The greater the work of literature and the greater the skill and wisdom of the author, the more levels of meaning we discover in the work. By analogy, we would not expect the Bible to yield all of her secrets upon a simple reading. We would expect that the Bible calls out to us for minute and careful examination. The Torah will reward her ardent suitors for the attention they lavish upon her. The reward: insight, wisdom, virtue, a path of life consistent with the higher meaning of all that exists, and ultimately, we pray—salvation.

Loose Construction and Strict Construction

All the laws of the United States of America are guided by the Constitution. Our president and other elected officials and our judges swear loyalty to the Constitution. No law may exist that contradicts the meaning and intent of the Constitution. It is the task of the Supreme Court of the United States of America to determine the meaning and intent of the Constitution by analyzing cases appealed to that court because they raise constitutional issues.

Some judges on the Supreme Court are "strict constructionists." These judges try to read the Constitution as narrowly as possible, to get it to mean exactly what it seems to be saying. Strict construction-ists are generally interested in "original intent." They try to interpret the Constitution according to the thoughts and intentions of the Founding Fathers who wrote it, as determined by their other writ-ings, by the plain sense of the words, and by the historical record. Usually, strict constructionists are political conservatives. They often represent the vested interests of the more privileged members of soci-ety, who are the ones most likely to want to keep things just as they used to be.

Some Supreme Court justices are "loose constructionists." They believe that the Constitution must be interpreted according to the changing needs of the age. These judges believe that the meaning of the Constitution goes well beyond the original intent of the writers. Loose constructionists tend to be political liberals. They tend to sup-port the interests of the lower social classes of society. Loose con-structionists have discovered in our Constitution, for example, the obligation of law enforcement officers to read a criminal suspect his rights at the moment he is arrested, the so-called Miranda rights. The loose constructionists know, of course, that the right of the accused to hear these words is not stated in the Constitution, but they would argue that this right is inherent in the Constitution and this right becomes apparent as the meaning of the Constitution unfolds through time.

A person plants an acorn. It grows into an oak tree. What did that person plant, an acorn or an oak tree? The strict constructionist would say the former, the loose constructionist the latter. Neither one would be wrong, but they would draw different conclusions because of their different approach to the facts.

The Torah is the "Constitution" of the Jewish people. During the centuries of the second Jewish state (530 BCE–70 CE), from Ezra to the Roman destruction, the Torah was literally the Constitution of that state. The ancient rabbis served as judges and teachers of Torah law. Some of the rabbis were strict constructionists, and others were loose constructionists. Then as now, the strict constructionists tended to come from and represent the Judean aristocracy. The loose con-structionists represented the larger number of Jewish peasants and

artisans and ordinary folk. In the unfolding of the Jewish interpretation of Torah, the loose constructionists won a victory over the strict
constructionists at every stage along the way.

Pharisees and Sadducees

Shortly after the successful revolt of the Maccabees against the
Syrian Greek Empire (165 BCE), the Jewish religious leadership
divided into sects. The two major sects were the Sadducees and the
Pharisees. The Sadducees represented the views of the ancient hereditary priesthood, including the high priests, who had been ruling the
Jewish people for centuries.[14] The Sadducees were conservative in
their interpretation of Torah. Historians suppose that the Sadducees
were sticking close to the high-priestly traditions that predominated
in the centuries before the Maccabean revolt initiated radical changes
in Judean society and culture. The Pharisees initiated the new
approach to Torah, but in their time they denied this. The Pharisees
claimed that they were following ancient tradition going back to
Moses. They accused the priestly Sadducee party of being the inno-
vators. This claim is to be expected. Every sect in antiquity claimed
for itself the mantle of true and ancient tradition. Despite Pharisaic
claims, the Sadducees, as the party of the priesthood, were the party
most likely to have preserved ancient traditions unchanged.

The Pharisees were the loose constructionists of the late Second
Temple period. The later Rabbis saw the Pharisees as their historical
predecessors. The Rabbis inherited the loose-constructionist methods
of the Pharisees. In their time the Pharisees were distinguished from
the Sadducees by two articles of faith, both of which demonstrate
their loose way of reading the Torah: the doctrine of the bodily resurrection of the dead and the "traditions of the elders" from which
they derived Torah law.

The doctrine of resurrection is a good example of a teaching that
loose constructionists discovered in the Torah though it is never

---

14. The Maccabean revolt led to the replacement of the ancient Zadokite high-
priestly line by the upstart Hasmonean priestly family. The rise of a new, less clearly
legitimate leadership was one of the prerequisites for the breakdown of Jewish leadership into sects and factions.

explicitly mentioned. This doctrine was under constant attack by the strict-constructionist Sadducees, who did not believe in life after death. Rabbi Simai claimed, "It would be possible, if we were wise enough to interpret every single letter in the Torah, to reveal the doctrine of the resurrection of the dead. We are unable to demonstrate this only because of our own deficiency in properly interpreting the Torah" (*Sifre Deuteronomy, Ha'azinu* 306). The positive statements about the Pharisees in the New Testament are largely due to the fact that Christian doctrine depended on the truth of the Pharisaic doctrine of resurrection.[15]

The traditions of the elders, the body of law for which the Pharisees were renowned, were the forerunner of the rabbinic oral Torah. The Pharisees did not think they needed to quote Torah text in order to determine Torah law. They believed that they could teach Torah law by true tradition, that they could quote a law in the name of a revered teacher from whose mouth they had heard it, that we could count on our teachers to faithfully transmit an oral tradition that goes back to the time of Moses. This did not have to mean that every word spoken by the Sages had actually been spoken by Moses. Returning to the analogy above, Moses planted the acorn, and the tradition of the Sages was the oak that grew from it.

In addition to the traditions of their teachers, the Pharisees had another way to determine Torah law. They had rules of logical interpretation by which they could derive new law from the written Torah. The Pharisees used their loose reading of the Torah, along with their line of authority and their rules of interpretation, to apply the Torah to the new conditions of life in the Hellenistic world—the world of Greco-Roman culture. The Torah, written in an ancient Near Eastern culture and canonized in the era of the Persian Empire, now, thanks to the oral Torah, became relevant to life in the Hellenistic world of the eastern Roman Empire.

Rules of logic permitted the derivation of law from the Torah when new situations arose for which no tradition was available. The earliest set of logical rules for interpreting Scripture are ascribed to

---

15. The positive statements of the New Testament are counterbalanced by criticism because after the year 70 the newly empowered Pharisees attempted to suppress other Jewish sects, including the young Christian church.

the great Pharisee leader Hillel. Jewish tradition records the Seven Principles of Scriptural Interpretation of Hillel. Tradition ascribes Thirteen Principles to Rabbi Ishmael, a first-century CE Sage. The thirteen include Hillel's seven. Thirty-four principles are attributed to the second-century Rabbi Yose the Galilean. We note a trend here: in each succeeding century the logical principles for deriving new law from Torah expand. The oral Torah expands in form as it grows in content.[16]

In the traditional printed prayer book, the Thirteen Principles of Rabbi Ishmael are included in the daily morning prayers. This assures that every Jew will read this passage every day and be familiar with the idea of expounding the Torah through logical reasoning. For those who might be interested, these are the Thirteen Principles (*Sifra* 1):[17]

1. Inference from minor to major, or from major to minor (*kal v'homer*).
2. Inference from similarity of phrases in different texts (*gezerah shava*).
3. A comprehensive principle derived from one text or from two related texts (*binyan av*).
4. A general proposition followed by a specifying particular (*k'lal u'perat*).
5. A particular term followed by a general proposition (*perat u'k'lal*).
6. A general law limited by a specific application and then treated again in general terms must be interpreted according to the tenor of the specific limitation.
7. A general proposition requiring a particular or specific term to explain it and, conversely, a particular term requiring a general one to complement it.
8. When a subject included in a general proposition is afterward particularly excepted to give information

---

16. Gentile Greek scholars of the same era used similar rules of logical interpretation to derive relevant lessons from Homer's *Iliad* and *Odyssey*. These classics required interpretation even back then to save them from obscurity and oblivion.

17. Translation based on Morris Silverman, *Weekday Prayer Book* (Hartford, CT: Prayer Book Press, 1956), 110. Note that nos. 6–11 are variants on the principle of general and particular.

concerning it, the exception is made not for that one instance only but is to apply to the general proposition as a whole.

9. Whenever anything is first included in a general proposition and is then excepted to prove another similar proposition, this specifying alleviates and does not aggravate the law's restriction.

10. But when anything is first included in a general proposition and is then excepted to state a case that is not a similar proposition, such specifying alleviates in some respects, and in others aggravates, the law's restriction.

11. Anything included in a general proposition and afterward excepted to determine a new matter cannot be applied to the general proposition unless this be expressly done in the text.

12. An interpretation may be deduced from the context or from what follows after it.

13. Two texts contradict each other until a third text is found that reconciles the contradiction.

Hillel and Shammai

Hillel and Shammai flourished in Judea during the reign of Herod the Great, about 40 BCE to 10 CE. They lived before the title "rabbi" had come into existence and are known simply by the honorific "the Elder." Rabbinic tradition says that Hillel and Shammai ruled the Jewish people in their day, holding the offices respectively of president of the Sanhedrin (nasi) and vice-president of the Sanhedrin (av bet din). Nineteenth-century historians accepted this tradition. They surmised that Hillel and Shammai were the respective heads of the Pharisee and Sadducee parties. These historians, living at the dawn of the great age of democracy, saw the Torah debates of the ancient Jewish Sages as the debates of a Jewish parliamentary democracy. These historical guesses about the identity of Hillel and Shammai have been copied and repeated in later works. As a result, many people today are still learning that Hillel and Shammai were the political leaders of the Pharisee and Sadducee parties in a parliamentary Sanhedrin.

Contemporary historians, however, believe that Hillel and Shammai were both Pharisees. They most likely did not hold high office or wield governing authority in their own time. Their influence was like that of the great Greco-Roman philosophers in the Gentile world. Hillel and Shammai were the founders of the two great schools of Pharisaic thought and Torah interpretation. The Pharisees who were followers of Hillel and Shammai became the rulers of the Jewish people a generation later, after the Romans destroyed the Temple in 70 CE. Some historians believe that Hillel and Shammai preserved the Pharisees through the difficult years of Herod's reign by drawing them out of politics and focusing instead on the development of their program for Judaism, their particular vision of how to live the life of Torah.

Shammai was the strict constructionist of the Pharisees whereas Hillel was the loose constructionist. They founded two schools, called Beit Shammai, the "house" or "school" of Shammai, and Beit Hillel.

The Mishnah contains many disagreements between Beit Hillel and Beit Shammai. In almost every instance, the Hillelites give a lenient interpretation to Torah law, and the Shammaites give a stringent interpretation. The Mishnah records only nine disagreements between Hillel and Shammai themselves. Most of the conflicts are between their schools in a later generation. Tradition says that the conflict between the two schools increased as time went by.

One disagreement between the schools concerns Hannukah candles. According to Beit Shammai, we kindle eight lights on the first night, seven on the second night, and so on until on the eighth and final night we light one candle. Beit Hillel says that we light one candle on the first night, two on the second night, and so on until we light eight candles on the eighth and final night of Hannukah. The reasoning of Beit Hillel is that "in matters of holiness we increase, not decrease." As anyone who has celebrated Hannukah knows, Jews today follow Beit Hillel.

Whenever there is a disagreement between the teachings of Beit Hillel and Beit Shammai, Jewish law follows Beit Hillel. This may be because the Hillelites predominated in the rabbinic Sanhedrin at Yavneh. The Hillelites may have outnumbered the Shammaites. The historian Jacob Neusner believes, on the basis of a careful analysis of historical layers in the Mishnah text, that the Shammaites predominated at first in the rabbinic Sanhedrin but when the Hillelites later took control, they suppressed the legal rulings of Beit Shammai. Rabbi Akiva was a disciple of the school of Hillel. His influence may have been what sealed the victory of the Hillelites when Rabbi Judah the Prince composed the Mishnah.

Whatever the cause, Jewish law from the second century on follows the teachings of Hillel, the liberal interpreter, the loose constructionist, the one who nearly always gives the more lenient interpretation to the law. A later generation of Sages said of Hillel and Shammai, "The words of this one and the words of that one are both the *word of the living God*. But the law follows Hillel because he was kindly and modest" (Talmud *Hagigah* 10a).

Multiple Truths

Eilu v'eilu divrei Elohim hayyim—"These and those are the word of the living God." From the debates of Hillel and Shammai, the Jews learned and accepted as a general principle that two contradictory readings of Scripture can both, paradoxically, be true. Nevertheless, the law follows the majority vote of the Sages. The divine word can be paradoxical, but the divine law must be directive. The minority opinion is true as Torah, but we do not live by it. Whenever two great Jewish scholars disagree on a point of Torah and their disagreement is not over egos or personal politics but over the honest attempt to discern the will of God, Jews say of these scholars, as they say of Hillel and Shammai, "The words of this one and the words of that one are both the word of the living God."

Rabbi Akiva and Rabbi Ishmael

By around the year 100 CE, the scholars of Beit Hillel had won the day, and the two schools of Hillel and Shammai faded into history. Then, in the council of the seventy-one rabbis who sat in the Sanhedrin, a new split developed between liberals and conservatives, loose constructionists and strict constructionists. Among the Rabbis, Rabbi Akiva represented the loose constructionists, and Rabbi Ishmael represented the strict constructionists.

Akiva rose to prominence from the lower classes. In early adulthood he was an illiterate shepherd, but in midlife he began to study. He became the universally acknowledged greatest Rabbi of his time. More Talmudic laws are quoted in the name of Akiva than in the name of any other Rabbi. Akiva's intellectual opponent in the Sanhedrin was Rabbi Ishmael, an aristocrat from a priestly family. Rabbi Akiva was a populist. He understood the life and the mind-set of the common folk. He used his loose way of reading Torah to adjust the law to the needs of the people. He wanted the law to be livable, an acceptable and welcome burden.

Despite their greatness, Rabbis Akiva and Ishmael came to a terrible end. They were arrested by the Romans during the Jewish rebellion led by Simon Bar Kochba in 132–135 CE, in the reign of the Roman emperor Hadrian. They were tortured to death in the arena in Antioch. Jews retell the heart-rending story of their martyrdom every year in the liturgy of Yom Kippur.

Akiva's and Ishmael's Way of Reading Torah

Rabbi Akiva taught that there is no extraneous word in the entire Torah. Every repetition, every phrase or letter that is, strictly speaking, extraneous, was placed in the Torah by God to invite an interpretation. Nearly every sentence in the entire Bible begins with an extraneous "and." The grammatical reason for this is not known to us, nor was it known in Greco-Roman times. Readers of the old King James Bible are familiar with this affectation of biblical Hebrew, since every "and" was translated into English in that translation.

The Hebrew language, unlike English, contains a preposition for the direct object of a sentence. This preposition, *et*, is not translatable. It merely indicates which noun is the object, and not the subject, of the sentence's verb. In English we might say, "The dog bit the boy." In Hebrew one would say, "The dog bit *et* the boy," indicating that it was the dog that did the biting and the boy that was bitten.

In the beginning God created et *the heavens and* et *the earth* (Gen. 1:1).

Rabbi Ishmael asked Rabbi Akiva: Since you have studied twenty-two years with Nahum of Gamzo, (you teach the principle that) every "thus" (akh) and every "only" (rak) in the Torah comes to limit something, while every "et" and every "also" (gam) in the Torah comes to add something. What, then, is the meaning of the two examples of "et" in this verse?

He replied: Had the Torah been written without the "et", heretics might claim that the heavens and the earth were also creative powers [that is, they could be included in the subject of the sentence along with God.] . . . Here is another explanation: "et the heavens" is given to include the sun and moon, the stars and planets. Et the earth is to include trees and plants and the Garden of Eden. (Midrash *Genesis Rabba* 1:14; also in variant form in Babylonian Talmud *Hagigah* 12a)

In this text we see the interpretive method of Rabbi Akiva. If every extraneous particle in the Torah comes to add something, what is the something that it adds? Truly, whatever Rabbi Akiva wishes to say that it adds.[18] It is a very open system of interpretation. Seven of the twenty-two letters of the Hebrew alphabet are written in the manuscript Torah scroll with little decorations on top, called crowns. Later tradition claims that God placed the crowns on the letters just so that someday Rabbi Akiva could interpret them to make new Torah laws.

Rabbi Ishmael took a commonsense approach to the reading of the Torah. His view was that "the Torah speaks in human language." When human beings speak, they repeat themselves. They generate awkward usages and grammatical oddities. People use lots of extraneous words. When the Torah is repetitive or awkward, Rabbi Akiva seeks a hidden message, but Rabbi Ishmael sees only normal speech patterns. Rabbi Ishmael believed in the divine origins of the Torah. But he took the point of view that when God speaks to human beings, God chooses to use normative human patterns of speech. Rabbi

---

18. In our example from *Genesis Rabba*, the first explanation for the *et* raised objections, and so a second rationale is presented.

Ishmael takes the Torah pretty much for what it seems to be saying. He is a narrow constructionist.

Jewish tradition shows a preference for the view of Rabbi Akiva over that of Rabbi Ishmael. In the Torah there is an emphatic form of the verb in which the verb is repeated twice, first in infinitive form and then in conjugated form. In Hebrew poetry every idea is stated in couplets, first in one set of words and then in the next line with a different set of words. Following the principles of Rabbi Akiva, the Jewish Sages made new lessons and newly revised rules for living out of all of this scriptural word repetition.

Rabbinites and Karaites

The Babylonian Talmud is the fulfillment of the oral Torah. Once the Talmud became normative for Jews all over the world, a faction arose who objected to the great liberties that rabbinic tradition takes with the Torah. These sectarians called themselves Karaites, which means "Scripturalists." The Karaites rejected the entire rabbinic tradition of biblical interpretation, the whole oral Torah. They attempted to live literally by the word of the Torah. For example, the Karaites did not light Sabbath candles, nor did they allow the hearth fire to burn on its own as talmudic law permits. The Karaites sat in the cold and dark on Sabbath eve.

The Karaite movement arrived on the historical scene in ninth-century Babylon. The Karaites rebelled against the authority of the gaonim, the heads of the Babylonian academies. It is interesting to speculate on the prehistory of Karaism. Did the Karaites arise as a new movement, in reaction to current Jewish political rivalries in Babylon? Or does Karaism reflect a quiet undercurrent of biblical literalism that went underground for nearly a thousand years, from the decline of the Sadducees, only to resurface in the Middle Ages? The Karaites are the ultimate strict constructionists.

For a few centuries, Karaites and Rabbinites conducted a fierce intellectual battle as they sought to convince the Jewish masses of the rightness of their opinions. The Rabbinite leaders defended the Talmud and the concept of oral Torah, and the Karaites supported their more-or-less literal reading of the Bible.[19] Ultimately the Rabbinites triumphed and the Karaite movement shrank into obscurity. After this controversy died down, virtually all Jews recognized the sovereignty of the Talmud in questions of Jewish law and practice until the rise of Reform Judaism in the nineteenth century.

A Karaite Response to the "Messianic Verses"

In the sixteenth century, Isaac of Troki, a Lithuanian Karaite, wrote a Jewish response to every verse in the Bible that Christians interpret christologically. He was defending Judaism against Christian missionaries who used these verses to try to convert Jews by convincing them that Christians have the proper way of reading the Bible. Isaac of Troki's book is entitled *Hizzuk Emunah*, "Faith Strengthened." In the nineteenth century, an English Jew translated the book into English, but he did not publish it at first for fear of offending Christians at a time when the Jews of England were seeking civil rights. The work has since been published in America.[20]

Trude Weiss-Rosmarin points out that Isaac of Troki's Karaism gave him a unique qualification to engage in Jewish-Christian disputation. He based his responses completely within the Tanakh, the common heritage of Jews and Christians. A Rabbinite Jew would have resorted to quoting from Talmud and Midrash, which Christians do not acknowledge as Sacred Scripture. Isaac of Troki's arguments would probably not convince a faithful Christian, but that is beside the point. His arguments were accepted by Jews, who felt confirmed in the scriptural interpretations of their own faith tradition thanks to his book.

I politely decline here to engage in Jewish-Christian debate over the meaning of specific biblical verses, as such debate is not in the modern spirit of mutual acceptance. Also, modern historical study of the Bible has made the traditional arguments for both sides of the

---

19: Although biblical literalists claim to reject all interpretation, in the eyes of their opponents their literalism seems to be another form of interpretation. This is an argument that the Rabbinites made against the Karaites and that modern-day religious liberals make against fundamentalists.

20. Isaac of Troki, *Faith Strengthened*, trans. Moses Mocatta (New York: Ktav, 1970).

debate into a moot point. My self-appointed task is limited to explaining—to Christians, Jews, and whoever may be curious—how Jewish people interpret the Scriptures for themselves. For those who wish to know how Jews interpret biblical verses in which Christians discover Christ, Isaac of Troki's *Faith Strengthened* is a good reference work.

Rabbinic Deconstruction of the Torah:
600,000 Messages

We have seen that from Beit Hillel to Rabbi Akiva to the Rabbinites, the loose constructionists prevailed in Judaism throughout late antiquity and into the Middle Ages. The Rabbis taught as a principle of Torah interpretation that "there is no before and after in the Torah." That is, every verse in the Torah stands as an independent message from God, unrelated to its context in the five books. Even a single phrase or word or letter may be interpreted independently.

We recall that in Roman Judea, from 70 CE to about 400 CE, the central institution of rabbinic rule was the Sanhedrin, the high court of seventy-one Rabbis. The Rabbis taught that whenever there is a disagreement over the proper interpretation of Torah law, the law follows the majority vote of the scholars in the Sanhedrin. They justified this democratic viewpoint with a phrase from the book of Exodus, *ahare rabim l'hatot*—"After the majority must one incline" (Exod 23:2). In its wider context this phrase says something quite different: "After the majority one must incline *not* in the doing of evil." That is, one may not do wrong just because everyone else is doing it. The Sages did not feel they were doing any violence to the text of the Torah in pulling this phrase out of context to teach a lesson in the civics of democracy. As they saw it, God gave the Torah to be deconstructed. God intended the minilessons that can be drawn from Torah phrases and words when they stand independently.

According to the story in the book of Exodus, 600,000 Israelites stood at the foot of Mount Sinai to hear God reveal the Torah. The rabbinic Sages taught that there are 600,000 letters in the Torah, one for each Israelite who stood at the foot of Mount Sinai. (There are 5,845 verses in the Torah.) Just as each human being has an existence, a soul, an integrity of his or her own, so each and every letter of the Torah has an integrity of its own.

This legend reveals how the Jews see the Torah. The Torah is not a continuous narrative that one reads as one would read a novel. The Torah is a collection of individual verses, words, and letters. Each one has a message of its own. Every verse in the Torah has a soul as complex as the soul of a human being. One has to become acquainted with it on its own terms if one would get to know it and learn from it.

The Seventy Faces of Torah

We have learned that a verse in the Torah may serve as a locus classicus for an important theme in Jewish teaching. The verse Numbers 7:19 is the location for the rabbinic discussion on the unity of the oral Torah with the written Torah—tradition and Scripture. The context of this verse is the description of the gifts that the princes of the twelve Israelite tribes presented for the dedication of the worship tabernacle in the desert. As the author of our *Zohar* passage at the opening of this chapter might say, of what interest is it to us how much gold and silver and other precious items were used in the construction of an ancient tent that no longer exists? We must look to the inner meaning to find a reason that this passage is in the Torah. The verse reads:

> He presented as his offering: one silver dish weighing 130 shekels and one silver chalice of 70 shekels by the sanctuary weight, both of them filled with fine flour and mingled with oil.

The midrash Numbers Rabba here interprets this verse as follows (loosely translated for clarity):

> The prince of the tribe of Issachar gave a gift which symbolizes the Torah, because the tribe of Issachar had a particular love for Torah....
>
> The silver dish weighed 130 shekels, equal to the number of all the books in the written and oral Torah, to teach you that they are all part of the divine revelation....

*The chalice weighed 70 shekels. The chalice is used to hold wine. The Torah is likened to wine, which refreshes the spirit. The chalice was given the number 70 to teach us that **there are seventy faces to the Torah**....*

The fine flour symbolizes that the Torah is all complementary, no part contradicting another part. The oil symbolizes good deeds, for the study of Torah must be accompanied by good deeds which are in accordance with what has been learned.

Shiv'im panim laTorah—"There are seventy faces to the Torah." Every single verse in the Torah yields seventy different interpretations. Each interpretation teaches something new and different. They may even contradict one another, like the teachings of Hillel and Shammai. Yet each one of the seventy interpretations is the true word of God.

The image of the seventy faces may be taken from the imagery of the jeweler's art. Each side of a cut gem is called a facet, a little face. A light sparkles within every fine gemstone. We know that this light is a reflection, but the ancients thought of the light in a gemstone as originating from within the stone. The beauty and fascination of a fine gem is that the one stone sparkles in so many different ways. We know that there is a single light within the stone, but we see that light differently depending upon which face we gaze upon. One diamond is like seventy different diamonds as we turn it, but of course it is one. In the same way there is only one God, whose light shines forth from every verse in the Torah. We see that light differently depending upon how we interpret the verse. The unitary light of God's Holy Spirit is fully revealed in many sparkles and flashes, as we seek God through a multitude of interpretations on every single verse of Scripture.

Chapter Four

Jewish Education and Torah

Rabbi Judah ben Tema used to say: At five one is ready for the study of Scripture, at ten years for the Mishnah, at thirteen one is responsible to observe the commandments, at fifteen for Talmud, at eighteen for marriage, at twenty to earn a living. (Pirke Avot 5:24)

These are the commandments for which one receives a reward both in this life and the next life: honoring one's father and mother, performing deeds of loving-kindness, attending the house of study morning and evening, hospitality to wayfarers, visiting the sick, dowering the bride, attending a funeral and consoling the bereaved, devotion in prayer, and making peace where there is strife; but the study of Torah is equal to them all.

(Mishnah Peah 1, recited in the daily morning prayers)

Literacy in the Ancient World

In ancient society literacy was limited. Those who were able to read and write guarded and limited access to this skill, which was a source of power and authority. In societies that developed a written language, literacy was limited to the temple priesthood and the government civil servants—the scribes. Royals and nobles did not bother learning to read. When a king needed to hear a document, his scribes read it to him; when he needed to compose a document, he dictated to the scribes.

Temple priests kept the myths of the gods and of the origins of the world and the nation in written form. They read the appropriate myths to the people on the various national festivals when people gathered at the temples. The priests were revered as the keepers of knowledge and tradition. The scribes who served in the king's employ kept track of mundane matters that required documentation, such as treaties and deeds and tax records. The scribes glorified the ruler by recording his great deeds in the annals.

Many societies had complex writing systems that took years of study to master. Children of priests and scribes were schooled from early childhood so that they would be prepared to inherit their task and its attendant social status from their fathers. The Phoenicians, neighbors of the Israelites, invented an alphabet that reduced the symbols for written language from thousands to about two dozen. This could have led to a democratization and expansion of literacy, but it did not.

The Pharisees and Rabbis Expand Literacy

When it came to literacy, the people of biblical Israel were like all of their neighbors. The priests kept the sacred traditions. Ezra and his group, who edited and published the Torah, were priests. So were most of the literary prophets. The prophet Jeremiah had a personal scribe, Baruch ben Neria, to whom he dictated his words.

We do not know much about secular scribes in the biblical era. Ezra held the title "scribe," but he was also a priest. The party of the Pharisees who gained prominence after the revolt of the Maccabees probably arose among professional scribes. One piece of evidence for this is that in the Christian Gospels Pharisees are associated with scribes. Rabbinic traditions portray the Pharisees serving as government officials and court judges, which would be consistent with their role as literate laypersons.

The Pharisees and their successors, the Rabbis, evolved into an ideologically motivated party that challenged the priesthood for leadership of the Jewish people. The Pharisees held as an ideal the priesthood of all Israel, which made the professional hereditary priests of Judaism extraneous. This ideology is reflected in the constant conflict between the Pharisees and the priestly Sadducees, until the ultimate victory of the Pharisees. Once Pharisaic doctrine became the standard for all Jews, the separate sect of Pharisees disappeared.

The Pharisees took seriously the Torah's promise that Israel would be "a kingdom of priests and a holy nation" (Exod 19:6). To fulfill this injunction, the Pharisees behaved like priests. They could not eat the tithes that were reserved for the priesthood, but they could be exceedingly careful about tithing. (A tithe is a tenth part of a farmer's produce that is donated to the priests as a holy contribution.) The Pharisees formed brotherhoods that only ate food known to be properly tithed. The New Testament condemns the Pharisees for being overly concerned with tithing. It is typical, when one sect in a religion is in conflict with another, to challenge the other not on its essential doctrines but on its rites of identification. True to the historical pattern, the early Christians criticized the Pharisees for tithing. It's not that the Pharisees were concerned only with the externals of tithing and ritual purity law but rather that the observance of these rules identified one as a Pharisee. Behind these observances lay a noble purpose, to live as a priest of God.

Literacy and knowledge of sacred writings were a distinguishing feature of a priest, in Judaism as in all ancient societies. To be a kingdom of priests, every Jew had to be literate, and so the Pharisees established an ideal of universal male literacy for the Jews. What began as an ideal was then put into practice, as the Pharisees were able to influence the social structure of Jewish communities. During the Greco-Roman era the Jews established elementary schools in every Jewish community. The goal was to enable every Jewish male to read the Torah. One Jewish tradition ascribes the establishment of the schools to Simon bar Shetach in the first century BCE. It probably took some time for the Pharisaic goal of universal education of male children to become a reality. Sooner or later it did happen, nearly two millennia before any other society on earth established schools for universal literacy. That goal was next fulfilled in America in the mid–nineteenth century after the passage of child labor laws removed young children from the workplace.

The Rabbinic Torah Curriculum

The ancient Rabbis established a curriculum that was so suitable for its purpose that it continued virtually unchanged for nearly two thousand years, from Roman times until the eighteenth-century European Enlightenment. This curriculum was encoded in Jewish law and reiterated in Jewish legal texts throughout ancient and medieval times. Every father was responsible for the elementary education of his son. The community obligated him to pay tuition, but free school was provided for the children of the poor. Higher education was supported through community funds. In antiquity the most distinguished rabbis established schools for the training of rabbinic disciples. Some rabbis charged tuition, but others did not. Rabbi Akiva, who remembered the difficulty of acquiring an education in his early years of poverty, held his academy in the open under a fig tree. Jewish elementary school came to be called *heder* (*HAY-dur*), the one-room schoolhouse. The school for higher education leading to rabbinic ordination was called a *yeshiva* (*y'-SHEE-vah*), meaning a place where one "sits down" in order to learn at the feet of the wise.

As soon as a boy could speak, his father taught him two Torah verses. First, "The Torah commanded us by Moses is the heritage of the house of Jacob." Then, "Hear, O Israel, the Lord is our God, the Lord is One." The ordering of these two verses is probably intentional. Monotheism, the faith in one God expressed in the "Hear, O Israel," is important in Judaism, but according to Judaism, one acquires salvation through observance of the commandments in the Torah, not through faith. First the Jewish child learns to revere the Torah with its commandments. He learns that Torah is the special heritage of the Jewish people, which makes them unique. Only then does the child learn the unity of God.

At the age of five or six, as soon as the child is ready, his father introduces him to the heder. There he sits and learns the alphabet. Then he learns the Torah and all the books of the Bible, reading them through until he knows them almost by heart. The curriculum begins not with the creation story in Genesis but rather with the book of Leviticus. The ancient Rabbis said, "Since the child is pure, let him learn the laws of ritual purity." This cute saying probably disguises a more serious agenda. The Rabbis wanted the children to think of Torah not as a book of ancient stories but as a book of rules for living. Torah is the source of the 613 mitzvot, the "commandments" by which a Jew lives his life and guides his every deed. The book of

Leviticus, as a book of laws and not stories, gave the child the right Jewish idea about what is important in the Torah.[21]

By the age of ten the child had learned the Torah and the twenty-four books of the Bible. At this point religious education ended for most children, who went to work in their father's profession. Promising students, and the children of the wealthy, continued their education to study the Mishnah. At the age of fifteen the best students were selected to go on to the study of Talmud. In the time of Rabbi Judah ben Tema, who is quoted at the beginning of this chapter, "Talmud" meant the laws of logical interpretation by which law is derived from Scripture. After the publication of the Babylonian Talmud, "Talmud" meant to study this book, a task that could easily occupy a lifetime. Those who mastered Talmud were ordained as rabbis to function as leaders and teachers in the Jewish community. A rabbi, from the seventh to the eighteenth century, was defined as a person sufficiently learned in Torah to be able to derive new law from the Talmud.

Torah Service as Reenactment
of the Revelation at Mount Sinai

A Jew who would attend synagogue worship services for a year on all Sabbaths and holidays would hear a lot of Scripture recited aloud. The entire Torah is read in the weekly allotments of the *parashat ha-shavua'*, the weekly portion.[22] On every festival and holiday relevant selections from the Torah are recited. To accompany every weekly and festival Torah reading, there is a reading from the books of the Prophets. This reading is called the haftarah, "conclusion," because it concludes the scriptural lesson for the day. The haftarah serves to acquaint the listener with a large and representative selection from the books of the Prophets. Many psalms are included

---

21. By contrast, American Protestant Sunday school puts the emphasis on Bible "stories," which teach the lessons of faith. American Jewish religious school, following this model, initiates young children into Judaism through stories from the Bible, Midrash, and Talmud.

22. In modern times most Reform and many Conservative congregations read only a selection from the weekly portion, primarily to shorten the worship service.

in the liturgy. On the festival of Purim the book of Esther is recited in public, and on the Fast of the ninth of Av the book of Lamentations is read aloud. On the Sabbaths during Passover and Sukkot it is Jewish custom to read Song of Songs and Ecclesiastes, respectively, while on Shavuot Jews read the book of Ruth.

The public reading of Scripture provides a passing knowledge of Torah and the other books of the Bible. The public reading must be supplemented with formal and informal study. In ancient times the public reading of the Torah helped to familiarize the Jewish public with their Scriptures, but this need was superseded by the introduction of universal schooling and literacy.

One function of the public reading of the Torah is to ritually reenact God's saving act of giving the Torah to Israel. When the time comes in the service for the reading of Scripture, the worship leaders remove the handwritten scroll of the Torah from the ark (this sacred closet for Torah scrolls sits at the front and center of every synagogue) and parade the scroll around the synagogue with great ceremony. The congregation members demonstrate reverence toward the divine word by the respect they grant to the scroll. Then the scroll is unrolled on the bimah, the reading table, and the reader recites from the weekly or festival portion assigned to that day. Before and after the reading a member of the congregation receives the honor of being called to the bimah to recite the blessings over the reading of Scripture. The reading of the day is divided into sections—three sections for a weekday, more for a festival or holy day, up to seven sections on a Sabbath. A blessing over the recitation of Torah is said before and after each section. As the congregation members observe the reader reciting from the scroll, it is as if they are standing in the place of their ancestors at the foot of Mount Sinai, a people newly released from slavery in Egypt by the power of their God, listening to the divine revelation of Torah to Moses and the Israelite assembly.

Jews revere Torah, with its commandments, as the means to personal, national, and universal salvation. In that sense, the scriptural reading in the Sabbath morning service is not really equivalent to the scriptural reading in Christian worship. The Torah service is more parallel to the communion service, a ritual enactment of God's act of saving grace.

Informal Jewish Education: Shul and *Bet Midrash*

Only the fortunate few were qualified to master Talmud and attain rabbinic ordination, but the Jewish masses were not deprived of continuing Jewish education once their formal schooling in heder came to an end. There were plenty of opportunities for lifelong learning. When the synagogue was not in use for prayer, it doubled as a place for informal study. Thus the Yiddish term for a synagogue is *shul*—from the same root as the English *school*. Every Jewish community had at least one *bet midrash*, a library where Jewish men could gather in small groups for informal Torah study. Unlike the hushed American library, the *bet midrash* was a noisy place where the men engaged in lively dialogue, even excited shouting, as they attempted to unveil the seventy faces of the Torah.

Although women were excluded from the formal educational system, Jewish women were naturally eager to participate in the Jewish virtue of learning Torah. Some Jewish fathers educated their daughters at home. Rashi's daughters were famously brilliant. In Europe girls were often taught to read and write Yiddish, the Jewish dialect of Medieval German. Men and sometimes women wrote learned books in Yiddish especially for women. The most famous of these books, *Tsena U'Rena* ("Go Forth and See"), contains translations of portions of the Torah, laws and rules for the conduct of a kosher Jewish household, and wise advice for the pious Jewish wife.

The Torah was read aloud in the synagogue in the hearing of the gathered community. There is a Torah portion, called the *parashat hashavua'*, "portion of the week," for every Sabbath in the Jewish year. In the ancient land of Israel the portions were short, and it took about three and a half years to read through the five books of the Torah. Every community followed its own pace. In Babylon they read the Torah annually, beginning and ending in the fall on the Jewish festival of Shemini Atzeret. The Babylonian custom became normative. Every Jew hears the Torah recited aloud annually in the synagogue. As one cannot learn Torah from the public reading alone, tradition held that every Jewish man should read the coming week's Torah portion to himself three times in the week, once in Hebrew and twice in the Aramaic translation. In this way a man would be intimately familiar with the Torah all of his days.

Since adult males came to know the Torah by heart, Jewish legal codifiers recommended that once a man had mastered the written Torah, he might better spend his study time focusing on the oral Torah. Talmud study was the most revered form of Jewish learning, but Talmud was too difficult for those without higher education. In the Middle Ages scholars wrote anthologies of oral Torah for Jewish men to study in their groups in the *bet midrash*. The *Ein Yaakov*, "Well of Jacob," contains the legends of the Talmud, which are easier to learn than the legal portions. The *Menorat HaMaor*, "Candelabrum of Light," of Rabbi Isaac Arama contains moral lessons from the Talmud, the midrash, and Jewish law codes. Men could study these works in small groups on a Sabbath afternoon or weekday evening and get a good general Jewish education while they got a feel for what their rabbis and scholars were studying in the Talmud and technical legal literature.

After Rashi published his commentary to the Torah in the twelfth century, it became popular to study Rashi's comments on the weekly Torah portion. Rashi is challenging enough for the greatest scholar, but the common man could also glean much wisdom from Rashi. Since Rashi often quotes the midrash and Talmud, the ordinary Jew could get a feel for the entire Torah, written and oral, by studying the *parashat hashavua'* with Rashi's commentary.

After the publication of the Talmud, a prohibition arose against studying Mishnah without the Gemara or some kind of commentary. Learning Mishnah by itself could lead one in a direction not countenanced by later Jewish tradition. Many rabbinic contracts in the medieval and premodern period called for the community rabbi to teach a lesson on one paragraph of the Mishnah every morning after morning prayers, before the men went off to work. The learned rabbi could present the Mishnah within the context of his broad rabbinic knowledge. From the rabbi's little daily lectures the men of the community would grow in familiarity with the teachings of oral Torah.

Oral versus Written Torah

The Jewish educational system created a prejudice favoring study of the oral Torah over the written Torah. This prejudice grew and increased over time. The fact that every man studied the Bible in his childhood led to the conception that the Bible is child's play. Men took knowledge of the Bible for granted while they yearned for the status that came with knowledge of the Talmud and Jewish law.

In the Middle Ages the Jews divided into two primary ethnic divisions that persist to this day. In the twelfth century the major centers of world Jewish population were *Ashkenaz* (France and Germany, the Rhineland) in the Christian world and *Sepharad* (Spain) in the Islamic world. Jews are considered Ashkenazic if their ancestors lived among Christians and Sephardic if their ancestors lived among Muslims. Significant social and cultural differences arose between Sephardic and Ashkenazic Jews. These differences were reflected in the distinct formal and informal educational systems that arose in the two communities.[23]

Sephardic Jews retained a greater respect for the intellectual challenges presented by the written Torah. In the Ashkenazic world of Christian Europe, the preference for Talmud study became more and more pronounced, with correspondingly less emphasis on Bible study.

Ashkenazic Jewry and Universal Study

Christian law prohibited Jews from living on the land, and so Jews turned from farming toward the urban occupations of artisan, shopkeeper, trader, and banker. These occupations afforded Ashkenazic Jews the opportunity to earn enough income to meet the needs of their households with a minimal amount of labor. Excess free time was used not to earn more income but to learn more Torah. A poor man who worked hard all day had only a brief hour every evening for study in the *bet midrash*. A man who could earn his living in half a day was free to go to the *bet midrash* in the afternoon and spend three or four hours a day in study.

---

23. After the Spanish expulsion of Jews in 1492, many Sephardic Jews ended up in Christian lands. Most Dutch Jews and many Jews in England, Italy, and southern France were Sephardic. Most American Jews are Ashkenazic, though there are significant Sephardic communities in Seattle, Long Island, Los Angeles, and Deal, New Jersey. In Israel there are approximately equal numbers of Sephardic and Ashkenazic Jews. Because of Ashkenazic domination of the yeshivot in Israel and America, many Orthodox Sephardic Jews are taking on Ashkenazic customs and attitudes.

From the fifteenth century on, the center of Ashkenazic Jewry moved eastward, from France and Germany into Poland. Polish Jewry built their entire society around the study of Talmud. In many Polish communities, they skipped the study of Bible in elementary school. Children of five years would be immersed directly in the deep sea of Talmud study. The Polish legal codifiers rationalized that since the Talmud contains many quotes from the Bible and Mishnah as well as the Gemara, one could fulfil the ancient mandate to learn Bible, Mishnah, and Talmud from the Babylonian Talmud alone. They punned that the Talmud of Babel (Babylon) was so named because it contained a babble of the written and oral Torahs.[24] This preference for Talmud study over Bible study persists to this day in the yeshivot of the Orthodox world in America and Israel, which are based on the Polish-Lithuanian model.[25]

Growing anti-Semitism in modern Poland led to increasing Jewish unemployment and impoverishment in the decades leading up to the Holocaust. Widespread Jewish unemployment did not lead to a street corner society in the Jewish ghetto. The men put their enforced leisure to better use, hanging out in the *bet midrash,* learning an extra page of the Talmud.

Even people in the lower social classes who held low-paying, rough-and-tumble, mind-numbing jobs revered learning and participated as they were able. In his post-Holocaust paean to the lost world of East European Jewry, *The Earth Is the Lord's,* Rabbi Abraham Joshua Heschel writes:

> "Once I noticed" writes a Christian scholar, who visited the city of Warsaw during the First World War, "a great many coaches on a parking-place but no drivers in sight.

---

24. A Jewish joke: Someone shows a yeshiva student a copy of the Bible. Amazed, he later tells his friends, "Guess what—someone collected all the 'verses' in the Talmud and put them together into a single book!"

25. As demanding as the Polish Jewish educational system was upon young minds, the intellectual training produced scholars of extraordinary brilliance. Many young men who grew up in a Polish yeshiva but then went off to a German university earned their doctorates in just a few years and went on to great scholarly achievements. The high proportion of Jews who have won Nobel prizes in the sciences is largely due to the intellectualizing influence of the Polish yeshiva.

In my own country I would have known where to look for
them. A young Jewish boy showed me the way: in a court-
yard, on the second floor, was the *shtibl* (Hasidic synagogue) of the Jewish drivers. It consisted of two rooms:
one filled with Talmud-volumes, the other a room for
prayer. All the drivers were engaged in fervent study and
religious discussion.... It was then that I found out and
became convinced that all professions, the bakers, the
butchers, the shoemakers, etc., have their own *shtibl* in the
Jewish district; and every free moment which can be taken
off from their work is given to the study of Torah. And
when they get together in intimate groups, one urges the
other: *Sog mir a shtickl Torah*—Tell me a little Torah."

An old book saved from the countless libraries recently
burned in Europe, now at the Yivo Library in New York,
bears the stamp, "The Society of Wood-Choppers for the
Study of Mishnah in Berditchev."[26]

In America it is usual to think that intellectual conversation belongs to
high culture, reserved for the highly educated few. Intellectualism is as
likely to be mocked as admired. College education is too often thought
of as a ticket of admission to a good job and a higher salary, rather than
as training to prepare a person for a fuller life of the mind. In the Jewish
shtetl, by contrast, even those who worked in the most physical, low-
paid, and unskilled professions eagerly approached the intellectual
challenges of Torah study. Learning was universally admired. Not only
the Jewish cab drivers but even the woodchoppers, the lowest of all
professions, engaged in higher learning in their spare moments.

Torah Learning in the Sephardic World

In the Islamic world the Jews filled a fuller social pyramid.
Among Sephardic Jews there was a greater gap between the intellectual aristocracy and the minimally educated masses than among the

---

26. Abraham Joshua Heschel, *The Earth Is the Lord's* (Cleveland, New York,
Philadelphia: Meridian & J.P.S., 1963), 46–47.

Ashkenazic Jews of Eastern Europe. Yet the Sephardim also revered learning at every level of society. My friend Ibrahim Nabatian tells of his grandfather, a Persian Jew who lived in a small village an hour's drive north of Teheran. He was a merchant who made his living from what he could buy and sell off the back of a donkey. Yet he was also sufficiently educated to function as the rabbi of his Jewish community.

The Sephardic intelligentsia of medieval Spain developed a step-by-step, progressive elementary curriculum that approaches modern ideas of education. Children were taught Hebrew language and grammar before moving on to the study of biblical literature, whereas in the Ashkenazic world children learned Hebrew word for word, directly from the Torah. The Sephardim excelled in Talmud study, but their interest also extended to biblical commentary, codification of Jewish law, mysticism, and ethical treatises. Sephardic scholars wrote systematic philosophical treatises on Judaism in the Middle Ages. The Sephardic interest in philosophical ethics and mysticism influenced Ashkenazic Jewry, first in the mystical Hasidic revivalist movement of the eighteenth century and in nineteenth-century movements for educational reform aimed at broadening the curriculum of Jewish education. Also, the great Sephardic law codes became normative for Orthodox Ashkenazic Jews after being amended by commentaries providing for the differences in Ashkenazic legal custom. The law code *Shulchan Aruch*, "The Set Table," of Joseph Caro, a Spanish Jew living in Safed in Galilee in the sixteenth century, became the basis for Jewish Orthodoxy up to this very day. The Polish rabbi Moses Isserles wrote *The Tablecloth*, explaining where Ashkenazic law and custom differ from Sephardic Jewish law. All rabbinic legal decisions of the past few centuries are indexed according to the topical outline of the *Shulchan Aruch*.

Modernity Diminishes Torah Learning

Judaism evolved as a religion in which learning is the primary virtue. An unlearned Christian or Muslim could still be devout, but Hillel's ancient maxim that "the ignorant cannot be pious" (*Pirke Avot* 2:6) became a self-fulfilling prophecy in Jewish society. The Rabbis formed Judaism into a religion in which Jewish faith and virtue are based upon knowledge of the sacred texts that unfold the meaning of the divine commandments. The continuity of Judaism came to depend upon the Jewish educational system.

Modernity created a disruption in Jewish education from which the Jewish people have yet to recover. The grant of civil rights and citizenship to Jews in modern nation-states brought Jews into intimate contact with the broad society around them. The need to acculturate and adjust to new economic opportunities in science, technology, law, and medicine meant that Jews could no longer focus all of their intellectual energy on sacred subjects. Many Jews in Western countries attended public schools where Jewish subjects were not taught at all. In Eastern Europe Jews kept their own schools into the twentieth century, but many Jewish parents who wanted their children to succeed in the secular world sent them to modern schools where only a portion of the students' time was spent on Torah-oriented learning. Even the most rigidly antimodernist Jews found it necessary to educate their children to survive in the new society, which meant time taken away from Talmud study for practical subjects.

As the ancient Jewish educational system began to break down, the old yeshiva system was best preserved in the country of Lithuania, between northeastern Poland and Russia. In the towns around the city of Vilna, great yeshivot arose. As a concession to modernity, these yeshivot allowed the study of subjects such as mathematics, which did not undermine traditional piety. They broadened the Jewish curriculum to include the great ethical writings of the medieval Sephardic scholars. Despite these changes, they retained their emphasis on mastery of the Talmud. The Lithuanian-style yeshiva is the model for most modern-day yeshivot in Israel and in America. In fact, Orthodox Jews in the early twenty-first century can boast that there are more students learning in Lithuanian-style yeshivot today than there were during Vilna's heyday in the late nineteenth century.

For all of its importance, the traditional yeshiva reaches only a small minority of Jewish students in the modern age. A great many Jews grow up and go out into the world without the educational preparation needed to live a meaningful Jewish life. This lack of education has accelerated the rate of secularization and assimilation among modern-day Jews.

Jewish Learning in America

Until the mid–nineteenth century there were no rabbis at all in the United States. The state of Jewish learning was abysmal in early America, and very few Jewish pioneers were successful in transmitting Judaism to the next generation. The thriving Jewish day school and yeshiva movement in America, which still touches only a small percentage of young Jews, did not get off the ground until after the Second World War. Unlike Catholic immigrants to America, who established their own educational system, Jews availed themselves of the public schools. This pattern helped Jews adjust quickly to life in America. But it led to a secularization of the Jewish passion for learning, which is revealed in high college attendance figures for Jews. This trend did not bode well for Jewish knowledge of Torah, as Jewish children sat passively through public-school Christmas holiday programs while learning little about their own cultural heritage.

Most Jewish children in America, from the mid–nineteenth century to the present day, learn what they know of Torah and Judaism from supplemental schools. These schools followed two patterns that have subsequently merged, the Sunday school and the afternoon Hebrew school.

The Sunday School

The American Jewish Sunday school was the creation of Rebecca Graetz, a daughter of German Jewish immigrants to Philadelphia. She was the model for the heroine Rebecca in Sir Walter Scott's novel *Ivanhoe*. Graetz based her curriculum on the pattern of American Protestant Sunday schools. The children learned Bible stories and a Jewish catechism. In the 1880s the Reform movement of Judaism came into being with the establishment of the Union of American Hebrew Congregations (UAHC). The UAHC has a depart-

ment of education that worked to improve the curriculum of the
Jewish Sunday school, developing and publishing textbooks. The
emphasis until the 1970s was on customs and holidays, Jewish history, and stories from the Bible, Talmud, and Midrash. This curriculum, with its focus on stories and customs, reflected an intentional
turning away from laws and commandments as the definition of
Jewish living. The vision of what sort of Jew this new curriculum
would generate was never well articulated. Jewish leaders were themselves unsure of how to be modern, American, and Jewish.

Hebrew School

Eastern European immigrants to America established after-
school Hebrew schools based upon the model of the Polish heder.
Unfortunately, the absence of systematic instructional methods in the
old Polish system made it difficult to teach children within the
American context of limited instructional hours and diminished student motivation. In Eastern Europe, children learned to read Hebrew
with comprehension, translating from the Bible one word at a time.
In America, children came to Hebrew school already tired from a day
of public school. The students wanted to be outside playing baseball
like their non-Jewish classmates. The Hebrew school succeeded for
the most part only in training children to recite the prayer book by
rote, without comprehending the Hebrew, in preparation for a bar
mitzvah observance at the age of thirteen. Few Hebrew school children continued their Jewish education beyond bar mitzvah.

Jewish Education in America Today

In our times the Sunday school and the Hebrew school have
been integrated. Most American Jewish children who receive some
religious education go to supplemental school for two to six hours a
week, on some combination of weekday afternoons and Sabbath or
Sunday morning. Many Jewish children also get a more intensive
Jewish learning and living experience at summer camps that include
an educational component. The UAHC and its Conservative Jewish

counterpart, the United Synagogue, strive to develop curricula better suited to the practice of Judaism in America and to the learning styles of American children. Recent textbook publications demonstrate a commitment to Jewish religious faith and spirituality, to the practice of Judaism as a way of life, and to the ethical virtues of the commandments. Also, in response to the serious diminution of Jewish knowledge and practice, contemporary religious-school textbooks begin at the beginning, teaching elementary aspects of Judaism that can no longer be taken for granted, such as how to observe the Sabbath in the home on a Friday evening.

The traditionalist and modernist wings of Judaism could probably improve the state of Torah knowledge by learning from one another. Traditional Jews master large amounts of text from the Talmud and other classic rabbinic writings, but they engage in little analysis. There is a tendency in the traditionalist Jewish world to respect volume of knowledge over content. The good and the bad of this approach are both represented by the "daily *daf*," the popular method of reading one's way through the Talmud in seven years by covering a page, or *daf*, every day regardless of randomness of subject matter.

The modernist wing of Judaism has developed an incremental curriculum and a topical approach to learning. Unfortunately, most modernist Jews have not studied enough of the texts of Judaism to give substance to their learning. Outside Orthodoxy, *Talmud* is a mere word to most Jews. Many modernist Jews are not equipped to handle the literary genres of Talmud, Midrash, and commentary. Talmud is neither poetry nor prose, neither fiction nor nonfiction. A public-school education does not prepare one to swim in the sea of Talmud study.

Many of the Jewish writers and intellectuals who opened up the entry of Jews into modern society were horrified when they observed the relative ignorance of the next generation. To remedy this, many of these pioneers turned, in their later years, to creating anthologies that would reintroduce the classics of Jewish sacred literature to a new generation. For example, the story writer Micah Josef Berditchevsky wrote *Mimekor Yisrael*, a compendium of Jewish folktales. The famous poet Haim Nachaim Bialik composed *Sefer HaAggadah*, the *Book of Legends*, a collection of inspiring scriptural interpretations and historical tales from the Talmud and midrashic works. The essayist Ahad Ha'am created the first Jewish encyclopedia. Despite such works, knowledge of the Bible and of the works of oral Torah has diminished in each modern generation.

Institutions such as the Shalom Hartman Institute in Jerusalem and the Leo Baeck School in Haifa are working to bridge the gap between traditionalists and modernists, to join modern methods of study to a serious encounter with sacred Jewish texts. May their labors bear fruit.

Chapter Five

Levels of Torah

Our masters taught: Four men entered the "Garden" [literally, PaRDeS, root of the English word Paradise]. *They were Ben Azzai, Ben Zoma, Aher[27] (Elisha ben Abuya), and Rabbi Akiva.... Ben Azzai cast a look and died: of him Scripture says, "Precious in the sight of the Lord is the death of His saints" (Ps 116:15). Ben Zoma looked and became demented; of him Scripture says, "Have you found honey? Eat only so much as you can digest, lest you be over-stuffed and vomit it" (Prov 25:16). Aher cut off the young shoots [that is, he became a heretic and misled the young with his teachings]. Rabbi Akiva entered in peace and departed in peace.*

(Babylonian Talmud, hagigah 14b)

"My teaching shall drop as the rain" (Deut 32:2). Even as one rain falling on various trees gives to each a special savor in keeping with its species—to the vine the savor of grapes, to the olive tree the savor of olives, to the fig tree the savor of figs—so the words of Torah are one, yet within them are Scripture and Mishnah, Halakhot and Aggadot. (Sifre Deuteronomy 206)

Rabbi Abbahu and Rabbi Hiyya bar Abba happened to come to a certain place where R. Abbahu lectured on Aggadah while R. Hiyya bar Abba lectured on Halakhah. All the people left Rabbi Hiyya bar Abba and went to hear Rabbi Abbahu, so that R. Hiyya bar Abba was greatly upset. To comfort him, R. Abbahu said: May I tell you a parable to illustrate what each of us represents? Two men came to a certain city, one to sell precious stones and pearls, and the other to sell different kinds of [cheap] notions. To whom will people run? Will they not run to him who sells the different kinds of notions?

(Babylonian Talmud, sotah 40a)

---

27. Aher means "other." Because he departed from the parth of Torah, Jewish tradition calls Elisha ben Abuyah by this nickname.

Halakah and Aggadah

We have learned that the Jewish term *Torah* applies to much more than just the written words of the first five books of Scripture. All the books of the written and oral tradition, and all conversations and further writings based on these books with holy intention, are included in Torah. The words and writings of Torah fall into one of two categories. They are either halakah or aggadah.

- Halakah is Jewish law. Aggadah is everything else, all of the nonlegal teachings of Judaism. Halakah includes rules and directions for righteous living. Aggadah is the language of faith, hope, and comfort.

- Halakah literally means "the way." Judaism is a behavioristic religion. Jewish is as Jewish does. Halakah teaches a Jew the way to live—the way of righteousness by which a person, like Father Abraham, can walk before God and be perfect.

- Aggadah literally means "the telling." Aggadah is Judaism as story, parable, legend. Underlying every act of obedience to the sacred law is the faith that there is a God who commands the law, who is pleased by our obedience, and who grants reward for righteousness. As the tradition teaches, "There is no commandment unless there is One who commands" *(Sifra)*. The aggadah teaches faith in God. Judaism is not, for the most part, a religion of systematic theology. The aggadah provides, in piecemeal fashion, the theological underpinning of the Jewish way of life.

Halakah

Halakah exists on three levels. The first level of the halakah is that of **mitzvah,** a commandment of God. A mitzvah is an explicit statement in the written Torah. Jewish tradition says that there are 613 mitzvot (plural of mitzvah) in the Torah; 613 is a symbolic number. There are 365 instances of "thou shalt not," one for each day of the year. Every day says, "Please do not sully me with sins." There are 248 instances of "thou shalt," one for each bone in the human body (according to the ancient count). Every limb of the body cries out, "Please use me for the performance of a mitzvah."

The second level of the halakah is specific laws and rules. While the totality of the Jewish way of life is called "the" halakah, each specific Jewish law is called "a" **halakah**. For example, it is a mitzvah in the Torah that one should refrain from work on the Sabbath. The halakah lists thirty-nine activities whose performance on the Sabbath would constitute work.

Halakot (plural of halakah) are based upon the Mishnah and Gemara of the Babylonian Talmud and secondarily upon other rabbinic books of halakic literature (halakic midrash, the Tosefta, the Jerusalem Talmud). After the publication of the Talmud, great rabbis wrote legal opinions on specific halakot. This halakic legal literature is called *responsa*. The halakic literature is continually evolving. For a new legal ruling to be accepted as true Torah, the rabbinic judge must demonstrate that it is grounded in the Talmud. There is no need to demonstrate a basis in the written Torah, the Bible.

Occasionally a great Sage would try to simplify Jewish observance by summarizing all of Jewish law in a code organized by topic. The greatest codes are the Mishneh Torah of Maimonides (thirteenth century), the Arba Turim of Jacob ben Asher (fifteenth century), and the Shulchan Aruch of Joseph Caro (sixteenth century). The law codes never achieved the status of the Talmud itself, which remains the ultimate authority. Jewish law was never fully codified; there are always a variety of opinions on any given topic.

The Mishnah and the Talmud are not books of laws and rules. They are collections of rabbinic discussions about divine laws and rules. The tradition preserves a variety of opinions on every matter of the law. "Both these and these are the word of the living God."

Even though the mitzvot in the Torah are the basis for all halakah, halakic literature does not center around discussion of biblical verses. Midrash, the literature of verse-by-verse interpretation of the Bible, is almost entirely aggadah. The books of halakic midrash—*Mekilta, Sifra,* and *Sifre*—are secondary works created to prove that the laws in the Mishnah could be derived from Scripture if we had to demonstrate this fact.

The halakic discussions of the Rabbis are organized around rabbinic traditions rather than scriptural verses. The topical organization of the Mishnah provides the basic framework, though the discussions in the Talmud usually range far from the original topic, in the manner of human conversation, so that any topic could arise anywhere in the Talmud.

In the legal literature of contemporary American law, cases are argued and decisions are rendered through reference to other cases and seldom through direct reference to the statutes passed by legislatures. Similarly, the halakah is determined through precedent and tradition, with little direct reference to the mitzvot in the Torah.

The third level of the halakah, after mitzvah and halakah, is the level of **minhag**, "custom." A social custom that becomes widespread and is observed over a period of time acquires the force of law. For example, in ancient times, when the Jewish calendar was uncertain, Jewish communities outside the land of Israel observed an extra day of every holiday just to be sure they hit the right day. The publication of the calendar in the fourth century obviated the need for the extra day, but since it had already been observed for centuries, the rabbis of the time decreed that this was a minhag that had acquired the force of law. Except for Reform Jews, Jews outside Israel observe the extra day even in our times, sixteen centuries after the publication of the written calendar. The social customs of the Jewish people are a source of Torah; custom is one way that the voice of the living God continues to speak in the life of the Jewish people.

Aggadah

The most common format for aggadah is **midrash**, the symbolic interpretation of a biblical verse or phrase. Because most midrash is aggadic and most aggadah is midrash, Jews often use the terms *midrash* and *aggadah* interchangeably, as if they mean the same thing. Technically, though, there are other forms of aggadah that are not midrashic interpretations of Scripture. Although the Talmud is essentially a halakic work, about a third of the Talmud is aggadah. Besides

midrash, the aggadic portions of the Talmud include proverbs, para-
bles, and tales of the Sages.

The lives of the great rabbis, their deeds and their responses to
great historical events, are teachings of Torah. After the close of the
Bible, the Jews ceased to write systematic history, but the tales of the
Sages and the lineage of masters and disciples constitute a form of
historical memory, albeit in legendary form and presented in dis-
jointed bits and pieces. More significant than the mere recalling of
historical facts, the tales of the Sages show us by example how to live
the life of Torah. When a rabbinic disciple adopted a master, he not
only learned oral Torah from the master's mouth; he imitated the master's way of life. The tales of the Sages teach one how the Torah comes
to life as it is internalized by great personalities.

Although the Rabbis did not use the midrash form for the development of halakah, midrash continued to evolve in the oral traditions
of synagogue preaching. Eventually the greatest midrash interpretations of Scripture were put into writing. The great age of midrash literature is the fourth through the ninth centuries. In that era,
particularly in the land of Israel, oral traditions were gathered and
published in many classic midrashic texts. One can fill a small book-
case with midrashic works that have come down to us from this time
period.

Around the year 1500, Rabbi Jacob ibn Habib selected and published just the aggadic portions of the Talmud with a commentary
designed to promote simple faith and religious purity. This work,
titled *Ein Yaakov*, was republished again and again. It became one of
the most popular Jewish works for study in the *bet midrash*. Halakic
study requires mental training and intense focus, which are reserved
for dedicated rabbis. Aggadah is entertaining, educational, and inspirational. So common Jews found great solace in the study of talmudic aggadah in the *Ein Yaakov*.

The Superiority of Halakah

In ancient times different rabbis specialized in different realms
of Torah teaching. Some focused on practical laws and rules, others
on more theoretical aspects of Torah. Some were experts in halakah,

others in aggadah. Over the course of time, halakic scholarship acquired a higher status than knowledge of midrash and aggadah. Aggadah was popular among the common folk. Much of the aggadic literature developed out of popular preaching. Halakah, however, was the province of the intellectual aristocracy. Halakah seemed to have more significance, since it is the practice of Judaism, observance of the mitzvot, that acquires for a Jew ultimate entry into the world-to-come. Aggadah seemed like the appetizer, but halakah was the main course. Aggadah inspired and comforted, but halakah led to right-eousness and salvation.

The preference for halakah over aggadah was exacerbated by the shift of rabbinic authority from the land of Israel to Babylon in late antiquity. All of our great works of midrash were composed in the land of Israel, but the greatest Talmud derives from Babylon. The Babylonian rabbis seemed to have a decided preference for halakah.

The intellectual demands of halakic study served to raise its stature. Although aggadah draws on the poetic imagination and is very intellectually engaging, no realm of Jewish study places a higher demand on the pure intelligence than the study of halakah. The great-est Jewish minds were drawn to the challenge of becoming a scholar of halakah.

The aggadah received a further blow in the thirteenth century. Nahmanides (1194–1270, not to be confused with Maimonides), the great Spanish rabbi from Gerona (in Catalonia, near Barcelona), was forced into a public interfaith debate with a Christian scholar, Pablo Christiani (1263). Previous disputations centered around the inter-pretation of messianic biblical verses, as we have discussed above in relation to the Karaites and Isaac Troki. The Jews had ready responses to the customary Christian arguments, but Pablo Christiani had a new tactic. A scholarly convert from Judaism, Pablo had a list of midrash texts that seemed to confirm a Christian reading of Scripture. Backed into a corner by Pablo's unanticipated arguments, Nahmanides responded by denigrating the midrash. Midrash, he claimed, was merely inspirational literature, lacking authority and full of meaningless contradictions and inconsistencies. Any midrash that disagreed with mainstream Jewish teaching could be dismissed out of hand. After the disputation Nahmanides found himself in an uncom-fortable position among the Christians and his own Jewish commu-

nity, and he retired to the land of Israel. Unfortunately for the repu-
tation of aggadah, Nahmanides' negative claims about the midrash
outlasted the Spanish persecutions. After the time of Nahmanides,
Jewish scholars generally became dismissive of the great body of
midrashic literature, which fell into neglect. Many of the midrash
texts known to us today had to be recovered by modern scholars
from obscure manuscripts hidden away in old libraries.

Some modernist Jews have attempted to revive the aggadah as a
source of authentic Judaism not based on laws and rules that modernists are reluctant to observe. In non-Orthodox rabbinical seminar-
ies, courses on midrash are among the most popular, easily rivaling
courses in Talmud. One great modern advocate of aggadah was the
national poet of the Zionist movement, Haim Nachman Bialik
(1873–1934). In his later years, Bialik worked with his scholarly friend,
Ravnitsky, to create a compendium of aggadah suitable for the modern
taste and translated when necessary from Aramaic or from archaic
Hebrew terminology into modern Hebrew. This book, *Sefer
HaAggadah,* has been translated and published in English as *The Book
of Legends.*[28] In Hebrew or in English, it is an excellent resource for anyone who desires an introduction to the aggadah.

Halakah and *Torah Lishmah*

As we have noted above, the Mishnah and Talmud are not
books of law but of discussions about the law. For every legal topic,
the Mishnah and Talmud provide a variety of rabbinic opinions. The
Talmud yields actual laws and rules only through the later interpretations of the rabbinic scholars.

One might study the Talmud in order to have a basis for knowledge of the practical halakah, the laws and rules of Jewish living as
unfolded in the law codes and late rabbinic writings. A rabbi who
functions within the community must know the practical halakot relevant to his function. In traditional Jewish society there were a number of professions that required rabbinic training. A *shoket,* a ritual

---

28. Haim Nachman Bialik, *The Book of Legends,* trans. William Braude (New
York: Schocken Books, 1992).

slaughterer, must know the halakah about kosher animals. A *dayyan*, a communal judge, must know Jewish civil and criminal law. A neighborhood rabbi must know the halakah of family purity and the rules of daily life and observance, for the sake of the local Jews who seek his guidance.[29]

Although practical halakah is respected, there is a higher level of halakic study. This is *Torah lishmah*, literally, "Torah for its own sake." At this level one studies the halakic opinions of the Sages not in order to learn the law but just for the sake of engaging in the study of Torah. One tries to understand the logic of the Sages and the reasons for their disagreements, without regard to the practical application of the halakah. Some study groups in the *bet midrash* would make a point of studying only the sections of the law that were no longer current, such as those governing agricultural offerings that apply only in the land of Israel, so that their Torah study would be *lishmah*, purely for its own sake.

Although *Torah lishmah* is without pragmatic application, it is not without consequence. By learning *Torah lishmah*, one enters into intimate communion with God. One is symbolically dipped in the mikvah, the baptism of Torah that purifies the soul. *Torah lishmah* makes the soul worthy of salvation and brings closer the redemption of all the world.

PaRDeS, Walking in the Garden of Torah

The Talmud tells a story about Rabbi Akiva and three of his disciples who took a strange journey into the *pardes*, a Persian word for "garden." One disciple died, one went insane, and one lost his faith. Only Rabbi Akiva entered and exited the *pardes* in wholeness. For centuries Jews wondered, "What is this *pardes* that is so rewarding and yet so dangerous?" Recent discoveries of obscure texts have taught us that Rabbi Akiva and his disciples were engaging in mystical speculation of the type called *hekhalot*—palaces. The *hekhalot*

---

29. The Nobel Prize–winning author Isaac Bashevis Singer was the son of a neighborhood rabbi in Warsaw. In Singer's memoir, *In My Father's Court*, one can read how a traditional rabbi functioned as an arbiter of Jewish law and practice.

mystic goes on a spirit journey to visit the divine palaces in the seven levels of heaven. The talmudic tale warns us that spiritual attainment is dangerous unless one is firmly grounded. Because Rabbi Akiva was knowledgeable and faithful in the observance of halakah, he was able to journey safely in the heavenly realms.[30]

Previous generations did not know the original symbolism of the *pardes* in the talmudic tale and speculated about the symbolism of the garden. In the Middle Ages, mystically minded Jews began to apply the term *pardes* to the four levels on which one can read the Torah for meaning.[31] The four levels correspond to the four Hebrew consonants in the word *PaRDeS*:

> P = *peshat* (sounds similar to *fur shot*), the literal or simple meaning. Halakah and actual historical events are aspects of peshat.

> R = *remez,* the allegorical meaning according to the way philosophers read the Scriptures, in which every story is an allegory for a philosophical truth.

> D = *derash* (rhymes with *wash*), the rabbinic way of interpreting scriptural verses through midrash.

> S = *sod* (rhymes with *load*), the secret, mystical message of the Scriptures, which is available only to the initiated adept. This level is revealed through study of the Kabbalah, medieval Jewish mysticism. The *Holy Zohar* reveals Torah on this level.

The four levels are stepped, each one considered superior to the level that precedes it. The mystics put their speculation at the highest level of Torah, above practical law, philosophical study, and the sermon lessons of ordinary simple faith. At the level of *sod* the letters of the Torah unite to form the true name of God. Thus the Torah is more than just a revelation from God; at the level of *sod* the Torah is the

---

30. This is a lesson that is equally relevant to our own times, when many people wish to become spiritually enlightened without doing their homework first and getting their life in order.

31. Historians speculate that the concept of these four levels was borrowed from Christian scholars in Spain.

self-revelation of God. One who knows how to read the Torah in this manner comes to a direct meeting with God. By speculating that the ultimate level of *pardes* is mystical speculation, the medieval mystics brought the talmudic story of the *pardes* close to its original sense.

In order to understand better the four levels of Torah, let us examine one text from the Torah in all four ways. We choose for our text the mysterious "law of the red cow," which describes the ritual of purification for one who has become ritually impure through contact with the dead. A person who is ritually impure cannot attend sacrifices nor eat sacrificial food until he or she is purified:

> *The Lord spoke to Moses and Aaron saying: This is the ritual law that YHWH has commanded: Instruct the Israelite people to bring you a red cow without blemish, in which there is no defect and on which no yoke has been laid. You shall give it to Eleazar the priest. It shall be taken outside the camp and slaughtered in his presence. Eleazar the priest shall take some of its blood with his finger and sprinkle it seven times toward the front of the Tent of Meeting. The cow shall be burned in his sight—its hide, flesh and blood shall be burned, its dung included—and the priest shall take cedar wood, hyssop, and crimson stuff, and throw them into the fire consuming the cow. The priest shall wash his garments and bathe his body in water; after that the priest may re-enter the camp, but he shall be impure until evening. He who performed the burning shall also wash his garments in water, bathe his body in water, and be impure until evening. A man who is ritually pure shall gather up the ashes of the cow and deposit them outside the camp in a pure place, to be kept for sprinkling water for the whole Israelite community. It is for purification. . . . One who touches the corpse of a human being shall be impure for seven days. He shall purify himself with it on the third day and on the seventh day, and then be pure. . . . Whoever touches the water of sprinkling shall be impure until evening.* (Num 19:1–22)

Curiously, the sprinkling water makes impure one who is pure, and makes pure one who is impure.

Peshat

Despite the step-by-step instructions in the Torah, we do not have adequate information on how to perform the ritual of preparing the sprinkling water. Tradition claims that the ceremony was performed only seven times in all history. To make matters more complicated, Jewish legal tradition says that the term "without blemish" refers not to the cow itself (sacrificial animals all had to be unblemished) but to the cow's color. The cow had to be entirely red. The halakah says that "even two hairs that are not red disqualify the cow from use for this purpose." No entirely red cow has ever been seen, and attempts to breed one in contemporary Israel have not been successful.

The *peshat* of this chapter is not so simple as it may seem. At a glance we may say that the procedure is very simple. Human remains are the most potent form of ritual impurity. One who comes into contact with them requires a full week to return to the status of purity. Twice during that week the person must be sprinkled with the water of purification. In principle this is just another of many rules of purification, just like the rule that requires a knife that has touched unkosher meat to be stuck in the earth up to its hilt for three days, and then it is pure once again.

The details of the preparation of the red cow and the sprinkling ceremony complicate the matter. The Talmud states (*Yoma* 67b) that this is one of the mitzvot over which Satan and the Gentile nations mock Israel, saying, "What is this ceremony and what does it accomplish?" (That is, this rule causes Jews to doubt the divine origins of the Torah, and it exposes Judaism to mockery from non-Jews.) Because of this, says Rashi in his commentary, the Torah calls this mitzvah a *hoke*. This Hebrew word means a law or rule that is a decree of the ruler. It is a law because the king says so, not because there is any rationale or sense to it. The divine King has decreed the ceremony of the red cow and the water for sprinkling, and therefore "you are not permitted to speculate on the matter," says Rashi.

A contemporary Jewish modernist would give a historical and anthropological explanation for the ritual of the red cow and the sprinkling of water. Some of the texts in the Torah reflect prehistoric memories. The Torah's historical myth is that pure monotheistic religion arose full-blown from the time of Moses at Mount Sinai, but there are many texts in the Bible suggesting that the pure monotheism we find in Second Temple Judaism arose only gradually from the mythology and magic of primitive Israelite religion, which resembled in many ways the magical pagan practices of Israel's neighbors.

Prehistoric man feared and revered the spirits of the dead. The ancestors could intercede for one in the world beyond, but the dead could also return to do harm to the living, as in modern-day horror movies. The ceremony of the red cow may have its origins in ancient rites designed to placate the spirits of the dead and shield the living from their envy. The ancient prophets and scribes who copied this still-living ceremony into the Torah text may have been conscious of the pagan origins of this rite. They may have been anxious to disguise the original nature of the rite. This may account for the mysterious gaps, the lack of rationale, and the fact that this ritual is described as a *hoke*, an inexplicable divine decree.

Historical study thus illustrates the prehistoric roots of Israelite religion in paganism and magic, and it chronicles the struggle of the prophets and biblical scribes to purify Israelite religion according to their transcendent notion of a single deity who rules the world with justice, not by whim. We get a glimpse of the evolution of Western religion from spirit worship to paganism to monotheism. The historical analysis transmits a religious message of its own even if the methodology of text analysis derives from the secular social sciences.

Remez

Remez is the allegorical interpretation of the philosophers. When the ancient and medieval philosophers of religion confront a text like this, nonrational and devoid of philosophical content, they read it as an allegory of a philosophical lesson. The philosophers were the rational scientists of their day. They perceived the world as modern scientists do, as the result of a chain of material cause and effect. The philosophers object to the concept of magic. They give rational explanations for the biblical miracles, denying the existence of the supernatural.

Premodern philosophers understood that, as men of wisdom and discernment, they were "lonely at the top" of the social heap.

They understood that their insights were not welcomed by the unlearned masses, who preferred the certainties of simple piety. The philosophers assumed that God used allegory in giving the Torah to Moses in order to teach the people philosophical lessons that were above their comprehension. In this way God turned Israel into a nation of philosophers, even without their conscious acquiescence.

Anyone who touches human bones or graves must undergo this uncomfortable sprinkling ritual of purification. This should be enough to discourage people from using relics and human remains for the performance of magic or for other undignified purposes that resemble the pagan religions. God has given this rule to wean Israel away from consulting the spirits of the dead and from other practices that are not consistent with pure monotheism.

Also, the philosophers note, the water of purification is made up of ashes and water, the matter of which the human body is made. One who undergoes this ritual is reminded of the passing nature of the mortal body as opposed to the eternal nature of the human spirit, which consists of wind and fire. At a time of death and loss, the ritual of purification reminds us to focus our life on matters of eternal significance that strengthen the soul—matters such as philosophical knowledge and right living.

Derash

The midrash relates the following aggadah about Rabban Yohanan ben Zakkai:

> *A certain heathen came to Rabban Yohanan ben Zakkai and said to him, "Your ceremony of the red cow looks like witchcraft to me."*
>
> *Rabban Yohanan answered him, "Have you ever seen a man possessed by a demon being exorcised?"*
>
> *"Yes," replied the heathen.*
>
> *"What did they do to him?"*
>
> *"We burn herbs beneath him and he breathes the smoke, and we throw water on him, and then the demon goes away."*

> "Well," said Yohanan, "the spirit of defilement is the same as
> your demon. We sprinkle the waters of purification, and it goes
> away."
>
> The heathen went away, content with this answer. When he
> had gone, Rabban Yohanan's disciples said to him, "You pushed
> him away with a broom straw, but what will you say to us?"
>
> Yohanan replied, "By your life, the dead do not really defile
> and the water does not actually purify. Nevertheless, this is a
> decree laid down by God and we must observe it." (Tanhuma
> Buber, Hukkat #26, Numbers Rabbah 19:8)

One may derive a number of valuable lessons from this story. An
Orthodox Jew may learn that reasons for commandments are only for
the faithless. The faithful are content to observe the mitzvot, confident that God has a purpose even if it is beyond our comprehension.
A modernist Jew might learn from this story that some religious
observances do not relate to objective reality but to psychological
states. Sometimes people must perform religious rites not to change
the world but to change themselves. Some rites are not sacramental
but are nevertheless worthwhile because they enhance our relationship with God. If Rabban Yohanan were speaking to his disciples in
modern terminology, he might say that there is no actual status of
defilement but people feel defiled by contact with the dead. They
need a ritual after an intimate encounter with death to help them feel
that they have rejoined the world of the living.

Sod

Hasidism arose in the Ukraine around the year 1750. This
charismatic sect of Judaism, which thrives to this day, was the last
great movement of Judaism to base its doctrines upon the mystical
system of the Kabbalah. Hasidic Jews gathered around a spiritual
leader and guide, whom they addressed as rebbe, not to be confused
with rabbi. Many rebbes were Talmud scholars, but their status as
rebbe depended upon their intimacy with the divine rather than their
Torah knowledge. The Hasidic rebbe David of Tolnye interpreted the
law of the red cow thus:

What does the Torah have to do with a cow? It raises this subject only to teach us that, just as the cow defiles and makes pure [as we have noted, the sprinkling water purifies one who is defiled, and defiles one who is pure], so too does the Torah both defile and make pure. We have learned in the Mishnah (Yadaim 3:5) that "the Scriptures render the hands impure."[32] ...A person who has learned much Torah and then became arrogant, this is the person who has been defiled by contact with the Torah. If a person has learned much Torah and still does not think too much of himself, the Torah likens him to water which is the source of purification. This person will be cleansed from all his impurities.[33]

The mystic denigrates the *peshat* of the text. Why would the Blessed Holy One be concerned with cows? That would be beneath God's glory. The text is symbolic of the relationship between the human soul and the Torah. The two are really one. The real human being is not the material person but the spirit that comes from God. Similarly, the true Torah is not the written words but the divine spirit that breathes within the Torah. The bodily Jew and the scroll of the Torah are both earthly expressions of the divine spirit. The human soul is divine and pure, and yet the human being is capable of doing evil. Similarly, the pure spirit of Torah can be used for good or ill as it enters into a person. This is the solution to the paradox that the waters of sprinkling can both purify and defile. The paradox is symbolic of the Torah, which purifies a person if it makes him humble, but paradoxically the pure Torah distances a person from God if it makes him arrogant. Good and evil are always in the power of human choice. Even Torah, the most divine thing on earth, when placed into human hands, can be used for good or ill.

The mystic desires to live his life in an *unio mystica*, constant sacred communion with God, which is called in Hebrew *d'vay-koot*.

---

32. The term in the Mishnah for a book of Holy Scripture is that it is a book that "renders the hands impure." Whoever touches a scriptural book is in a state of ritual impurity for the remainder of the day, which prevents that person from eating sacrificial offerings. This is a mysterious ruling, but we note that in practice it would prevent the priests from studying Scripture, leaving that role to their rivals, the rabbis.

33. Quoted in Lawrence Kushner and Kerry Olitzky, *Sparks beneath the Surface* (Northvale, NJ: J. Aronson, 1993), 192.

In order to invite God's presence into his soul, the mystic must make room for God by suppressing his own ego. As one Hasidic rebbe said, "Where is God? Wherever we let God in." Arrogance drives God away, but a humble soul invites God's presence. To be learned and yet humble, that is the goal. Here is the mystical lesson of the waters of purification.

Chapter Six

Midrash

"Zee meed-rash eez so bee-u-tee-ful. You must pr-r-r-obe zee meed-rash."
(often said by Prof. Dr. Eugene Mihaly,
Hebrew Union College, Cincinnati, in class)

Introduction to the Midrash

Eugene Mihaly (died 2002) taught midrash to generations of rabbinical students at Hebrew Union College in Cincinnati. An immigrant from Hungary, he actually bore a slight resemblance to the Hungarian "Count" of Sesame Street. He encouraged his students to appreciate the wisdom, the cleverness, and the intellectual exuberance of midrash. Among his disciples was my own midrash teacher, Professor Dr. Norman Cohen. Norman helped us to see that when we learn midrash, we are learning our own lives even as we study the word of God.

Midrash is the interpretation of biblical verses in the manner of the rabbinic Sages of Roman and Byzantine times. Most midrash works on two levels at once. On the first level, the Sages note a grammatical complexity or unusual word usage in the Hebrew text of the Bible. The midrashic interpretation explains or validates the unusual or incongruous Hebrew. On the second level, the grammatical opening allows the Sages to raise a Jewish theme relating to the context of a scriptural verse, phrase, or word. In our survey of the midrash, we will give two explanations for each text. The first will explain to the English reader the problem or issue in the Hebrew text. The second explanation will explore the symbolic language of the midrash and the Torah lesson that the Sages wish to teach. Our translations will not be literal but phrased to give the English reader a sense of the flow and meaning of the Hebrew original.

There are many published books of midrash. We will not attempt here to review them all. Our intention is to enable the reader to develop a positive appreciation of midrash as a literary genre of Scripture interpretation. Midrash arose out of popular preaching as the Torah was read and interpreted to the public by Sages. Midrash is theologically profound, but it speaks to the concerns of the ordinary individual. The wit of the preacher in interpreting the Scriptures, the fun of midrash, is evident in the written record. In ancient times midrash was the public entertainment of the Jewish masses, even as it was their way of learning how to live faithfully by the Torah. We too will, it is hoped, enjoy the midrash as we learn from it.

The True Shepherd of Israel

> **Torah:** God spoke to Moses and Aaron in the land of Egypt, saying...(Exod 12:1)

> **Midrash:** I hear the Torah saying that the divine speech went to both Moses and Aaron.
>
> But when the Torah says: "On the day that God spoke to Moses in the land of Egypt..." (Exod 6:28)
>
> I learn that the divine word went to Moses and not to Aaron.
>
> If so, then why does our text say "Moses and Aaron"?
>
> To teach you that both Moses and Aaron were worthy to receive revelation.
>
> Why, then, did God not speak to Aaron as well?
>
> For the sake of the honor of Moses.
>
> God excluded Aaron from hearing revelation except in three instances when the situation required his presence. (*Mekilta, Bo, Pischa* 1)

> **Grammatical Commentary:** We call the Torah the Five Books of Moses. Numerous paragraphs in the Torah begin with the phrase "God spoke to Moses, saying...." How do we explain the incongruous presence of Aaron, the brother of Moses, alongside Moses in this passage?

Lesson Commentary: The rabbinic form of Judaism, which arose after the destruction of the Second Temple in 70 CE, is a different religion from that described in the Bible. The biblical religion is a religion of sacrifices presided over by priests. The rabbinic religion is a religion of worship, study, and mitzvot, presided over by wise men called rabbis. For centuries, in the last years of the Second Temple and in the years that followed the destruction, priests and rabbis were rivals for leadership of the Jewish people. That struggle is reflected in the conflicts between priestly Sadducees and rabbinic Pharisees recorded in the Talmud and in the New Testament. The rabbis ultimately prevailed, and the rabbinic Talmud established the agenda for Judaism ever after. The priests (*cohen,* pl. *cohanim*) became irrelevant as Jewish leaders.

The rabbis discovered in the Torah a precedent for the preference of rabbis over priests. Aaron, the brother of Moses, was the first high priest of the Jewish religion. Moses, the greatest Jewish leader, has no formal title. In rabbinic lore Moses becomes *Moshe Rabbenu*—our Rabbi Moses. Though the appellation is anachronistic, it fits well. Moses, like the later rabbis, is a teacher of Torah, a judge and guide for his people, a transmitter of mitzvot.

The superiority of Moses to Aaron symbolizes the superiority of rabbis to priests as Jewish leaders. We respect Aaron, but only Moses is a conduit for revelation. We learn from this midrash that we respect priests, but we learn how to live the life of Torah only from rabbis.

A Lesson for Religious Leaders

Torah: The above discussion of Moses in Midrash *Mikilta* leads to a general discourse on prophecy.

Midrash: There are three kinds of prophets.
One is equally concerned for the honor of the father (God) and the son (Israel).

One is more concerned for the honor of the father than the son.

One is more concerned for the honor of the son than the father.

Jeremiah was concerned for both father and son. He said:

"We have sinned and rebelled and You have not forgiven" (Lam 3:42).

[Jeremiah equally rebukes Israel for sinning and God for not forgiving.]

As a reward, God granted him a double portion of prophecy....

Elijah was more concerned for the honor of the father than the son, as he said:

"I have been extremely zealous for God, the Lord of Hosts" (1 Kgs 19:14).

God therefore commanded him to pass the mantle of prophecy to Elisha.

Jonah was more concerned for the honor of the son than the father, as Scripture says:

"Jonah rose up to flee to Tarshish" (Jonah 1:3).

Why? Because he feared that if the Assyrians listened to his prophecy and repented it would make Israel look bad in comparison.

God granted Jonah a double portion of prophecy, as Scripture says:

"God spoke to Jonah a second time..." (Jonah 3:1).

We learn that all the patriarchs and the prophets sacrificed themselves for the sake of Israel. (*Mekilta, Bo, Pischa* 1)

Lesson Commentary: Here is a message for all religious leaders. You must represent God to the people, and you must represent the people to God. Often it is difficult to balance the two. This is the challenge that faces the clergy of every religion in every time and place.

It is best to represent both God and the people equally, but sometimes this is hard to do. If one is to err, the Rabbis teach that the leader should err in the direction of indulgence toward the people. God punished Elijah for preferring God and being harsh toward the people, but God rewarded Jonah for disobeying God for the benefit of the people. In the spirit of true prophecy, a religious leader must always put the welfare of the people not only above his own welfare but even above his or her noble passion for God.

What It Means to Be a Chosen People

Torah: I have *set you apart* from all the other peoples to be Mine. (Lev 20:26b)

Midrash: (A) If you set yourselves apart from all the other peoples, then you belong to me.

And if you do not set yourselves apart, then you belong to Nebukadnezzer, King of Babylon, and his companions.

(B) Rabbi Eliezer ben Azariah says:

Whence do we know that a person should not say,

"I do not want to wear clothes made from a linen-wool mixture. I do not want to eat pork. I do not desire that prohibited woman"?

Rather one should say,

"I desire to do these things, but what can I do? My Father in Heaven has commanded me not to."

We learn this from the text: "I shall set you apart from all other peoples to be Mine."

"Apart" means "separated from sin and consecrated to the Kingdom of Heaven." (*Sifra, Kedoshim* 22)

Grammatical Commentary: The Torah says that God will "set apart" the Israelites. The Hebrew verb is *avdil*. The Midrash wishes to define this term. In what manner and for what purpose does God distinguish the Jews from all other peoples?

Lesson Commentary: The Jews are distinguished from all the peoples of the earth, in the twenty-first century as much as in the past. This people of only ten million members receives inordinate attention at the United Nations, in the world press, and in the focus of nations and peoples. The so-called Jewish question, concerning the role of the Jews in a modern nation-state, was first raised in the Estates General of revolutionary France. The Holocaust was proposed in Nazi Germany as the "final solution" to this question. Anti-Semitism and anti-Zionism are still shockingly motivating forces in world affairs today. Many Westerners, often motivated by their Christian faith, rise to the defense of the Jews, convinced that the Jewish people have a special role in God's plan and a special place in God's heart. The Jews are the "Chosen People" of the Bible, which is accepted as Scripture by all the world's Christians and Muslims. To be a Jew is sometimes to benefit, often to suffer, from the world's attention. It is both wonderful and fearsome.

The anonymous author of part A of our midrash acknowledges that the distinctiveness of the Jews is a mixed blessing. He has a pious response to the history of persecution. The Jews are subject to persecution when they *fail* to remain distinctive. When the Jews set themselves apart, they are subject to God, but when the Jews assimilate, God turns them over to the power of the world's rapacious empires. The nations punish the Jews not for being "a people apart" but for failing to remain distinctive. Theodore Herzl, the very secular father of modern Zionism, made a similar point. He noted that anti-Semites in nineteenth-century Europe hated assimilated Jews more than they hated religious Jews. Assimilation is not a cure for anti-Semitism. The Jews must accept their unique role among humankind.

Rabbi Eliezer ben Azariah has a different view of Jewish separateness, one that may be more amenable to the acculturated Jews of contemporary America. To him the distinction of the Jews is not social or cultural but only in being faithful to the divine commandments, the mitzvot. Moral purity that comes from obedience to the Torah is the distinguishing feature of the Jew. A Jew may live as a member of the wider society as long as that Jew remembers and observes the commandments.

In promoting this view of Jewish distinctiveness, Rabbi Eliezer ben Azariah reiterates one of the central tenets of rabbinic Judaism: obedience to the mitzvot is the highest possible ethical level for a human being. One who does good out of obedience to the commandments, while acknowledging his evil urges, is on a higher ethical level than the person who voluntarily does what is right and good. As the Sages taught, "one who is commanded and performs is higher than one who is not commanded and performs," and "the greater the evil urge, the greater the saint" who has overcome his or her evil urge.

Who Is a Jew?

Torah: When *a person from you* presents an offering... (Lev 1:2b)

Midrash: "a person"—to include converts
"from you"—to exclude apostates
How do we know it isn't the other way around, to exclude the converts and include the apostates?
The text says "B'nai Yisrael," "children of Israel."
Just as the children of Israel are those who observe the covenant, so do converts, thus excluding apostates who do not accept the covenant. (*Sifra* ad loc., Midrash *HaGadol Vayikra* 2)

Grammatical Commentary: There is an unusual preposition in this phrase. We would expect the Torah to say "any one of you" or "any of your people," but the Torah says a person "from" you. The preposition *from*—the prefix *mi* in Hebrew—when taken literally, is generally used to exclude something. The unusual use of this preposition here hints that the Torah is interested not only in who may offer a whole offering (*olah*) as a sacrifice but also in who may not present this sacrifice.

Lesson Commentary: According to halakah, only a Jew may present an *olah* offering at the Jerusalem Temple. The determination of who may or may not present such an offering gives us a functional definition of who is a Jew.

Christians pride themselves on being an "Israel of the spirit." They are a religious people united by faith, not nationality. Christian community is determined by communion, the recognition of one another's baptisms and Holy Eucharist. Whoever can share communion is part of the same Christian community.

Judaism is the religion of a people. Conversion to Judaism is a citizenship ceremony in which one joins the nation of Israel. "Catholic Israel" (*Klal Yisrael*) consists of all the members of the Jewish people. It is essential to define who is "in" and who is "out" as a Jew.

The halakic definition of a Jew in the Talmud is well known— the child of a Jewish mother is a Jew. This definition is not as complete as most people imagine. Having a Jewish mother merely creates a presumption of Jewish identity.

This midrash from the *Sifra,* the halakic midrash to Leviticus, tells us who is within what we may call the Jewish communion. Lest we think that Jewish identity is defined by birth, the halakah excludes the apostate from offering a sacrifice. A born Jew who adopts another religion is no longer permitted to offer sacrifices. The born Gentile who converts to Judaism is included in the Jewish communion. The convert may offer sacrifice. Religious affirmation, not birth, ultimately determines who is a member of Israel.

The second half of our midrash acknowledges that there is something arbitrary in the logic of the law. Linguistically, the text could lead us to conclude the opposite, that birth is what counts and that the apostate is included while the convert is excluded. The midrash affirms that we rely on tradition to teach us the true law. Tradition teaches us that "children of Israel" means not literal children but adherents to the covenant. Faithfulness to the covenant of Israel makes one a member of Israel. Therefore "a person" includes the convert who lives by the covenant, but "from you" excludes the apostate who was born Jewish but now rejects the covenant.

To Serve God with All Your Heart

> **Torah:** You shall love the Lord your God with all your heart *(levav-cha),* with all your soul, and with all your might. (Deut 6:5)
>
> **Midrash:** *With all your heart* means with both of your hearts, the two impulses of the human heart. Love God with your good impulse and your evil impulse.
>
> Another interpretation: *With all your heart* means with all the heart that is within you. Do not be divided within yourself over the service of God, but give God your all. *(Midrash HaGadol, Vaethanen 5)*

Grammatical Commentary: The Hebrew word for "heart" comes in two forms, with a single letter v *(lev)* or with a double letter v *(levav)*. In this verse the word appears in the doubled form.

Although technically the word for heart belongs to a class of words that behave in this manner, the midrash chooses to draw a lesson from the doubling of the letter. The Torah must be referring to two different hearts within man.

Note that the word "heart" in the Bible does not mean what it means in modern English. To us the heart is the seat of the emotions, but in the Bible the heart is the seat of the mind, the intellect. To love God with all your heart means with your mind, not with your passion.

Another interpretation: This phrase often appears in the midrash, introducing a new idea that is unrelated to the previous interpretation. Following the concept that there are seventy faces to the Torah, we can follow up one interpretation with another new and different one. Our second interpretation teaches the lesson of wholeheartedness in the service of God.

Lesson Commentary: The rabbinic psychology is that the human psyche is made up of two conflicting forces, which the Rabbis called the good impulse and the evil impulse. From these names one might assume that the goal of righteous living is to strengthen the good impulse and suppress the evil impulse. The Rabbis offer a different lesson. One must yoke both impulses to the mitzvot in order to guide and direct them toward goodness. Without the mitzvot, one could be misled into evil by either impulse.

How could one do evil with the good impulse? The altruistic desire not to use any earthly resource that another person could better use could lead one to commit suicide.[34] How could one do good with the evil impulse? One could direct one's lust toward the mitzvah of marriage and raising a family. One could direct one's greed toward the mitzvah of honest labor to earn an income.

To love God with all of your heart means, in rabbinic Judaism, to train your entire psyche to observe the mitzvot that are found in the Torah.

---

34. The William Saroyan play *The Time of Your Life* explores this possibility. The "hero" of the play ultimately chooses murder over suicide.

The Purpose of Creation

> **Torah:** In the beginning God created the heavens and the earth. (Gen 1:1)
>
> *Bereshit*—in the beginning, at first
>
> *Bara*—(he) created
>
> *Elohim*—God (In poetic Hebrew the subject may follow the verb, as here.)

> **Midrash:** BERESHIT BARA' ELOHIM,
> Read it as BARA' SHEIT BARA' ELOHIM.
> Six things preceded the Creation.
> Two were created at that time, and four arose in the mind of God.
> The Torah and the Throne of God were created;
> The patriarchs and the people Israel and the Holy Temple and the Name of the Messiah arose in the intention of God.
> Rabbi Ahava ben Zeira said: also repentance.
> And some say: also Heaven and Hell. (*Genesis Rabba, Bereshit* 1:4)

Grammatical Commentary: The very first word of the Bible is grammatically incorrect. The first word ought correctly to be *bareeshona*, not *bereshit*. It is indeed surprising that the very first word of the Torah is incongruous. Here is a text that virtually screams, "Please interpret me!" The Sages do this with cleverness and wit. They divide the first word into two words. *Bereshit* becomes *bara sheit,* which means "He created six things." (In Aramaic, not Hebrew, but the Rabbis spoke Aramaic.) Now the Rabbis are free, in the open spirit of midrash, to tell us what six things preceded the creation of heaven and earth and why God created them.

Lesson Commentary: God created six things before creation.

Torah: God would not create a world of moral relativism. God first defined right and wrong, then created the world according to the moral pattern of the Torah. As the Gospel of John sees Christ as the *logos* of the universe, the Rabbis saw Torah as the *logos* of the universe.

Throne: God did not create the world and then abandon it. God rules over the world of creation. God is watching. God cares.

Patriarchs and Israel: Having created the world according to the moral pattern of the Torah, God needed a means to transmit the Torah to the world. The Jewish people are that means. God would not have created the world without the intention that someday the descendants of righteous men and women would stand at the foot of Mount Sinai to bring the Torah from heaven to earth.

Temple: God provides humankind with a means for atonement and communion, the Temple sacrifices.

Name of the Messiah: God created the world with the intention of redeeming it. We can be confident that the teleology of creation— its ultimate purpose—is the redemption of all being. As for why the midrash says "the name of the Messiah" rather than just "the Messiah," we do not know. Most likely it says this in defense against the Christians who would claim, "It is Jesus."

The last two additions spoil the balance between text and lesson. They bring the count of pre-creations to more than six. The authors of these additions must have believed that the lesson required them even if the text did not. Rabbi Ahava ben Zeira lived after the destruction of the Temple. In rabbinic theology, repentance replaces Temple sacrifice as the means of atonement. The final comment came from those who believed that God would not create a world without justice. Since there is no justice in this life, there must be justice in the world-to-come, in heaven and hell. Although hell plays no role or very little role in later Judaism, some groups of Jews in the rabbinic era believed in the existence of a heaven for reward and a hell for punishment in the afterlife.

The Name of God: Justice and Mercy

Torah: On the day that the Lord God (*YHWH Elohim*) created earth and heaven... (Gen 2:4b)

Midrash: A parable of a king who had fine glassware.

The king said: If I put hot water into them they will crack.

If I put cold water into them they will crack.

What did he do?

He mixed the hot with the cold and poured it lukewarm into the glasses, and they held.

Thus said the Blessed Holy One:

If I create the world with the Attribute of Mercy it will not stand.

If I create the world with the Attribute of Justice it will not stand.

I will create the world with a mixture of Mercy and Justice. Perhaps it will then stand! (*Genesis Rabba, Bereshit* 12:15)

Grammatical Commentary: The Torah has two different names for God. Sometimes the Torah calls God Elohim, which means "the Deity." Sometimes the Torah calls God by the four consonants YHWH, which Jews call "the ineffable name of God." This is God's personal name, too holy to pronounce. Bible scholars often pronounce this name "Yahweh," which is a historical conjecture, and some Christians pronounce it "Jehovah." Rather than say the holy name, Jews say "Lord"—in Hebrew *Ah-do-nai*. Because this name too has acquired holiness, pious Jews will often say *Hashem*—"the name."

Some sections of the Torah use one name exclusively for God, and other texts use only the other name. The first creation story, the seven days of creation, uses the name Elohim. The second story of creation, the story of Adam and Eve, combines the two names. This is cause for comment.

Lesson Commentary: In rabbinic theology, God is radically One, yet from the perspective of human experience, there are two aspects to God's being, the aspect of justice and the aspect of mercy. Sometimes, to avoid speaking as if God were divisible, the Rabbis speak of God possessing two thrones, one for justice and one for mercy. God sits on one to judge the world, the other to forgive the world. In human life it is difficult to know when to demonstrate justice and when to show mercy. We cannot acquit every criminal defendant, nor can we condemn them all. The monotheistic faith of the Jew teaches that in God this seeming duality disappears in a higher unity. The Rabbis taught that the divine name YHWH refers to the aspect of mercy and the divine name Elohim refers to the aspect of justice. The creation story combines the two names to teach us that the world cannot endure on mercy alone or on justice alone. God had to mingle justice with mercy for the world to endure. In our attempt to live righteously, we too must always mingle justice with mercy in proper proportion. We should never, even temporarily, set aside one and function only by the other.

The modern historical study of the Bible began with the Documentary Hypothesis of the German scholar Julius Wellhausen. Wellhausen suggested that the different names for the deity in the Torah come from different source texts. There was a Jehovah document, which Wellhausen called "J." There was an Elohist document, which he called "E." The final editors combined these two documents with "P," the priestly source, and "D," the book of Deuteronomy, to create the Torah.

The ancient Rabbis had their own version of the Documentary Hypothesis. They believed that the entire Torah had only one source and author, God. Nevertheless, they were so tuned in to the voice of the Torah that they were aware that the texts that use the divine name YHWH have a different voice, a different style, contradictory content, and often a different theology than the texts that use the other divine name, Elohim. The Rabbis' solution to this problem is that sometimes God was speaking to Moses from the aspect of mercy and at other times from the aspect of justice.

The Wedding Day of God and Israel

Torah: On the day that Moses concluded (*kallot*) the erection of the Tabernacle... (Num 7:1)

Midrash: "I have come into my garden, my sister, my bride" (*kallah*) (Song of Songs, 5:1).

Rabbi Azariah told a parable of a king who was so angry with his wife that he deposed her and cast her out. Some time later he regretted his action and invited her back.

She said: First let my husband resume his former practice of accepting gifts from me, and then I shall return to my proper place. [The king built a wedding canopy to meet his wife, where she offered him gifts. When he accepted the gifts from her, they renewed their wedding vows.]

[When God desired to forgive the sins of humankind and enter into intimate communion with them, Moses said, "First accept our gifts, and then let us renew our relationship." God then commanded Israel to build the Tabernacle as a place of sacrifice, and God renewed the covenant with Israel in this tent.] So the Torah says: On the day that Moses became a bride (*kallot*) through the erection of the Tabernacle. (*Pesikta D'Rav Kahana, Piska* 1:1)

Grammatical Commentary, the *Petichta* Format: Imagine that you are a Jewish peasant in the land of Israel sometime around the third century. Six days a week you labor in your fields. Your life is not much better than that of your animals. But on the seventh day, the Sabbath, you are free to rest and to develop your mind and spirit. You go to the town square, where after morning prayers a learned Sage reads the weekly parasha from a Torah scroll. Thanks to your elementary schooling and your faithful attendance at Sabbath worship, you know the Torah by heart. You know the opening words that you will hear in this week's Torah portion.

Before the Torah reading, the Sage rises on a podium to preach to the gathered crowd. Instead of quoting from the weekly Torah portion, the Sage quotes a biblical verse seemingly at random from Psalms, or Proverbs, or Job, or perhaps from the Song of Songs or another book from the third section of Scripture, the Writings. Now your interest is piqued. You know that the preacher has to conclude his sermon with the opening verse of the weekly parasha. You are anxious to hear what clever interpretations and wise teachings the preacher will share as he winds his interpretation from his introductory biblical verse to the opening verse of the weekly portion.

This midrash format is called *petichta*, the Aramaic word for "opening" or "introduction." The *petichta* text from the biblical Writings introduces the sermon, which in turn introduces the weekly parasha.

In our midrash above, the *petichta* text is related to the Torah text by a play on words. The word for "concluded," *kallot*, sounds similar to the Hebrew word for "bride," *kallah*. The play on words leads to an association of ideas. The tent in which Israel served God through sacrifice is similar to the wedding bower, the *huppah,* under which a Jewish bride and groom marry.

Lesson Commentary: The midrash reconceives the sacrificial service in the Temple as a wedding ceremony. When Israel brings gifts to God in the Temple, they are united with God in a loving communion just as husband and wife are united on their wedding day. By the time this midrash was published, the Temple service had long since been replaced by the prayer service conducted in the synagogue. The listener understood that when the preacher spoke of the desert tabernacle or the later Jerusalem Temple, he was really referring to the synagogue. The synagogue offering of prayer and Scripture study reestablishes a marital bond between God and Israel.

When the Good Die Young:
A Lesson for the Day of Atonement

Torah: The Lord spoke to Moses after the death of the two sons of Aaron who died when they drew too close to the presence of the Lord. The Lord said to Moses: Tell your brother Aaron that he is not to come at will into [the Holy of Holies, before the ark] lest he die, for I appear in the cloud over the cover. Thus only shall Aaron enter the Holy of Holies: with a bull of the herd for a sin offering and a ram for a burn offering.... And from the Israelite community he shall take two he-goats for a sin offering and a ram for a burnt offering....

Aaron is to offer his own bull of sin offering, to make expiation for himself and for his household. . . .

Thus he shall purge the Holy of Holies of the impurity and transgression of the Israelites, whatever their sins. . . .

And this shall be a law for you for all time: In the seventh month, on the tenth day of the month, you shall practice self-denial.... For on this day atonement shall be made for you to cleanse you of all your sins; you shall be clean before the Lord....

This shall be to you a law for all time: to make atonement for the Israelites for all their sins once a

year. And Moses did as the Lord had commanded him.
(Lev 16:1–34)

Midrash: On "After the death of the two sons of Aaron..."
(A) THE SAME HAPPENS TO GOOD AND BAD ALIKE
(Eccl 9:2)

Abraham was righteous, Nimrod was wicked yet both
grew old and died.

David was pure, Nebukadnezzer was impure yet both
ruled for forty years.

Solomon sacrificed to God, Jeroboam to a golden calf
yet each got to rule as king.

Moses was good, the twelve spies were bad yet neither
got to enter the Promised Land.

Sampson lived up to his vows, Zedekiah broke his vows
yet both were blinded.[35]

Aaron's sons were good, Korah's company were evil yet
both were burned, as it says:

After the death of the two sons of Aaron.

(B) Nadab and Avihu, Aaron's sons, turned their eyes
away from the divine Presence and would not enjoy its
radiance, therefore Scripture states:

AND THEY DIED BEFORE THE LORD. .

R. Yohanan said: Literally, "before" the Lord? At God's
instance? [Surely not!]

Rather, the Torah comes to teach you that it is so painful
for God when the children of the righteous die in their lifetime.

And how do we know that the death of the righteous
atones for the world?

As it is said:

"And they buried the bones of Saul and Jonathan his
son in the territory of Benjamin, in Zela, in the tomb of
their father Kish, and they did all that the King com-

---

35. Sampson's long hair was part of his Nazirite vow to God. King Zedekiah of
Judah made a vow of fealty to King Nebukadnezzer of Babylon, which he broke, and
he was put to death for his rebelliousness when the Babylonians conquered Jerusalem.

manded, and God responded to the plea of the land thereafter" (2 Sam 21:14). (*Tanhuma D'fus, Ahare Mot,* 1,8)

Grammatical Commentary: Leviticus 16 gives a complete
account of the rituals that the high priest is to perform every year
on Yom Kippur, the Day of Atonement. The passage incongruously
begins with a reference to an unrelated story: the two older sons of
Aaron, the first high priest and brother of Moses, made an inap-
propriate offering of incense on the day of their ordination, and
they were killed by heavenly lightning. This seemingly out-of-place
reference provides an opening for the midrashic interpretation of
this chapter. How does the death of the young and innocent before
their time relate to the subject of sacrificial atonement for sins?
What does the death of Nadab and Abihu have to do with Yom
Kippur?

Lesson Commentary: (A) The Yom Kippur observance of
rabbinic Judaism has a different character than the Temple era
observance of the Day of Atonement. While the Temple stood, Yom
Kippur was primarily an observance for the high priest. His many
sacrificial offerings on that day cleansed the Temple of accumulated impurity from sins and atoned for the sins of every Jew. The
Rabbis reconceived Yom Kippur as a day of intense personal intro-
spection for every Jew. Repentance, prayer, and charity are the
order of the day. Every Jew hopes that by his good deeds of the past
year and his repentance for his sins he will be found worthy for
God to write him into the Book of Life for the coming year.

We seek divine mercy to temper divine judgment so that we will
be worthy of God's blessing. We like to think that a combination of
good deeds and sincere repentance would assure us a long and com-
fortable life. We are aware, though, that life is often unfair. This is the
central paradox of monotheistic religion: we worship a God of justice,
but we experience life's injustice when we observe the death of the
innocent before their time. What benefit is there in our repentance if
the good often die young?

We might imagine that in our day God is insufficiently attentive
to the world but that things were better back in the Bible days, when
God was close to humankind and God spoke to us all the time
through the prophets. Not so, says our midrash! By cleverly juxta-

posing characters from different biblical stories, the author of this midrash demonstrates that the heros and villains of the Bible experienced the injustice of life as much as we do. Our first midrash establishes that we have a problem that we cannot evade. The injustice of life is real, not imaginary.

(B) This midrash draws a lesson by means of a grammatical analysis of the Hebrew term *lifnay YHWH*, "before the Lord." The Hebrew preposition *lifnay* is ambiguous. It could mean "at the behest of," as our first, anonymous interpreter suggests. This would mean that Nadab and Abihu died because God determined that they should die. The interpreter suggests a rationale that would justify their death: they did not appreciate God's presence as they served in the sanctuary. They were not sinners, but even so there was a good reason for their death. This anonymous opinion represents the point of view that life really is just; we are merely limited in our understanding of God's wise actions.

The midrash raises this possibility only to reject it. Rabbi Jonathan has the final word. He is horrified to think that one would interpret the ambiguous phrase in the above manner. Rather, Rabbi Jonathan teaches us, *lifnay* means "in front of," "before the eyes of." God did not will the death of Aaron's sons. Accidents happen. But God is not indifferent. God cannot stop "seeing" the death of the innocent; it is constantly before God's eyes. God responds by accepting their death as a sacrifice of atonement for the sins of all humankind. As compensation for their undeserved death, God rewards the human brothers and sisters of the innocent with forgiveness and blessing. The scriptural text that proves this is that after the death of King Saul's sons, who all died with their father at the battle of Gilboa, Israel experienced an era of peace. This peace was God's reward to Israel for the undeserved death of King Saul's sons.

Chapter Seven

Mishnah and Talmud

It is taught: On that (certain) day Rabbi Eliezer brought forward every imaginable argument, but the Sages did not accept any of them. Finally he said to them, "If the halakah agrees with me, let this carob tree prove it!" Sure enough, the carob tree was uprooted [and replanted] a hundred cubits away from its place. "No proof can be brought from a carob tree," they retorted. Again he said to them, "If the halakah agrees with me, let the channel of water prove it!" Sure enough, the channel of water flowed backward. "No proof can be brought from a channel of water," they rejoined. Again he urged, "If the halakah agrees with me, let the walls of the house of study prove it!" Sure enough, the walls tilted as if to fall. But Rabbi Joshua rebuked the walls, saying, "When disciples of the wise are engaged in a halakic dispute, what right have you to interfere?" Hence, in deference to R. Joshua they did not fall, and in deference to R. Eliezer they did not resume their upright position; they are still standing aslant. Again R. Eliezer said to the sages, "If the halakah agrees with me, let it be proved from Heaven!" Sure enough, a divine voice cried out, "Why do you dispute R. Eliezer, with whom the halakah always agrees?" But R. Joshua stood up and protested, "It [the Torah] is not in heaven" (Deut 30:12). We pay no attention to a divine voice, because long ago, at Mount Sinai, You wrote in the Torah, "After the majority must one incline" (Exod 23:2). Rabbi Nathan met [the prophet] Elijah and asked him, "What did the Holy One do in that moment?" Elijah replied: "He laughed [with joy], saying, 'My children have defeated Me, My children have defeated Me.'"

(Babylonian Talmud, *Baba Metzia* 59a-b)

The Format of the Talmud

The two Talmuds, the Talmud of the land of Israel and the Talmud of Babylon, are both built around the core text of the Mishnah. In volume, the Mishnah is about the same size as a Bible. The Mishnah contains rabbinic opinions on matters of Jewish law, organized by topic. There are six books in the Mishnah: Seeds (agriculture), Set Times (Sabbath and holidays), Women (matters of personal status), Damages (civil and criminal law), Holy Things (rules for the disposition of items that have been dedicated as offerings to the Temple service), and Purities (ritual purity and impurity). The six books, called orders, are themselves topically divided into a total of sixty-three *tractates*. For example, there is a tractate on prayer in the book Seeds; the topic of blessing God for food that is grown leads to the topic of prayer in general. Each tractate is divided into chapters. The chapters contain individual paragraphs that provide rabbinic opinions on a specific topic. Each of these paragraphs is called "a" mishnah.

According to Jewish tradition, the Mishnah was edited by Rabbi Judah the Prince and his court. Judah the Prince was the Jewish ethnarch, the ruler of all the Jews in the eastern Roman Empire, around the year 200 CE. Though his authority to rule was absolute and derived from the Romans, Judah surrounded himself with rabbinic Sages, and he deferred to their wisdom. He based his work on a set of written notes on the oral Torah that he had inherited from the great Rabbi Akiva. Within a few generations after its publication, the rabbinic scholars were using the Mishnah as a cornerstone of their learning, which centered on the divine law. The Mishnah is not a code of laws, but ultimately the Mishnah became the foundation text for halakah, Jewish law.

To get a sense of the form and content of the Mishnah, we will study one individual mishnah from each of the six orders of the Mishnah.

The Six Orders of the Mishnah

Seeds: If one sees shooting stars, earthquakes, lightning, thunder, and storms, one says, "Blessed is the One whose power and might fill the world." If one sees mountains, hills, seas, rivers, and deserts, one says, "Blessed is the Source of Creation."...For rain and for good news one says, "Blessed is the One who is good and does good." For bad news one says, "Blessed is the Lord, the true Judge." (Mishnah, *Berachot* 9:2) [Mishnah texts are identified by name of the tractate, the chapter, and the number of the individual mishnah.]

Commentary: The Bible makes no mention of a formula for blessing, but in the Mishnah the Jewish form of blessing is taken for granted. It must have arisen sometime after the close of the Bible and well before the publication of the Mishnah. There are blessings for different kinds of food and for every type of human experience. Notice that there are two different blessings for two different types of natural wonders. One might say, "Would not one blessing suffice?" Perhaps, but the type of awe we feel in the face of sudden, dynamic natural wonders is different from the type of awe we experience at the sight of permanent fixtures of nature. The halakah takes into account the psychology of the human experience of the divine. Note that just as one blesses God for the good, so does one bless God for the bad. In this we imitate the example of the righteous biblical character Job. The blessing over bad news is recited, for example, when we hear of the death of a loved one.

> **Set Times:** Four times in the year the world is judged: on Passover for grain, on Shavuot (Pentecost) for the fruits of the tree; on Rosh Hashanah all that came into the world pass before God like flocks of sheep; and on Sukkot all are judged for water. (Mishnah, *Rosh Hashanah* 1:2)

Commentary: The Jewish calendar was a matter of controversy in the centuries before and after the destruction of the Temple. Each Jewish sect had its own calendar. The right to impose one's calendar on the general populace represented the authority to lead the Jewish people. Once Rabban Gamaliel, leader of the Rabbis and head of the Sanhedrin at Yavneh, forced a dissident Rabbi to appear before him with his wallet and walking stick on the day that Rabbi had calculated to be the holy Day of Atonement. The Essenes hated the Temple leadership in part because the Essenes had their own sacred calendar, which the high priests did not accept. This prevented the Essenes from offering their sacrifices on what they considered to be the true holy day.

Ultimately the rabbinic luni-solar calendar was accepted as the calendar of the Jewish people. This is the calendar that is familiar to the Jews of today. In the rabbinic calendar, Rosh Hashanah, in the fall, is the primary new year, the day on which God judges the world. Nevertheless, other new years remain, partly as holdovers from other Jewish calendars. Passover marks the grain harvest and Pentecost the fruit harvest. These species of produce stand for judgment on their own new years. The festival of Sukkot, coming two weeks after Rosh Hashanah, is the beginning of the six-month rainy season in Israel. The ability of the land to feed its populace depended upon the rains; a dry season led to drought and mass starvation. The end of the Sukkot festival began a period of fervent prayers for rain. Rosh Hashanah, as the rabbinic new year, is the primary festival of divine judgment. On this day Jews acknowledge God as Ruler and Judge of the earth. Jews pray to God to write them down for good in the heavenly Book of Life. The rabbinic Rosh Hashanah is based on a saying of Rabbi Judah the Prince: "Know what three things are above you and you will keep far from sin—an eye that sees, an ear that hears, and all of your deeds written in a book" (*Pirke Avot* 2:1).

> **Women:** The Sages have said: There are four kinds of vows that a person is not required to fulfill—vows made in excitement, vows of exaggeration, vows made in error, and vows in which circumstances prevent [the person from fulfilling the vow]. (Mishnah, *Nedarim* 3:1)

Commentary: The Torah says that if a person makes a vow, he must fulfill it and if he does not, then God will "require it of him, and it will be accounted to him as a sin" (Deut. 23:22–24). Despite this, the Rabbis recognized that people are not responsible for matters outside their own control. For example, the Torah mediates the ancient law that "one who sheds human blood, by man shall his blood be shed" by distinguishing between intentional murder and careless manslaughter. Just so, the Rabbis recognized that there are states of emotion and consciousness in which a person speaks without genuine intention.

Rabbinic law reflects a revolution in the understanding of human consciousness that took place between the end of Hebrew biblical times and the origins of Christianity and rabbinic Judaism. The Rabbis came to understand that a person has an inner life of the mind that is not always the same as what a person says and does. Ancient man did not distinguish between speech and thought, but the Rabbis now recognized that a person can say one thing but mean another. The Rabbis graciously allowed that people should not be held to account for vows made with less than full intention. They should also not be held to account if their best intentions come to naught after honest effort. Results are important, but intention also counts.

We note a similar recognition of the complex relationship between intention and deed in Jesus' statements on hatred and murder, lust and adultery. Jesus is speaking in this instance of moral accountability before God. Christian law, like Jewish law, does not punish people for unfulfilled evil intentions but only for wrongful deeds.

> **Damages:** If two people each lay hands upon a piece of cloth and they both say, "I found it!" or they both say, "All of it is mine!" they must each make an oath [in court] that at least half of it belongs to him. Then they divide the cloth between them. (Mishnah, *Baba Metzia* 1:1)

Commentary: Jewish civil law begins with a basic rule of fairness. When two people claim the same item and there is no clear title, so that it is one person's word against the other, the judge splits the item or its value evenly between them. Note the form of the oath. If each claimant were to swear what he believed to be true, that all of the item is his, then the dispute could not be resolved by dividing the item. The claimants swear only that the half they are going to receive does, in fact, belong to them. The oath and the ultimate resolution are therefore not in conflict.

Holy Things: [A priest] who desired [the honor of] clean-
ing the ashes from the altar rose up early and immersed
himself in the *mikvah* [the ritual path of purification]
before the coming of the officer [in charge of the priests].
At what time did the officer come? Sometimes at cock
crow, sometimes a little sooner or later. The officer came
and knocked on the door of the place where the priests
were gathered, and they opened the door for him. He said,
"Let those who have immersed themselves choose lots!"
They chose lots, and whoever the lot fell upon was chosen.
(Mishnah, *Tamid* 1:2)

Commentary: This Mishnah gives a charming portrait of religious devotion. There is no task dirtier and more odious than shov-
eling ashes, but because it is an aspect of sacred service, priests vied
for the privilege, waiting up in the hours before dawn, hoping to be
selected.

The Mishnah is the blueprint for the entire postbiblical Jewish
way of life, but it is a puzzling blueprint. No one knows why the
Mishnah focuses a lot of attention on topics that may seem minor to
later Jews, and little attention to matters that might seem major to us.
The Gemara again shifts the focus of Judaism by discussing some
mishnayot (pl. of mishnah) extensively and others hardly at all and
by raising topics often unrelated to the mishnah under discussion.
The order Purities does not have a Gemara in the Talmud. This is a
subject that was left behind in later Judaism. The Mishnah gives a
detailed description of the daily functioning of the Jerusalem Temple.
This is surprising when we recall that the Temple was destroyed by
the Romans in the year 70 CE and the Mishnah was published
around 200 CE—a full 130 years and many generations later.

Why does the Mishnah present a detailed program for the conduct of the Temple and its sacrificial offerings? This is one of the historical mysteries of Judaism. One theory is that the Sages carefully
preserved the historical memory of the Temple's functioning in the
hope that someday the Temple would be rebuilt. The question-and-
answer format in this mishnah creates the sense of a young disciple
eager to learn a precious tradition about the Temple from an elder.
This could, of course, just be a literary device. Another theory is that

the Sages believed that studying about the Temple was equivalent to actually offering sacrifices. As the sacrifices once provided communion and atonement, so now learning halakot about the Temple sacrifices provides communion and atonement. Some scholars believe that the details about sacrifice in the Mishnah are actual historical memories. Others believe that the details represent a rabbinic fantasy, as in "This is how we would run the Temple if there were one and we were in charge." One theory is that the Mishnah represents the rabbinic response to the major religious question of late-first-century Judaism, "Now that the Temple no longer exists, what is different?" Some Jewish factions seem to have believed that, without the Temple, Judaism had ceased to exist. It is possible that the Romans believed that they had brought Judaism to an end by burning the Temple. The Christian response to the *hurban* (destruction of the Temple) was that God had replaced the Temple with the sacrifice of Jesus on the cross. This claim seems to have appealed more to Gentile Christians than to Jews. The Rabbis' response to the *hurban* was that "the destruction of the Temple changes nothing. Everything is exactly the same as it was before." If so, the Mishnah's interest in Temple and sacrifice is a message about continuity. Jews should go on living just as they always did. The relationship between God and Israel is unbroken and unbreakable.

> **Purities:** Judah, an Ammonite who had converted to Judaism, came before the Sanhedrin (the High Court). He asked them, "May I be counted as a Jew?" Rabban Gamaliel said, "You are forbidden." Rabbi Joshua said, "You are permitted." Rabban Gamaliel said to Judah, "The Torah says: An Ammonite or a Moabite shall not be admitted to the congregation of the Lord" (Dt. 23:4). Rabbi Joshua said to Gamaliel, "Yes, but are the Ammonites and Moabites of today the same people (as in biblical times)? Long ago, King Sennacherib of Assyria came and mixed up all of the nations...." And [the majority of the rabbis voted] to permit Judah to join the Jewish people. (Mishnah, *Yadaim* 4:4)

Commentary: The mishnah before us is typical in providing contrasting rabbinic opinions on an issue. Rabbinic sources and the

New Testament suggest that the Pharisees promoted conversion to Judaism. The Saducees, by contrast, did not seem to believe that there is such a thing as conversion. Religious conversion does not appear by name in the Hebrew Scriptures, though the book of Ruth, one of the later biblical books to be written, is clearly reaching toward the idea. Ruth the Moabite converts to Judaism, it seems, when she joins her Judean mother-in-law and goes with her to the land of Judah. The eventual Pharisaic-Jewish term for a convert, *ger,* comes from the biblical term for "resident alien." We see in the etymology of the term the evolution of a religious idea that eventually became even more central in Christianity and Islam than in Judaism. From the ancient geographic notion that a foreigner could immigrate to the land of Israel and live by Israelite law, there evolved the concept that one could acquire a Jewish soul by adopting the beliefs and the history of the Jews as one's own.

The Rabbis in the Mishnah all agree that there is such a thing as conversion. Their disagreement is over how far the permission to convert extends. The Torah specifically prohibits members of certain nations, ancient enemies of the Israelites, from joining the Israelite community. Can even a member of these nations religiously convert to Judaism? Notice how the Mishnah treats the word of the Bible. The Bible gets a vote but not a veto. Rabban Gamaliel quotes the Torah because it backs up his position, but Rabbi Judah trumps the Torah with rabbinic logic. He makes an appeal to history, claiming that because of the mingling of nations there is no longer such a thing as blood purity. Would that the racists in the world today accepted Rabbi Judah's logic! The religious principle of the Sages that all converts are welcome takes precedence even over an explicit biblical verse. The Bible is, one may say, another participant in the debates of the Sages. One talmudic story suggests that even when God speaks directly from the heavens, we do not listen. Only the logic and the traditions of the Sages may be heard in the debates in the academy. God gave the Torah to humankind so that the Sages could debate it and determine the halakah. That is the system. Since God created the system, even God has to live by it.

Talmud: Mishnah and Gemara

The Talmud consists of the Mishnah and the Gemara. The Gemara is a continuation of rabbinic discussion on subjects raised by the Mishnah. In the printed editions of the Talmud, each individual mishnah is followed by its gemara. The mishnah and gemara fill the center of the page. On the inside column of the page, Rashi's commentary is printed. On the outside column we find the commentary of the Tosafot, Rashi's students, sons-in-law, and grandsons who added their comments to his and presented their disagreements with his interpretations. In the margins are printed cross-references and additional commentaries in small print.

Whereas the Mishnah is concise and focused, the Gemara is extensive and wide-ranging. Sometimes the gemara to an individual mishnah may go for many pages and raise a variety of related or seemingly unrelated topics. While the Mishnah is about the size of the Bible, the Talmud, in its standard pagination, contains three thousand folio-sized sheets. Each sheet is called a page. The first side is "a" and the second side is "b." The Talmud of the land of Israel is printed in two columns, numbered "a" and "b" on the front side of the sheet, "c" and "d" on the back side. The Talmud is referenced not by the chapters and individual mishnayot under discussion but by the tractate, page, and side of the page.

The Rabbinic Authors of the Talmud

The Talmuds were composed by the scholars of the rabbinic academies in Israel and Babylon. In the late fourth century, the academies in the land of Israel ceased to function. The two chief academies at that time were in Caesarea and Tiberias. The scholars composed the Talmud of the land of Israel to preserve their oral traditions. In Babylon, the two academies at Sura and Pumbeditha thrived until the eleventh century. Sometime around the sixth or seventh century, the scholars of Babylon finalized their own Talmud. The Babylonian Talmud is more fully edited and is considerably longer than the Talmud of the land of Israel. A Jewish historical tradition states that anonymous scholars known as the Saboraim edited the Talmud over a period of perhaps decades or more.

A Rabbi who is quoted in the Mishnah is called a Tanna (pl. Tannaim). A Rabbi who is quoted in the Gemara is called an Amora (pl. Amoraim). Talmud scholars speak of Tannaitic authorities and Amoraic authorities. Besides their own opinions, the Amoraim also quote many rabbinic opinions from the Tannaitic period that are not included in the Mishnah. Such a mishnaic tradition found in the Gemara is called a baraita. Altogether there are six generations of rabbinic Tannaim quoted in the Mishnah, and seven generations of rabbinic Amoraim quoted in the Babylonian Talmud, followed by the anonymous editors, the Saboraim. With the editing of the Talmud, the Sages whom we call "the Rabbis" ceased to flourish. The title "rabbi" continues in use and designates a scholar who is sufficiently learned in the Talmud and halakic process that he can derive law from the Talmud.

The *Sugyah*

The basic unit of the Gemara is called a *sugyah* (pl. *sugyot*). Each *sugyah* is presented in the format of a roundtable chat between a group of Rabbis initiated by the subject of the relevant mishnah. As in real-life small talk, the topic often shifts as the discussion progresses, and something said by one participant raises a new issue in the mind of another party to the chat. These discussions are purely a literary device. In a talmudic *sugyah*, rabbis from different times and places present ideas as if they were all sitting together. A fourth-century Rabbi might ask a question that is answered by a third-century Rabbi. The editors of the Talmud are responsible for this discussion format. Do you find this description of the Talmud confusing? Do not worry about it! Talmud study is difficult and demanding. With practice one gets better. A Jewish joke: When you first start learning Talmud, it takes a whole day to get through a single page. Later, when you get better at Talmud study, it takes a whole day to get through just half a page. The humor depends on the idea that the better you get at Talmud, the more you find in it. At every level of knowledge and skill, Talmud study is slow going.

Most *sugyot* are too lengthy to quote in full. We will study selected portions of some *sugyot*. Also, since the language of the Talmud is highly elliptical—that is, written in a kind of shorthand—we will translate into complete sentences in order to make the text more understandable. Because of the elliptical style of the Talmud, a literal word-for-word translation would come out as incomprehensible gibberish.

The Oral Torah and the Written Torah

> [The rules concerning] release from vows, which have no basis in Scripture, hover in the air. The laws concerning the Sabbath, festal offerings, and misappropriation of holy things are as mountains hanging by a hair, for they have scant proof from Scripture but many halakot. The laws concerning civil cases, the offering of sacrifices, ritual purity and impurity, and forbidden sexual relations are firmly based in Scripture. Nevertheless, both kinds of laws are essentials of the Torah. (Babylonian Talmud, *Hagigah* 10a)

Commentary: The Talmud acknowledges an imbalance between the content of the written Torah—the Bible—and the content of the oral Torah. In direct contradiction to the written Scriptures, the oral Torah permits a person to go to a rabbinic court and be released from a vow. One famous talmudic story of release from a vow occurs after Rabbi Akiva's father-in-law disinherits his daughter Rachel for marrying Akiva, who was then a poor shepherd. Years later the father, Kalba Savua, regrets his words, and he goes to the great Rabbi Akiva to be released from his vow of disinheritance, not realizing that Rabbi Akiva is his own son-in-law. Akiva releases him, and the two embrace.

For some topics, many mitzvot back up the halakah, while in other cases huge amounts of halakah are based on just a few words of Scripture. According to the Sages, the quantity of scriptural backing should have no effect when we evaluate the significance of a particular halakah. It is all God's Torah.

To What Extent Does the Obligation of Charity Extend?[36]

> Our Rabbis taught: If an orphan boy and an orphan girl
> applied [to the communal charity fund] for maintenance,
> the girl gets first claim on the money [if there is not
> enough to support both], because it is not unusual for a
> man to go begging but it is unusual for a girl to do so.
>
> If an orphan boy and an orphan girl applied for a mar-
> riage gift, the girl orphan is married off first because the
> shame of a woman is greater than the shame of a man.
>
> Our Rabbis taught: If an orphan applied for assistance
> to be married, they must rent him a house, furnish it and
> supply it, and then he is given a wife in marriage, for it
> says in Scripture [that one must supply the poor with]
> "sufficient for his need in that which he wants." (*Ketubot*
> 67 a, b)

Commentary: The Talmud elsewhere establishes the rule that
all human life is equal in value. There is no objective criterion by
which one person can tell another person to jump out of an over-
crowded lifeboat. Age, profession, gender, and so forth are no meas-
ure of the value of a life. How, then, do we decide who has priority of
access to limited lifesaving resources? How, for example, do we
decide in our society which applicant is first in line for an organ
transplant? The Sages discuss who has prior claim upon limited charity funds. The Rabbis permit gender to be a determining factor, for
reasons that they supply. A woman is put to greater shame, and her
purity is endangered, if she has to wander the streets begging and if
she remains unmarried. In this case it is for the good of society to care
for indigent women first, then the men.

> **Talmud:** Our Rabbis taught: "Sufficient for his need"
> means you are commanded to maintain him, but you are
> not commanded to make him rich. "In that which he

---

36. The commentary is interspersed here between sections of a text that is continuous in the Talmud.

wants" [could include] even a horse to ride on and a servant to run before him. It was related about Hillel the Elder that he bought for a certain poor man of good family a horse to ride on and a servant to run before him. On one occasion he could not find a servant to run before him, so he himself ran before him for three miles.

Commentary: Our Sages establish the minimum obligation of charity and also the maximum response of one who wishes to go beyond the letter of the law, which the Rabbis called "going within the law." Minimally, one must meet the material needs of the poor. Maximally, one may fulfil the mitzvah by giving the poor person everything that he wants. The Talmud gives us an aggadah that demonstrates the exemplary behavior of the Sage Hillel. Hillel reaches the level of saintliness in charitable generosity. Notice how the topic of the *sugyah* has shifted. We have turned from the question of priority to the question of sufficiency in charity. This is typical of the topical shifts of the Gemara.

Talmud: Our Rabbis taught: It once happened that the people of Upper Galilee bought for a poor member of a good family of Sepphoris a pound of meat every day.

[An objection is raised.] A pound of meat! What is the greatness of this?

Rabbi Huna replied: It was a pound of fowl's meat.

And if you prefer, I might say: [A large quantity of] ordinary meat for a pound [of money].

Rabbi Ashi replied: "The place was a small village, and every day a beast had to be spoiled for his sake."

Commentary: We observe the conversational style of the Gemara. Another aggadah is brought to illustrate the point that one may go beyond the letter of the law in giving charity. Then we come to a later generation that is puzzled by the story. What is so special about a pound of meat? That does not seem especially generous. Two named Rabbis and one anonymous source "save" the story by providing possible explanations. Charity, to be deserving of praise, must be generous.

Talmud: A certain man once applied to Rabbi Nehemiah [to be maintained on charity]. "What do you usually eat?" the Rabbi asked him. "Fat meat and old wine," the man replied. "Will you consent to live with me on lentils?" asked the Rabbi. The man lived with him on lentils and died.

"Alas" [Rabbi Nehemiah] said, "for this man whom Nehemiah has killed."

[Another rabbi said:] On the contrary, he should have said, "Alas for Nehemiah, who killed this man."

However, [the man himself was to blame, for] he should not have cultivated his luxurious habits to such an extent.

Commentary: Here is a discussion that could be taking place today, on the subject of public welfare. Should the poor have to suffer want to assure that we do not overpay them? Or should the poor be privileged to determine their own level of need, including what we givers might consider luxury items? One recalls in our time the invidious mention by welfare critics of apocryphal "welfare queens" who live luxuriously on the public dole. The talmudic discussion presents both sides of this eternal debate. Some blame the man for living luxuriously on charity. Others blame Rabbi Nehemiah for taking it upon himself to force the man to live abstemiously. Who defines need, the donor or the recipient?

Talmud: Our Rabbis taught: If a man has no means and does not wish to be maintained [on charity, out of pride,] he should be granted [the necessary sum to maintain him] as a loan, and later it can be turned into a gift. So says Rabbi Meir.

The Sages, however, said: It is given to him as a gift, and then it is granted to him as a loan.

[An objection is raised.] As a gift? But he refuses to accept gifts!

Raba replied: It is offered to him in the first instance as a gift.

Commentary: We have discussed generosity on the part of givers who want to go beyond the minimum requirement. Now we turn to the recipient. What if the needy person refuses to accept the generosity of others? We have two opinions. One is that we lend him money and after he has accepted the loan, we turn it into a gift. The other opinion is that we urge him to accept the charity as a gift and later we make it a loan as a last resort. "The Sages" means the majority of the Sages, as opposed to the opinion of an individual Sage.

Talmud: When Mar Ukba was about to die, he requested, "Bring me my charity accounts." Finding that he had given seven thousand gold denarii as charity, he declared, "The provisions are scanty and the road is long." He immediately distributed half of his wealth [as charity].

But how could he do such a thing?

Has not Rabbi Elai stated: It was ordained at Usha that if a man wishes to spend liberally, he should not spend more than a fifth [of his wealth on charity]?

[They answered] This applies only during a man's lifetime, since he might thereby be impoverished [if he gave away his own means of support], but after death this does not matter.

Commentary: Mar Ukba is the example of the individual who is maximally generous in charity. Halakah places a limit on the person who is so charitable that he would give away everything. The maximum a person is permitted to donate in any given year is one-fifth of his net worth. This does not apply, however, to bequests. At the time of death a person may give away as much of his fortune as he desires. The journey of which Mar Ukba speaks is the journey to eternal life in the world-to-come. Charity buys one a share of eternity.

Honesty in Business
(*Baba Metzia*, Mishnah 4, Talmud 60a,b)

Mishnah: *Ona'ah* ("oppression") is an overcharge of one-sixth the standard purchase price. How long does a person have to demand a refund due to *ona'ah*? As long as it takes him to show the item to (another) merchant or to a friend. Rabbi Tarfon taught in Lod: *Ona'ah* is an overcharge of one-third the standard purchase price. The merchants of Lod rejoiced. He said to them: "The customer has the whole day to demand a refund." The merchants said: "Let Rabbi Tarfon leave things the way they are," and they followed the [majority ruling of the] Sages. (Mishnah *Baba Metzia* 4:3)

Commentary: Here is a fine example of the relationship between Scripture and Talmud. The Sages are interested in defining *ona'ah*, oppression, because the Torah says, "You shall not oppress your neighbor." But, the Sages do not quote the Scripture, nor do they demonstrate an interest in explaining or commenting on Scripture in the manner of the midrash. Rather, the unquoted Scripture becomes the basis for a rabbinic discussion of honesty in business. The subject of business ethics arises in the civil code, the tractate *Baba Metzia,* in its proper place in the topical ordering of the Mishnah. The Sages take it for granted, on the basis of their own traditions, that *ona'ah* refers to economic oppression. One would not naturally come to that conclusion from reading the written Torah; one might think that the Torah was referring to social or political oppression. Here we see the relationship of Talmud to Scripture: The Talmud explains how to live by the Torah, but it is not a commentary on the Torah.

On the topic, the Sages believe in fair pricing, which is also an issue in contemporary American economic legislation. We may recall the public outrage in the 1970s when the price of petroleum at the wellhead shot upward and the major American oil companies raised the price on stored oil they had already purchased at the former lower prices. Overcharging is unjust to the consumer. The Sages define unfair pricing as a charge of more than one-sixth above the customary price. (The Sages presume a social setting in which goods are sold in the bazaar and the price is determined by barter.) Fair-pricing laws are not useful unless the customer has an opportunity to compare prices and seek a refund if necessary. The Sages therefore set a limited time span during which the exchange is not final. Rabbi Tarfon introduced a novel rule: the merchant may charge up to one-third over the standard price, but the customer has all day to demand a refund. The merchants determined that their loss was greater than their gain under this new system, and by their request the traditional ruling of the Sages was restored.

> **Mishnah:** Both the buyer and the seller are subject to the laws concerning *ona'ah*. Both a non-merchant and a merchant can make a claim regarding *ona'ah*. Rabbi Judah says: The merchant cannot make a claim regarding *ona'ah*. The victim of *ona'ah* controls the situation. If he wants he can say, "Give me back my money [and take back your goods]." If he wants he can say, "Give me back the amount which you overcharged me." (*Baba Metzia* 4:4)
>
> Just as there is *ona'ah* in commerce, so too is there *ona'ah* in speech. A person should not say, "How much does this cost?" when he has no intention of buying. If a person is a penitent, do not say to him, "Remember your past actions!" If a person is a child of converts, do not say, "Remember the actions of your ancestors [who worshiped idols]!" For Scripture says: "You shall not oppress or wrong him" (Exod 22:20). (*Baba Metzia* 4:10)

Commentary: Mishnah *Baba Metzia* 4:3 defines "oppression." The next mishnah discusses the application of the rule. Here the Sages disagree: the anonymous opinion is that the merchant and the buyer are both subject to the rule. The Sages believe that underpaying is as oppressive as overpaying. Rabbi Judah believes that only the buyer is protected by the rule of *ona'ah*. Perhaps he believes that the merchant, as a professional, can take responsibility for himself. Or perhaps Rabbi Judah believes that the rule exists only for the protection of consumers. Next we learn of another refinement to the law: the victim of an overcharge has the right to choose whether to void the transaction or take a refund of the overcharge and keep the goods.

The tenth mishnah in *Baba Metzia* 4 broadens the concept of "oppression." Note how easily the Sages shift between specific legal rulings and broad ethical principles for righteous behavior. This is typical of talmudic thought. From the legal prohibition of overcharging we extend the principle to the ideal that we should never say something to another person that makes him or her feel oppressed.

Mishnah: Rabbi Judah says: A shopkeeper must not give to children popcorn and nuts, because that encourages them to come to his shop [which is unfair to his competitors]. But the Sages permit it. Nor should a shopkeeper sell below market price. But the Sages say: Good for him! A shopkeeper, says Abba Saul, should not sift crushed beans. But the Sages permit it. They all agree that he may not sift them only at the top, for this is nothing but deceit.

Talmud: What is the reason of the Rabbis? Because the shopkeeper can say to his competitors, "I gave them nuts. You can give them plums."

Commentary: The Gemara explores the reasoning behind the debate between Rabbi Judah and the Sages over the morality of giving treats to children who are sent to do the shopping. The argument of the Sages is that this is not unfair because all shopkeepers are free to compete in this way, to the ultimate benefit of the consumers.

Talmud: Nor should a shopkeeper sell below the market price. But the Sages say: Good for him! What is the reason of the Rabbis? Because he helps to make the price more flexible.

Commentary: The same debate over fair pricing arises in our modern society. Some say that low prices are a monopolistic practice designed to drive competitors out of business and reduce competition, ultimately raising prices. Others say that whoever wants to charge a lower price is only benefiting the consumer, which is surely permissible. In this text the Sages permit low prices.

Talmud: A shopkeeper, says Abba Saul, may not sift crushed beans. But the Sages permit it. Who are these Sages? It is Rabbi Aha. For it has been taught: Rabbi Aha permits it with regard to goods that can be seen.

Commentary: Someone wants to know who is the source of the tradition that disagrees with Abba Saul. Another identifies this person as Rabbi Aha on the basis of a tradition he has received in the name of Rabbi Aha, which he now repeats. Rabbi Aha permits dressing up the produce for sale as long as the customer is free to sort through it.

Have you ever purchased a bag of fresh vegetables, only to find that the produce not visible is of lesser quality than that which shows through the cellophane? Or maybe you have bought some meat packed on a Styrofoam tray and discovered at home that the bottom side of the meat was unattractive. The Talmud would permit the shopkeeper to put the best produce on top in a loose bin, but if the produce is bagged so that only the top shows, then what shows must be representative of the quality of the whole.

Religious Zealotry: Killing in the Name of God
(*Yoma* 23a, *Sanhedrin* 82a)

This topic may seem especially relevant after the September 11, 2001, attack on the World Trade Center towers and the Pentagon.

Mishnah: For the honor of removing the ashes from the altar [on Yom Kippur], the priests who so desire run a race. Whoever first arrives within four cubits of the ramp that leads up to the altar wins. It once happened that two priests were tied. One shoved the other and he fell off the ramp and broke his leg. After that the Sages decreed that the honor is determined by lot.

Talmud: Our Rabbis taught: It once happened that two priests were equal as they ran to mount the ramp and when one of them came first within four cubits of the altar, the other took a knife and stabbed him in the heart. . . . All the people burst out weeping. The father of the young man came and found him still in convulsions. He said: "May he be an atonement for you. My son is still in convulsions, and the knife has not become ritually impure." [The father's remark] comes to teach you that the purity of their implements was of greater concern to them even than the shedding of blood. Concerning this the Scriptures say:

"Moreover, Manasseh [King of Judah] shed innocent blood very much, until he had filled Jerusalem from one end to the other." (*Yoma* 23a)

Commentary: The Talmud tells us two stories of violence in God's holy Temple, at the very foot of the altar where sacrifices of atonement are offered. In the first story assault leads to a broken bone. In the latter—to murder! The first story is in the Mishnah. The second story, in the Gemara, is introduced with the phrase "Our rabbis taught," which means that this story is a baraita—a teaching from the mishnaic era that is not included in the Mishnah but recorded later in the Gemara. The Amoraim are confused by the similarity of the two stories. They discuss (not included in our quotation) which event might have happened first. The stories are similar in plot but different in substance. The murder story raises the topic of religious zealotry. The father of the murder victim steps forward to make a statement. He does not comment on the death of his son or on the evil deed of the perpetrator. He only wishes to remind the audience that since his son is not yet dead, the knife used to stab him is still ritually pure. (The technical significance is that the knife could be retrieved from his son's body before his son dies, and it would then still be suitable for use in the sacrifices.)

This story belongs to a genre of rabbinic literature that we may call "speculation on the sin that caused God to allow the Romans to destroy the Second Temple." This was the rabbinic way of exploring the question "What are the social conditions that make it impossible for a society to survive?" The biblical prophets had predicted the downfall of the First Temple on account of idolatry and massive social injustice. The Rabbis were aware that such conditions did not prevail in the last days of the Second Temple. The Rabbis sought more subtle clues to the withdrawal of divine protection from Jerusalem, for they were certain that God would not have permitted the Romans to destroy the Temple except to teach Israel an exemplary lesson. In this story the Rabbis teach us that a society is hopelessly corrupted when people care more for religious purity than for human life.

The man who symbolizes this perversion of religion in our story is the father of the murder victim. It would be forgiven us if we doubted the historical veracity of the tale. Surely, we pray, no father could be so perverse. Perhaps our tale is a fiction inspired by the mishnaic story of the broken leg? And yet the experience of our own age tells us that such a father indeed exists. A young man straps himself into a bomb belt and commits suicide in order to take the lives of infidels. The father speaks to the press: "I am proud that my son died as a martyr." Isn't this the father of our tale, who is more concerned for the purity of religion than for human life, even the life of his own son? The Talmud teaches us that to be worthy of divine protection, a society must place the ethical concern for human life above the passion for religious purity.

> **Mishnah:** One who steals [sacred vessels from the Temple] or curses with enchantments or who fornicates with a heathen woman, he is punished by zealots.

> **Talmud:** Rabbi Hisdah said: If the zealot comes to take counsel [with the legitimate government or religious authorities over whether to take vigilante .action], we do not advise or instruct him to do so. It has been stated likewise: Rabba bar Bar Hana said in the name of Rabbi Jonathan: If he comes to take counsel, we do not instruct him to do so. What is more, had Zimri forsaken his mistress and Phinehas had slain him [anyway, even though he failed to catch him in the flagrant act of fornication], Phinehas would have been executed [for murder] on account of [having killed him, even though he was motivated by religious zealotry]. Also, had Zimri turned upon Phinehas and slain him, he would not have been executed, since Phinehas was pursuing him [to slay him, and Zimri would have killed him in legitimate self-defense.] (*Sanhedrin* 82a)

Commentary: The Sages divide sins into crimes punishable by a human court and those over which the courts have no authority, for which we rely on punishment "at the hands of Heaven." That is, God will punish the person, or we might say the consequences of his own misdeed will come back to haunt him. The Rabbis here add a third category: sins that are not punished by the courts (because they are committed in secrecy) but that will be found out and punished by zealots, religious vigilantes. The Rabbis base their list of such sins on biblical tales, in particular regarding fornication with a heathen woman. Numbers 25 records that idolaters seduced the Israelites into idolatry by offering them their daughters for extramarital relations. Zimri, a tribal prince, brought a heathen woman into his tent. Phinehas, the grandson of the high priest Aaron, was so outraged that he grabbed his spear and thrust it through Zimri and his lover together. The Torah avers that God was so pleased with Phinehas's zealotry that God offered the high priesthood to him and his descendants forever.

The Sages cannot contradict the judgment of the Scriptures, but they interpret in such a way as to greatly restrict extralegal actions motivated by religious passion. The Sages clearly disapprove of zealotry. The religious zealot is merely a murderer if he acts with any forethought or if he has not caught the sinner in the flagrant act of sinning. Zealotry is justifiable, if at all, only as the immediate impassioned response to a blasphemous outrage that is being performed before one's very eyes. Not only that, but the victim of zealotry, though a sinner, is legally permitted to defend himself—fatally, if necessary.

The halakah prohibits religious and civil authorities from validating the actions of the religious zealot either before or after the act. It is difficult for a zealot to justify his actions to himself unless he is assured of the approval of the legitimate authority figures of his society. Religious terrorists in our time are encouraged by incendiary sermons that urge the faithful to act on their own. The Talmud prohibits this. The Talmud of the land of Israel adds: "Phinehas acted without the approval of the rabbis, and Rabbi Yehudah ben Pazi says they sought to excommunicate him except that the Holy Spirit leapt to his defense" (*Sanhedrin* 9:7). In other words, zealotry is prohibited unless God speaks from heaven to condone it in a specific case. It is more difficult for the would-be zealot to justify himself in his own eyes and in the eyes of society if he gains no moral support from those in authority in his society. The Talmud teaches us that the zealot, even when acting righteously, should be considered an outcast.

Chapter Eight

Commentary

Commentary Replaces Midrash

Around the eleventh century, with the rise of the High Middle Ages, the Jewish way of reading Scripture underwent a great transformation. The ancient process of Torah interpretation we know as midrash came to an end. Midrash was succeeded and replaced by a new process known as commentary. Commentary differs from midrash in a number of significant ways. Among them:

- Midrash evolves from folk tradition, primarily from interpretations that became prevalent in the preaching in the ancient synagogue. Many works of midrash present a variety of religious perspectives. Historical scholars find it difficult to date the classic works of midrash because they do not reflect any particular historical circumstance or school of thought except in the broadest sense. A commentary, on the other hand, is composed by an individual author. The commentator has a philosophy of Judaism that he transmits through his interpretation of Scripture. A commentary has internal unity. Having an author, a commentary reflects a particular time, place, and point of view.

- Each entry in a book of midrash is independent of each other entry. Many books of midrash focus on particular Torah verses, often the opening verses of the ancient Torah portions, and skip over other verses. Certain verses become the locus classicus for discussion of a particular topic. Commentaries, by contrast, present a continuous narrative on the Torah. The commentator goes verse by verse through the Torah, or sometimes unit of meaning by unit of meaning. The commentator comments at each point in the Torah where he feels he has something new to teach.

- Midrash is based on imaginative wordplay. The message of the midrash overrides the original context of the Scripture. Commentaries, however, demonstrate a renewed interest in *peshat,* the simple meaning of the Torah text. Of course, what seems like *peshat* to one commentator may seem like *derash,* interpretation, to another commentator. Commentators quote earlier commentators and express their disagreements in logical discourse.

- Midrash reflects the religious worldview of late antiquity. Commentaries, arising in the Middle Ages, reflect the religious and intellectual concerns of their own historical era.

The transition from midrash to commentary is a historical fact. We can only speculate on why this change took place. Some possible reasons are these:

- After a millennium, the creative possibilities of midrash may have been played out. The analytic system of Rabbi Akiva, in which every "and," "if," "also," and "but" came to teach something, created openings for new perspectives on the Torah. But by the Middle Ages the unusual words in the Torah had been assigned a meaning that became crystalized in tradition through written works of midrash. The system became closed. The theory of Rabbi Ishmael, that "the Torah speaks in human language," which was once a conservative point of view, now became a tool for reopening the Torah to new interpretive vistas.

- The Jews were living in a new intellectual environment, in the midst of Christian and Muslim neighbors. The budding Christian universities were developing the Scholastic method of interpreting Scripture. The Scholastic scholars used logic to eliminate, explain, or conciliate contradictions. They were interested in harmonizing human reason with divine revelation. In the Muslim world, Arab scholars applied the seven liberal arts of the ancient Greek curriculum to the study of Scriptures. Under Arab intellectual influence, Jews began to look for evidence of philosophical and scientific truths in the Bible. Especially influential was the Arab study of grammar. Muslims consider the beauty of the Koran to be a prime proof of the truth and superiority of Islam. The Arabs found that grammar, the scientific study of language, was a superb tool for demonstrating the beauty of Koranic Arabic. Arabic and Hebrew are both Semitic languages, constructed similarly. The Jews learned from the Arabs to use grammar as a tool to analyze the Bible. The study of grammar must be associated with the renewed interest in *peshat.*

- In Babylon (Iraq), the Karaites adopted philosophy from the Muslims as a tool in their ongoing debate with the Rabbinites. The Rabbinites responded with their own Jewish philosophy. Torah commentary became a tool for transmitting philosophical ideas. Some rabbinic scholars expressed their philosophy entirely through Torah commentary. Other scholars wrote philosophical treatises, which influenced other commentators. Still other philosophers did both, writing both systematic theology and Torah commentary.

Although grammatical and philosophical studies originated among the Sephardic Jews of Spain, North Africa, and the Middle East, these ideas gradually spread to the Ashkenazic Jews of France, Germany, and England. Spain was the fertile ground where Muslims, Christians, and Jews exchanged ideas. It should not surprise us that most of the top-tier commentators were Spanish Jews. But the greatest commentator of them all, Rashi, was an Ashkenazic Jew from the Champagne district in northeastern France.

The Great Commentators

Rashi (1040–1105): Rashi is the acronym for Rabbi Shlomo Yitzhaki. He is always known as Rashi. As a young man Rashi studied in the great talmudic academies that had arisen in the Rhineland as European Jews became independent of the scholars in Babylon. Rashi then went home to Troyes, in France, and established his own academy, which became the greatest of them all. With the help of his disciples Rashi composed commentaries on every book of the Bible and every tractate of the Talmud. In his Torah commentary Rashi carefully distinguished *peshat* from midrash. His interpretations reinforced traditional Jewish piety. Indeed, Rashi's Torah commentary became the virtual definition of Jewish piety. When the Hebrew Bible was printed in 1475, it was printed with Rashi's commentary. Most later commentators refer to him, and there are hundreds of commentaries on his commentary (supercommentaries).

Abraham Ibn Ezra (1092–1167): Born in Spain, Ibn Ezra traveled to North Africa, Italy, France, and England. A poor man despite his brilliance, he often made his living as a tutor for the children of the wealthy. His acerbic wit kept him in trouble with his employers, but his students adored him. Ibn Ezra was aware that he was one of the smartest people ever. The fact that his great scholarship did not help him rise out of poverty undoubtedly affected his profound comments on divine providence. In his commentary Ibn Ezra attempted to transmit the scientific rationalism of the Sephardic intelligentsia to his more pietistic Ashkenazic audience. He often tread lightly, couching his more radical statements in enigmatic language and concluding, "The enlightened will understand." Ibn Ezra commented on most of the Bible, writing two different commentaries to Exodus.

Nahmanides (1194–1270): This is the acronym for Rabbi Moses ben Nahman, also known as the Ramban, who is not to be confused with Maimonides, the Rambam, philosopher, and codifier. Nahmanides was renowned in Spain as a Talmud scholar and halakist. In our chapter on midrash we have discussed his 1263 disputation with Pablo Christiani. Nahmanides was an eclectic thinker. He critiques Rashi and Ibn Ezra, adding his own insights. While he expounds the plain sense of the text, he often reveals insights from the Kabbalah, Jewish mysticism. Nahmanides belonged to the earliest known circle of scholarly Kabbalists, in Gerona, Spain.

Don Isaac Abravanel (1437–1508): A true Renaissance man, Abravanel's education included all the sciences, Bible and Talmud, and Jewish and also Christian philosophy. In his lifetime he served as finance minister and chief advisor to five different kings: two in Spain, two in Portugal, and one in Italy. Abravanel convinced Ferdinand and Isabella of Spain to send Columbus on his voyage of discovery. In 1492 Abravanel joined the rest of Spanish Jewry in exile, though Ferdinand and Isabella begged him to remain as their advisor. As the leader of Spanish Jewry, Don Isaac felt that he must share the fate of his people. His Torah commentary summarizes the accumulated wisdom of the Jewish golden age in Spain. He refers often to Maimonides and other Jewish Aristotelian philosophers, but his commentary also reflects the return to piety and tradition that characterized Spanish Jewry in the era of persecutions. His method of commentary differed from the verse-by-verse method of most of the classical commentators. Abravanel's way was to isolate a unit of meaning, raise questions about it, and then answer the questions in a lengthy essay. Unlike most commentators, who began with Genesis, Abravanel first wrote on the book of Deuteronomy. He was able to apply the insights of his diplomatic career to this book, which contains most of the social and political legislation in the Torah. Whereas the other great commentators are often published together, the length of Abravanel's commentary requires that it be published separately.

Rashi, Ibn Ezra, and Nahmanides constitute the "big three" of Jewish Torah commentators. The greatness of their commentaries was immediately recognized, and they remain the most significant commentators even to the present time. As an introduction to medieval commentaries, we will focus on some key comments of Rashi and Ibn Ezra. You will find that these commentaries are difficult, and the subjects they raise are complex. They were written by scholars for scholars. It may be hard to believe that these commentaries achieved universal popularity among Jews, but they did. Ordinary working Jews would study Rashi's commentary on a Sabbath afternoon. In Orthodox day schools in our time, Torah with Rashi's commentary is often taught to elementary students. People draw from the commentaries according to their own level of understanding:

In the Beginning

> **Torah:** In the beginning God created the heavens and the earth. The earth was unformed and void, with darkness over the surface of the deep and the spirit of God was hovering over the water. God said: "Let there be light" and there was light. (Gen 1:1–3)

> **Rashi:** Rabbi Isaac said: The Torah [which is the law book of Israel] should have commenced with the verse: "This month shall be for you the beginning of the months" (Exod 12:1), because this mitzvah [to establish the calendar] is the first mitzvah given specifically to Israel. Why, then, does the Torah commence with the account of Creation [and all the history in Genesis and Exodus that precedes the giving of the Torah at Mount Sinai]? Because . . . should the nations of the world say to Israel: "You are robbers because you took the Land of Israel by force from the Canaanites," Israel may reply to them, "God created the entire world and gave it to whom God pleased. When God willed He gave it to them, and when God willed He took it from them and gave it to us."
>
> "In the beginning"—This verse shouts "please interpret me." Our Rabbis interpreted this verse that the Torah is the "beginning" of all, and for the sake of Torah God created the universe. If, however, you wish to explain it in its plain sense, it is that the world was in such and such a state and God said "let there be light!" Understand that the Torah does not wish to point out the actual order of the acts of Creation, for had that been the intent of Torah it would have said "at first" (barishona) rather than "in the beginning" (bereshit). The word "reshit" always exists in a construct state with the verb that follows—"In the beginning of God's creating...." Should you wish to argue that we should read the text in a way that proves that the heavens and the earth were created first, the text itself states that the water was created first. Also, the heavens are made of fire and water, so the creation of these must have preceded

the creation of heaven. Thus we have proven [on the basis
of both grammar and content] that the Torah is not telling
us the sequence of the acts of Creation.

Lesson: Rashi opens his commentary by asking why the Torah
begins as it does. In his answer Rashi responds to two primary questions: "What is Torah?" and "Who are the Jews?" Rashi teaches us that
"Torah is mitzvot, commandments to live by," and "the Jews are the
people of the Land of Israel." Rashi upholds the traditional Jewish view
of Torah, that Torah is the source of God's commandments, which guide
and direct the life of the Jew. Everything in the Torah other than mitzvot
is secondary and is intended to bolster our observance of mitzvot.

Rashi lived in the time of the First Crusade (1095). The overwhelming question of world politics in his day was, "Who owns the
promised land, the Christians or the Muslims?" Rashi's answer is,
"Neither Christians nor Muslims; God gave the promised land to the
Jews." The Jews in the Middle Ages had no military or political power
to assert their claim, but Rashi's claim, based on the authority of
Scripture, must have given great pleasure to his Jewish contempo-
raries. "They fight over it, but God gave it to us, and someday God
will give it back to us."

Rashi then comments on the difficult grammar of the opening
words of the Torah. We have already discussed this problem in our
chapter on midrash, which prepares us for Rashi's comments. Then,
as now, the relationship of science to the Bible raised issues for
people. Does human knowledge come from our own ability to reason
and discover, or do we learn truth only when God reveals it to us? Do
we learn about reality from scientific investigation and logical inference, or by reading divinely revealed Scripture? By denying that the
Torah gives the actual order of creation, Rashi is telling his readers
that the Bible is not teaching science. One need not try to harmonize
scientific theories of existence with the biblical creation story. This
answer may have satisfied people in Rashi's own time, but as the centuries passed, the conflict between science and revealed religion
became more acute. In our times this issue divides Christian fundamentalists from secularists and Christian modernists.

All the commentators, including Rashi, discuss at length the
grammar of the first two words in the Torah. Should they be read as

a construct verb, as Rashi believes ("At the beginning of the creating of the heaven and earth...")? Or should the verb be read as an active verb in the past tense ("In the beginning God created...")? This second translation is that of the King James Bible in English, but Rashi preferred the former. There is more at stake here than mere words. In Rashi's time as in our own (though not in biblical times), people felt a need to uphold the doctrine of *creatio ex nihilo,* "creation from nothing" rather than from pre-existent matter. The idea that God and matter coexisted before creation would seem to place a limit on God's control over the universe. Rashi believes that the Torah gives us no information one way or the other about the origins of the basic building blocks of matter. Rashi understands our desire to know, but he tells us that some kinds of knowledge will remain beyond us. This issue is as relevant to the quantum physics of our time as it was relevant to the Aristotelian cosmology of Rashi's own time. We also want to know—did God create the laws of physics, or was God constrained by the laws of physics in creating the universe? Physicist Steven Hawking's best-seller, *A Short History of Time,* argued that the universe was created not from within a black hole but on the edge of a black hole, which would mean that the laws of physics were already operative at the point of creation.

Note that Rashi quotes the midrash and the traditions of the Rabbis, but he distinguishes these from the plain meaning of the Torah text.

The Divine Image in Humankind

Torah: Let us make man in our image, after our likeness. (Gen 1:26a)

Ibn Ezra: There are those [who are troubled by the plural form of this sentence, which might imply the existence of more than one deity] who suggest that the verb is actually passive ["Let them be made in the divine image"]. And they say that "in our image, after our likeness" are the words of Moses [when he wrote down the Torah]. . . . This interpretation is senseless. We can see this in texts such as

"He who sheds the blood of man, by man shall his blood be shed," because man was created in the Image, that it is the image of God that is intended, not the human form. Every creature has a form of its own, [but that form is held sacred only in the case of man, because his image is a reflection of the divine image]. The Gaon (Saadia Gaon of Babylon) said that "in our image, after our likeness" refers to man's rulership over the earth. According to him the "image" refers to wisdom, and it is to honor man that he is likened to God. The plural form, according to him, is the royal "we," for it is the nature of kings to speak of themselves in the plural form. But all the proofs that he brings are false [for grammatical reasons that Ibn Ezra explains]. Rabbi Moshe Hacohen of Spain, in his grammar book, interprets this wrongly, because he takes examples from the Aramaic language which do not compare to the Hebrew.

Now I will explain it correctly: Know that all the act of Creation was done for the sake of humankind by God's command. The plants and animals were all put into place first, brought forth from earth and water. After all was ready, God said to the angels "Let us make man. We ourselves will make him, and he will not sprout from the elements of earth and water." We must remember that the Torah speaks in human language, for it was spoken by a human and it is intended for human hearing. A person is not capable of speaking words that are beyond his capacity or beneath it, but only words fitting to the human imagination. Thus we find much anthropomorphism in the Torah. Forbid it, forbid it, that anyone would ascribe an actual physical form to God! Because the soul of man is transcendent, because it is immortal, it is compared in its vitality to God. The soul is not a body, and it fills the body [as the spirit of God fills the universe]. The body of man is like a universe in miniature. [The "image of God" in man is the soul, which functions in the body as God functions in the universe.] . . . Our blessed God started with what is large and ended with what is small. The Prophet Ezekiel said, "I saw the Presence of God in the likeness of a human being" (Ezek 1:28). God is the One, God is the creator of all, and God is all, and I am prevented from explaining [what this means].

Lesson: Ibn Ezra deals with a number of religious problems in this comment. In doing so, he concisely presents virtually his entire theology. His main point is that there is only one deity, incorporeal and indivisible. Virtually all Jews and Christians take this for granted nowadays, but only because this was the outcome of a debate that raged in the Middle Ages, when many people still thought of God as a large man sitting on a cloud in the sky. The "we" who created humankind are God and the angels; there is no multiplicity in God. All anthropomorphism in the Bible is idiomatic language, not to be taken literally. Ibn Ezra is generally science-minded. He believes in material cause and effect. He apparently believes, though, that humankind was created by a special act of divine will. The human "image of God" does not consist in our physical form (Ibn Ezra would disapprove of Michelangelo's painting on the ceiling of the Sistine Chapel). Neither does the divine image lie in our ability to reason or our ability to rule all other living creatures. It is the soul—eternal, incorporeal, vital—that makes us in the divine image. The soul inhabits and rules the body as God inhabits and rules the universe.

The reader gets a sense of Ibn Ezra's acerbic personality. He considers his own opinion to be superior to that of all other scholars. He quotes famous scholars only to demonstrate how foolish or wrong-minded their opinions can be.

Ibn Ezra's final comment is enigmatic. He is apparently referring to the pantheistic doctrine that all that exists is a part of God. He does not wish to go into the matter, possibly out of fear that one might draw the ultimate conclusion of pantheism, that each person is a miniature deity unto himself or herself. Baruch/Benedict Spinoza, who studied Ibn Ezra's commentary, did draw this conclusion. One reason that Spinoza was excommunicated by the Jews and shunned by the Christians of Amsterdam was that he stated explicitly many ideas that Abraham Ibn Ezra was content to imply.

Who Wrote the Torah?

Torah: The Lord spoke to Moses on Mount Sinai: Speak to the Israelite people and say to them, "when you enter the land that I give you, the land shall observe a sabbath of the Lord. Six years you shall sow your field and six years you may prune your vineyard and gather in the yield. But in the seventh year the land shall have a sabbath of complete rest." (Lev 25:1ff)

Rashi: What does the Sabbatical year have to do with Mount Sinai? Were not all the commandments given on Mount Sinai? This text comes to teach us that just as the commandment of the Sabbatical year was given on Mount Sinai with every single one of its principles, its particulars, its details, and its rules, so also, every one of the commandments was given on Mount Sinai with their general rules and particular details.

Lesson: The Sabbatical year commandment is the only mitzvah in the entire Torah, other than the Ten Commandments, of which Scripture itself claims that it was given at Mount Sinai. That raises a possibility—perhaps *only* these eleven were given at Sinai, and the rest were given elsewhere? But that would undermine the basic premise of the dual Torah of the Rabbis, that all was spoken by God to Moses at Mount Sinai! Rashi's interpretation supports traditional Jewish piety. Mount Sinai is mentioned in this one case to let you know that this case is representative of every case. The entire Torah, written and oral, was given by direct revelation from God to Moses. We should note that Rashi's great piety was typical in the culture of medieval Christendom. Compare this to the view of Ibn Ezra, who lived in Christendom but came from the scientific and rationalist world of medieval Muslim Spain.

Torah: These are the words that Moses addressed to all Israel on the other side of the Jordan, through the wilderness, in the Arava near Suph, between Paran and Tophel, Lavan, Hazerot and Di-Zahav; it is eleven days' journey from Horeb to Kadesh-Barnea by way of Mount Seir. (Deut 1:1–2)

Ibn Ezra: "Across the Jordan." If you understand the secret of the final twelve verses [of the Torah, which describe the death of Moses], and also the verse "On that day, Moses wrote down this poem and taught it to the Israelites" (Deut 31:22), and the verse "The Canaanites were then in the land" (Gen 12:6), and the verse "And Abraham named the place Ad-nai Yireh, as it is said to this very day, 'On the mountain of Ad-nai it is seen,'" and the verse "Only Og, King of Bashan, was left of the remaining Rephaim. His bedstead was made of iron; it is now in Rabba of the Ammonites; it is nine cubits long…," if you understand the secret of these verses you will know the truth.

Lesson: What these verses have in common is that they are the internal proof within the Torah that the Torah was not all given at Mount Sinai but at least some of the Torah was written at a later time and place. The location of Moses' speech in the book of Deuteronomy, on the Plains of Moab, is "across the Jordan" only for someone who is living in the land of Israel, after the time of Moses. If this verse were given at Mount Sinai, it would not have been "across the Jordan," for the Israelites crossed the Jordan under Joshua after the death of Moses. Similarly, these other verses speak from the perspective of a later time and place. There was apparently a museum in Rabbat Ammon that had a giant bed purported to be the legendary bed of Og. This had to be considerably later than the time of Moses, who fought and defeated Og in battle.

The truth that Ibn Ezra dared not name is that the Torah was written over a period of time and in a variety of locations. It did not all come from Mount Sinai. Ibn Ezra believed, as he reveals in various places in his commentary, that the Torah was written in four parts. One part was written at Mount Sinai, one part during the forty years of wandering in the desert, and one part by Moses on the plains of Moab just before his death. The fourth part is the sections of the Torah that were written by someone else after Moses' death—"perhaps by Joshua," says Ibn Ezra, leaving open the possibility that it was written by someone who lived much later than Joshua. Even though Ibn Ezra's theory seems rather conservative, the idea that the Torah was written progressively, and not all in one time and place, undermines the idea of an eternal and unchanging halakah. If Torah evolves, then Torah can evolve also in our own time. This was the position of the radicals of the Enlightenment who claimed an authority for their own rational minds equal to that of tradition. Ibn Ezra was aware of the radical possibilities of his theory of the composition of Torah. Living in the conservative Middle Ages, where change was not welcomed and traditional authority was not challenged, Ibn Ezra could only hint at the truth. His fellow scholars would understand what he meant. They could be trusted to keep the secret amongst themselves. Spinoza became renowned as the first modern philosopher to say openly and in public what scholars had acknowledged for centuries—that there was a human element in the composition of the Scriptures.

Despite Ibn Ezra's radical view on the composition of the Torah, he did believe that it was divine and inerrant in all of its parts. He did not doubt that every personage mentioned in the Torah actually lived and every event reported in the Torah actually occurred, as we see in the next passage.

> **Torah:** Then Ad-nai opened the donkey's mouth, and she said to Balaam, "What have I done to you that you have beaten me these three times?...Look, I am the donkey that you have been riding all along until this day. Have I been in the habit of [disobeying] you?" (Num 22:23–30)

> **Ibn Ezra:** Our Rabbi taught (in the midrash) that God created ten things on the eve of the sixth day of creation [the mouth of the earth that swallowed up Korah, the mouth of the well that spouted water for Moses in the desert, the mouth of Balaam's donkey, Noah's rainbow, the manna, the rod of Moses, etc. (*Avot* 5:9)]. In my opinion, the meaning of this midrash is that God decreed these ten miracles, which are outside the pattern of nature [and only these ten]. The Gaon [Saadia] said that the donkey did not actu-

ally speak [but it was an angel that spoke, and also in the case of the snake that spoke to Eve]. Rabbi Samuel ben Hofni supports this view. Rabbi Samuel of Spain, the poet, backs them up. You should know that the rationalists are obligated to interpret the words differently from their plain sense because they believe that God cannot perform miracles, to upend the laws of nature, except to justify a prophet. They are wrong, because Daniel's three friends who were thrown into the lion's den were not prophets and yet God performed a miracle for them. Some say that Balaam was a prophet [worthy of a miracle] but in fact he was merely a sorcerer, and so the Torah calls him. Some say that Balaam was able to draw on his knowledge as an astrologer to perform magic. If you can believe this opinion, so be it. The truth as I see it, is that Balaam was an astrologer, and he was able to foresee when something bad would happen to a person, and Balaam would then curse that person. When the bad thing came to pass, people believed that Balaam's curse had caused the event [and so they ascribed to him powers to make things happen that he did not really possess]. This is why Balaam spoke slyly with Balak's ministers, telling them that he could not transgress the word of God. That which is created cannot change the word or the decree of its creator. This is the principle: one part cannot transform another part, only that which has power over the whole can transform a part of the whole. And I cannot reveal any more of this principle, because it is a deep secret. The truth is that the donkey did talk. If you will understand the secret of the angels who communicated with Abraham, and with Isaac, then you will understand the truth.

Lesson: Does God perform miracles to save righteous people? To put it on a personal level, if you are good, will God protect you? Well, yes and no, says Ibn Ezra. The only miracles are those that were foreordained at the time of creation. Other than those ten miracles, the world progresses by strict material cause and effect. It rains on the good and the bad alike. But God has granted humankind a form of special providence. The wise are able to gain insight into the mind of God. This enables them to foresee trouble and thus avoid it. As a man of his times, Ibn Ezra believed that the stars were intermediaries between God and humankind, messengers of truth. Above the level of the astrologer is the level of the Torah scholar who knows both secular science and the word of God. Such a person (of which Ibn Ezra considered himself to be the prime example) can achieve a blessed existence through his intellectual apprehension of God. This blessing will not be material, however, as evidenced to Abraham Ibn Ezra by his life of poverty.

Ibn Ezra is a modernist ahead of his time in that, like Galileo, he is an empiricist rather than a rationalist. He believes that truth is learned from demonstration, not logic. Unlike a modern empiricist, who demands reproducible experimental evidence, Ibn Ezra accepts the report of the Torah as reliable data.

Genesis 22: The Binding of Isaac

Torah: After these things, God tested Abraham.

Rashi: [After what things? Or rather words, since the Hebrew for "things" also means "words"?] Some of our Sages state (Talmud *Sanhedrin* 89) that this means after the words of Satan, who denounced [Abraham] and said, "Of every feast which Abraham made he did not offer before You one ox or one ram." God said to Satan, "He does everything only for his son; if I were to say to him 'Sacrifice him to me!' he would not object." Others say, after the words of Ishmael, who boasted before Isaac that he was circumcised when he was thirteen years old and he did not protest. Isaac said to him, "With one organ you intimidate me? If the Blessed Holy One said to me 'Sacrifice yourself to me!' I would not hold back."

Lesson: In the Middle Ages one demonstration of the validity of a religion was the willingness of its adherents to endure martyrdom. Rashi quotes sources to show that both Abraham and Isaac were willing to give all that they had, even their life and progeny, for the sake of God. The Crusaders murdered many Jews even though church law protected Jewish lives in theory. The Jews could have saved their lives by converting, but they chose to die loyal to their faith and their people.

Torah: God said to him "Abraham" and he answered *"Hineni"* ("here I am").

Rashi: This is the answer of the pious. It is an expression of humility and an expression of preparedness.

Lesson: In Hebrew there is more than one way to say, "I am here." When one says *hineni,* it means "Here I am, ready and willing to do your bidding." Rashi explains the sense of the word to his readers.

Torah: God said to him, "Please take your son, your favored one, Isaac, whom you love, and go to the land of Moriah, and offer him there as a burnt offering on one of the heights which I will show you.

Rashi: Moriah is Jerusalem. So we find in Chronicles (2 Chron 3) "to build the house of the Lord in Jerusalem on Mount Moriah." Our Rabbis explained that it is called Moriah because from there "instruction" (*morah'ah* in Hebrew) went forth to Israel. But Targum *Onkelos* calls it the "mountain of myrrh," associating the name of the mountain with the incense that was to be offered there at the Temple.

Lesson: We do not know the location where Abraham is said to have offered up Isaac. Jewish tradition associates the place of the binding of Isaac with the location of the holy of holies in King Solomon's Temple. This legend was already current in the time of the author of the biblical book of Chronicles, who calls the Temple Mount "Moriah" on account of the story in Genesis, whereas earlier sources call it "Mount Zion." Rashi also gives another midrashic etymology for Mount Moriah as the Temple Mount, this one from the ancient Aramaic Targum. Rashi often quotes Targum *Onkelos* as an ancient source of biblical interpretation. It is typical that holy places such as the Temple Mount attract associations with other religious events. A later Muslim legend says that Mohammed had a dream in which he ascended to heaven from the location of the Temple Mount, on which the Muslims built two mosques.

> **Rashi:** God says "offer him up," but God does not say "slaughter him," because the Blessed Holy One did not desire to slaughter him but only to bring him up on the mountain in order to prepare him as a burnt offering. But after Abraham had brought him up, God said to him, "Take him down."

Lesson: The medieval commentators were bothered by the question of how and why God would test Abraham. Does not God already know the hearts of God's servants? Also, how could God appear to be so fickle as to command something and then reverse the divine command? Rashi's solution is simple: God did not change his mind; God simply used ambiguous wording to test Abraham. God's command to "offer up" Isaac was fulfilled by placing him alive on the altar. The later great commentators are dissatisfied with Rashi's explanation here. Ibn Ezra says that God truly tested Abraham in order to reward him. Ibn Ezra, who prefers textual evidence to pure logic, avers that God can change his mind when he wishes. Nahmanides says that God tested Abraham to turn his potential righteousness into actual righteousness (as, for example, lighting a fire turns potential energy into actual energy.)

> **Torah:** On the third day Abraham looked up and saw the place from afar. Then Abraham said to his servant-lads, "You stay here with the donkey. The boy and I will go up there; we will worship and we will return to you."

> **Rashi:** Why did God wait until the third day? So that no one could say: "God confounded and confused him suddenly and distracted his mind, but if he had had time to

reconsider he would not have done it." The two lads are
Ishmael and Eliezer.

Lesson: The binding of Isaac is a troubling story. Many secularists in modern times use it as an example of the evils of religion,
which inspires parents to sacrifice their children as soldiers in times
of war. The suggestion that a loving father would not sacrifice his son
is a challenge to both Judaism and Christianity. Rashi says that
Abraham is not an exemplar of fanatical obedience to religious leadership; Abraham carefully considered God's commandment, and he
decided that obedience was proper in this case. Rashi upholds the
ideal that it is right to offer oneself and all that one holds dear for a
valid cause.[37]

The servant lads in the Genesis story are anonymous. Rashi identifies the two lads as Ishmael, Abraham's son by Hagar, and Eliezer of
Damascus, Abraham's chief steward. In medieval Judaism, Ishmael and
Eliezer are the archetypes of Islam and Christianity. Ishmael is symbolic of Islam. On the basis of the biblical story that Ishmael is the
father of the Arab tribes, Arabs claim descent from him. Eliezer is the
symbol of Christianity. Damascus, the town of his origins, was one
of the earliest centers of Christianity. Rashi is saying that Abraham
goes to the mountain with three lads, the representatives of Judaism,
Christianity, and Islam. Abraham then goes up the mountain with
Isaac while he leaves the other two behind. In Rashi's day as in our
time, the Christians and Muslims are numerous and powerful while
the Jews are a small and powerless minority in their midst. Rashi
assures his Jewish readers that despite their lack of earthly success
they are still the chosen ones of God. Rashi bolsters the faith and
self-confidence of the Jewish people in the difficult days of the
Crusades.

Torah: The two of them walked together. Then Isaac said
to his father Abraham "Father!" And he answered, "Yes,
my son." And he said, "Here is the firestone and the wood,

---

37. In truth, the secularists have their own causes for which devotion unto death
and sacrifice are deemed acceptable, such as making the world safe for democracy in a
war against totalitarian fascism. For a great modern exploration of the issue that Rashi
deals with here, read Søren Kierkegaard's *Fear and Trembling*.

but where is the sheep for the burnt offering?" And Abraham said, "God will see to the sheep for the burnt offering, my son." And the two of them walked together.

Rashi: "Together"—Abraham who was aware that he was going to slay his son walked along with the same willingness and joy as Isaac who had no idea of the matter.

"My son"—Although Isaac then understood that he was going to be slain, still "the two of them walked together"— with one heart.

Lesson: What was in the mind and heart of Abraham and Isaac as they went up the mountain? Rashi, with his fine sense for the text and his deep understanding of the human psyche, recognizes that the Torah tells us everything we want to know in the repetition of one phrase—"the two of them walked together." The story lets us know at what point Isaac learns of his father's plan. Rashi helps us in our literary appreciation of this well-told story. At the same time, he gives us a lesson in religious devotion. The father who goes to sacrifice his son, and the son who goes to be sacrificed, each walk with joy and pleasure in sharing the company of the other. They have complete confidence in one another and in God.

The Publication of the Jewish Bible: *Mikraot Gedolot*

The commercial printing press was invented in the fifteenth century. The Jews had a high rate of literacy, which attracted publishers both Jewish and Christian to Hebrew books. The first printed Hebrew book was the Torah with Rashi's commentary in 1475. A Christian publisher, Daniel Bomberg, created the standard for publishing the Jewish Bible and the Talmud. Bomberg published the Talmuds of Israel and Babylon in 1523. His Talmud pagination became the standard that is followed to this day. In 1517 Bomberg published the entire Hebrew Bible including the Aramaic Targum, Rashi's commentary, the Masora—the notes compiled over the centuries by Jewish scholars on the proper format of the Hebrew text— and some other commentaries on various biblical books. In

1524–1525 Bomberg published an expanded edition of the Hebrew Bible including the major commentators. It is called the *Mikraot Gedolot,* which means "The Expanded Scriptures." In English the *Mikraot Gedolot* is often called the Rabbinic Bible. Later versions of *Mikraot Gedolot* by other publishers added more commentaries but stayed with Bomberg's basic format.

The *Mikraot Gedolot* contains the Hebrew text of the Bible at the top center of the page, with the Targum below it. Surrounding the text, and often filling the facing page as well, are the various commentaries. The biblical text is distinguished from the commentaries by typeface. The Bible is printed in "square" letters, the ancient Aramaic alphabet, which is also used for the handwritten Torah scroll. The biblical text is punctuated with the Masoretic vowel markings and the Masoretic cantillation marks that preserve the traditional chant by which Scripture is recited aloud. The commentaries are printed in a medieval cursive alphabet that came to be known as "Rashi script." The commentaries are not vocalized.

The format of the *Mikraot Gedolot* promotes the Jewish concept that Torah study is a dialogue. One does not just read the Bible. Rather, one reads the Bible along with the various commentators, who disagree with one another on the meaning of each verse. The reader is drawn into the conversation, coming to his or her own opinion about who is right and who is wrong and what the Torah is really saying. Studying from a *Mikraot Gedolot* is like participating in a seminar led by a group of brilliant and contentious scholars.

The *Mikraot Gedolot* has been periodically republished with additional commentaries. In the 1870s two new editions, one from Warsaw and one from Vilna, became standard. Both featured the "big three" commentators—Rashi, Ibn Ezra, and Nahmanides—plus other commentaries, the Targums, and the Masora. For the next century, Jews had to content themselves with difficult-to-read photo reprints of these texts. In 1986 the *Mikraot Gedolot* was newly typeset and republished by the Mossad HaRav Kook[38] in Jerusalem. This work, entitled *Torat Haim* ("Torah of Life"), covers only the Torah, not the

---

38. The Mossad HaRav Kook was established in Jerusalem in 1937 to publish modern editions of the classic writings of Judaism. Many of the works of midrash, philosophy, and commentary mentioned in this book are available in quality Hebrew editions from the Mossad HaRav Kook.

Prophets and Writings. It includes the Torah text, the Targum *Onkelos,* and the commentaries of Rashi, Ibn Ezra, Nahmanides, Saadia Gaon, Rabbenu Hananel, Rashbam (Samuel ben Meir), David Kimhi, Hizkuni, Hinnuch, and Ovadia Sforno, and the Masora of Rabbi Meir of Rothenberg, altogether representing the ninth to the sixteenth century and countries from Iraq to North Africa to Italy to Spain to France and Germany. *Torat Haim* differs from the earlier *Mikraot Gedolot* in that the commentaries are printed in square letters. This is an important concession to the needs of the modern Israeli, who reads Hebrew with ease but is usually uncomfortable with the difficult Rashi script.

The modern Jew or non-Jew who reads English but little or no Hebrew can obtain a feel for the style of the *Mikraot Gedolot* by studying Torah from a book called the Humash (lit. "the Five," for the five books of the Torah). We will discuss the Humash in chapter 10 of this book.

Chapter Nine

Mystical Midrash

Kabbalah

In the Middle Ages a new Jewish mystical doctrine developed in Provence and Catalonia, in southern France and northeastern Spain, respectively. Known as Kabbalah, which means "tradition," this doctrine circulated at first among a small group of learned Rabbis. Like mystics of all religions, the initiates of Kabbalah were secretive about their doctrines, teaching them only to selected worthy disciples. The power of Kabbalah was such, however, that it attracted larger and larger numbers of Jews. By the seventeenth century, a majority of the world's Jews followed the teachings of Kabbalah.

The central text of Kabbalah is the *Zohar,* the "Book of Enlightenment." The *Zohar* was published around 1280 by Moses deLeon of Castile, in Spain. Most historians believe that Moses deLeon was the author of the *Zohar,* but Jewish mystics attribute authorship to Rabbi Simon bar Yohai, a second-century Galilean Rabbi who is the main literary character in the *Zohar.* The *Zohar* describes an ideal rabbinic world in which Rabbi Simon and his disciples travel around Galilee, encountering saintly people and acquiring insights into the profound secrets of the Torah. In the *Zohar* a donkey driver, a young boy, or an old man may reveal himself to be a Torah scholar and a hidden mystical master.

In form, the *Zohar* is a midrash to the Torah. The *Zohar* explains the mystical meaning of various verses and sections of the Torah, interspersed with stories and essays that develop the doctrines of the Kabbalah. It is written in a made-up language of its own, an artificial form of ancient Aramaic. The *Zohar* provides a powerful new justification for the observance of Judaism in even its smallest ritual details

158

by positing a cosmic chain of being in which the observance of mitzvot on earth generates positive reactions in the heavenly realm.

The central concept of the Kabbalah as developed in the *Zohar* is the doctrine of the *sefirot*. The ten sefirot (sing. *sefirah*) are emanations of God. God begins the act of creation within God's own being. From the Ein Sof, "Infinite Nothing" or "Endless Being," God creates the ten divine *sefirot,* each born from the one above it. The pattern of God's internal ten *sefirot* is then repeated in the creation of the spiritual realms and finally in the creation of the material world. Each human soul, as a universe in miniature, contains within itself the pattern of the ten *sefirot*. The doctrine of the emanation of the *sefirot* suggests a similar pattern within the being of God, the cosmos, the human social order, and the individual human psyche.

The ten *sefirot* are sometimes depicted as concentric circles and other times in a pattern of three descending columns called the "cosmic tree" with *sefirot* in the center, on the left, and on the right. Each *sefirah* has a multitude of names; they are commonly named Keter (crown), Hochmah (wisdom), Binah (understanding), Da'at (knowledge), Hesed (grace), Gevurah (judgment), Tiferet (beauty or compassion), Nezah (endurance), Hod (majesty), Yesod (foundation, the masculine principle), and Shekinah (presence, the feminine principle). Ein Sof is God in absolute transcendence, and Shekinah, the lowest sefirah, represents God in intimate contact with humankind. In many ways God's Shekinah is closer to humankind than to her source in the Godhead (ultimate divinity).

The ten *sefirot* provide a pathway between heaven and earth, a sort of great machine. The performance of mitzvot opens up the pathways between the heavenly *sefirot,* permitting a downflow of divine blessing and plenitude. Sins block the heavenly passageways, creating distance between God and humankind. The mystical adept, who practices the commandments and knows their mystical significance, is able to perform great acts of unification between God and humankind, acts that bring healing to the human condition.

According to the *Zohar,* the characters we meet in the Torah are actually symbols for the various *sefirot*. The things that befall the biblical characters in the stories of the Torah relate information about the interaction of the *sefirot*. For example, the three patriarchs—Abraham, Isaac, and Jacob—symbolize the *sefirot* of Hesed, Gevurah, and Tiferet. Since the *sefirot* exist first of all within the being of God, the stories of human interaction in the Torah symbolically reveal the inner life of God's own mind. In the Kabbalah the Torah is not just a revelation from God; it is the self-revelation of God.

Let us now examine some examples of how the *Zohar* interprets Torah according to the mystical doctrines of the Kabbalah:[39]

In the Beginning

When the King conceived ordaining, He engraved engravings in the luster on high.

A blinding spark flashed within the Concealed of the Concealed.

From the mystery of the Infinite, a cluster of vapor in formlessness, set in a ring.

Not white, not black, not red, not green, no color at all.

When a band spanned, it yielded radiant colors.

Deep within the spark gushed a flow imbuing colors below, concealed within the concealed of the mystery of the Infinite.

The flow broke through and did not break through its aura.

It was not known at all until, under the impact of breaking through,

one high and hidden point shone.

Beyond that point, nothing is known. So it is called the "Beginning,"

the first command of all....

Zohar, Concealed of the Concealed, struck its aura.

The aura touched and did not touch this point.

This Beginning emanated and made for itself a palace for its glory and praise....

The silkworm wraps itself within and makes itself a palace.

This palace is its praise and a benefit to all.

With the "Beginning" the Concealed One who is not known created the palace.

---

39. All translations are from Daniel C. Matt, *Zohar: The Book of Enlightenment*, Classics of Western Spirituality (New York: Paulist Press, 1983).

This palace is called *Elohim* (God).

The secret is, "With the Beginning, [the Infinite One] created Elohim."

Lesson: Many people think that mystics are rather crazy or even that mysticism is a form of insanity. The bizarre language of mystical expression can create that impression. The above text is a good example. In reality, mystics are quite sane. Societies that treasure mystical adepts also have insane people, and they know the difference. The far-out language of mystical literature is poetic metaphor, an attempt to express in words what is beyond words.

Our present text uses the following metaphors: an engraver engraving, a beam of light expanding through a prism into a rainbow, a point of light seen through a fog, a silkworm making a cocoon. These four metaphors describe God's work of creation as understood in the *Zohar*. Let us examine these metaphors for the quite rational lessons they transmit.

As an engraver draws lines in a stone to create a picture, so God functions as an engraver, drawing the universe, as it were, in three dimensions. We note in the *Zohar* a knowledge of and interest in geometry. The poem describes a buildup of the creative force until it explodes into a point, the original point of creation. Note that this poetic medieval image seems congruent with the modern-day big bang theory of the creation of the universe. The similarity between Kabbalah and contemporary scientific notions of creation and evolution has been noted by many contemporary Jews.

The *Zohar* attempts to resolve one of the main quandaries of monotheistic religion—how does a world of multiplicity derive from a Creator God who is absolutely One? Our world includes conflict, evil, and injustice. We experience existence as a series of sometimes antagonistic and sometimes complementary dualities. How does all this derive from one God who is good, just, and complete? The *Zohar* answers with a metaphor. It is like many colors of light expanding from a single beam of white light. God's creative force is the white beam, and as it expands into the created universe, it becomes multiple, like the multicolored beams of the rainbow. They are all rooted in the unitary white light. The *Zohar* tells us that the original expansion from unity to multiplicity takes place within the being of God.

Punning on the opening words of the Torah, the *Zohar* tells us that God's first creation was Elohim, God's own self. This refers to the emanation of the ten divine *sefirot* out of the Ein Sof. In our chapter on midrash we discussed the two names for God in the Torah. The *Zohar* teaches that YHWH is the Ein Sof, the ultimate unity of God, while Elohim refers to the ten *sefirot* that together make up the inner being of God, God's personality as it were.

The image of the point of light breaking through, like a candle seen in a fog, is most interesting. How can something come from nothing? Once God, the engraver of the universe, has a point of being to work with, God (like a human mathematician) can extend the point into a line, the line into a plane, and the plane into the three dimensions of a cube or sphere, the universe. Arguing backward, a three-dimensional object is created from two dimensions, the two-dimensional object from one, and the one-dimensional object from zero dimensions, the point. This point is the beginning of creation, and nothing can be said about what comes before it, but we can continue to argue backward that the object of zero dimensions, the point, is created by the being of less than zero dimensions, God. This is the light breaking through the aura. God is what precedes that which cannot be comprehended or explained.

One more image—the larva makes a cocoon, as God creates the universe. The larva makes a cocoon so that it can be transformed into a butterfly. What does this image suggest about God's reason for creating the universe? The universe is a palace for God's glory to be revealed, and that glory will be seen at the end of time, just as the butterfly will emerge from its cocoon when its transformation is complete. We learn elsewhere in the *Zohar* that the task of humankind is to assist God in that act of transformation through the fulfillment of Torah.

The mystical imagery of the *Zohar* is densely packed with meaning. Its allure has captivated many. Despite the difficult language, the *Zohar* has enticed multitudes of Jews to ignore Rabbi Akiva's warnings about the danger of mystical speculation and engage in Kabbalistic study.

The Source of the Soul

Torah: YHWH said to Avram: Go forth from your land, your place of birth, your father's house, to the land that I will show you. I will make you a great nation, and I will bless you; I will make your name great, and you will be a blessing. I will bless those who bless you and curse those who curse you, and all the families of the earth will bless themselves by you. Abram went forth as YHWH had directed him, and [his nephew] Lot went with him. (Gen 12:1–4)

Zohar: Rabbi Jacob son of Idi said: The souls of the righteous are all carved from the bedrock of the Throne of Glory, to guide the body as a father guides a son. Without the soul the body could not conduct itself [for the soul guides the body and responds to the divine Will]. When the Blessed Holy One sends the soul [into an earthly body] God blesses it with seven blessings. The soul is called Avram because it is *Av,* a "father" to the body and because it is *ram,* "elevated," for it comes from a high and holy place. God tells the soul to "go forth" from the heavenly realms "to the land I will show you," meaning, to the body of such and such a person. God promises to bless those souls that guide the body to do righteous deeds, and to curse those souls that guide the body to act perversely.

[Lot who went with Abraham symbolizes the evil impulse that enters a person when the soul enters the person, to mislead him into performing evil deeds.]

Lesson: When God created the world, God created one cosmic soul, the Primordial Adam. This soul is known also as God's Throne, for God rules the world through the spirit. Every individual human soul is a spark from this cosmic soul. The human person consists of body and soul. The soul provides consciousness, is able to comprehend the will of God, and is responsible to guide the deeds of a person to fulfill God's will. The soul has freedom and is able to obey or rebel. The evil impulse derives from the dark side;

it attempts to mislead the soul. The responsibility of every soul is to
fulfil its mission on earth by obeying the will of God. We learn elsewhere in the *Zohar* that when the individual soul does this, it
returns to its source and the soul of the first Adam is ultimately
reconstituted in its pristine unity.

The perspective of the *Zohar* is dualistic, both in its view of
body and soul (material and spiritual worlds) and in its view of good
and evil coming from two separate sources. This is in marked contrast
to the Rabbis of the talmudic era, who opposed all dualism.

The *Zohar* here interprets the story of Abraham in the book of
Genesis as a symbol for the travels of the soul in the material world of
human being. As Abraham is a resident foreigner in a strange land, so
is the divine soul a pilgrim here in the lower world of created being.

The Goal of All Creation

> **Torah:** YHWH called to Moses from the Tent of Meeting,
> saying: Speak to the Children of Israel and say to them,
> "When any of you brings a *korban* ["sacrifice," literally,
> "that which is brought near"] to YHWH.... (Lev 1:1–2)

> **Zohar:** Rabbi Hezekiah was in the presence of Rabbi
> Simon [bar Yohai]. He said to him: That which is called
> *korban,* should it not be called *keirub,* "drawing near," or
> *keribut,* "nearness"? Why is it called *korban* [that which is
> brought near—a noun, rather than a participle]? Rabbi
> Simon replied: This is well-known to the Comrades (the
> circle of disciples). Korban represents the drawing near of
> the holy crowns (the ten *sefirot*), drawing near to one
> another, connecting with one another, uniting into a com-
> plete oneness to perfect the holy Name. That is why it is
> written "korban to YHWH," and not to "Elohim," so that
> compassion will fill all the worlds. For this purpose we
> need compassion, which is YHWH, and not judgment
> which is "Elohim." Rabbi Hezekiah said: I am so glad that
> I asked this and gained clarity about what these words
> mean.

Lesson: Our world is broken and full of injustice. Israel is in exile from her land, oppressed and downtrodden. The fallen state of the world and the lowly estate of Israel in the material world below are reflections of the state of affairs in the heavenly world above. The ten divine *sefirot* are out of sorts with one another. The cosmic machine is broken, preventing the downflow of divine blessing into the world. Israel is in exile from her land because God is in exile from God's own being. When the ten *sefirot* are restored to harmonious relationship, then the overflow of divine compassion can fill the world with blessing and restore Israel according to all the biblical promises. God cannot accomplish this by God's own self. God requires the actions of humankind, specifically of the Jews who are devoted to mitzvot and who know the Kabbalistic meaning of each mitzvah, to accomplish the unification of God's being and thus of the universe. Every act of righteousness performed with proper intention is an act of *yihud,* of reuniting God with the world. Later Jewish mystics applied the term *tikkun olam,* "repairing the universe," to such actions. When the broken universe is fixed, "God will be One and God's name will be One," as promised by the prophet Zechariah. That will be the messianic age of a perfect world. God is in need of human obedience to bring this about. Every mitzvah plays a role in creating unity between the *sefirot.* Thus the Kabbalah becomes a powerful motivator for both ethical mitzvot and ritual mitzvot. It may be hard for a Jewish rationalist to believe that God cares whether there is pork on his dinner plate. But if keeping kosher is an act of *tikkun* that fixes our broken world and creates harmony on every level of being, then it is worth the effort. Faithful observance of God's mitzvot is the sacrifice that is called *korban,* "that which is brought near," because it reunites the *sefirot.*

The two divine names YHWH and Elohim function in this portion of the *Zohar* according to two different symbol systems. In the first symbolic pairing, YHWH represents God in ultimate unity, the Ein Sof, while Elohim represents God in the aspect of the ten *sefirot.* In the next sentence the name YHWH refers to the fifth *sefirah,* which is Hesed, or divine compassion, while the name Elohim refers to the sixth *sefirah,* which is Gevurah, or divine judgment. This constant shifting of metaphors is common in the *Zohar* and in mystical literature in general. Here the two divine names first represent the contrast between God's transcendence and God's presence, and then the dramatic tension between God's compassion and God's judgment.

Lurianic Kabbalah and Hasidism

The Kabbalah, like most mystical systems, was developed by and for a small group of learned initiates. The Kabbalists permitted the teaching of the secret doctrines only to an individual disciple and only if the disciple was married, mature, and learned in Torah, Talmud, and halakah. But the doctrines of Kabbalah were so compelling that more and more Jews studied it. During the Renaissance there were even Christians who learned Hebrew and Aramaic and developed a Christian version of the Kabbalah. Around the year 1580 a group of Kabbalists gathered in the city of Safed in Galilee, from where they could gaze at Mount Meron—burial place of Rabbi Simon bar Yohai, reputed author of the *Zohar*. For two years, until his untimely death, the leader of this circle of Kabbalists was Rabbi Isaac Luria. Luria developed his own reading of the *Zohar*, which became normative. We call it the Lurianic Kabbalah. Isaac Luria proposed that God created the world in three steps. The first is *tsimtsum*, "contraction." God diminished the infinitude of God's own being to create an empty space for the existence of the universe. Significantly, creation begins with an absence of God. The second stage is emanation. God creates the universe by exhaling, as it were, into the emptiness, one *sefirah* at a time, like a person with chewing gum blowing larger and larger bubbles. The third stage of creation is the disaster of "the breaking of the vessels." As God's holy light fills the universe, the lower and more material *sefirot* are unable to contain this light, like delicate glasses into which hot water is poured. The vessels shatter, breaking the pathway between heaven and earth and trapping the lowest *sefirah*, the Shekinah, in the material universe. As Israel is in exile from her land, so God is in exile from God's own being. Fallen sparks of divine light are captured in the shell of the material world. Going through the world performing mitzvot, Jews release these sparks so they can return to their source in the upper world. Israel is in exile in order to find and release the sparks wherever they lie. It is a descent for the sake of ascent, like the act of creation itself.

The function of the mitzvot is to repair the broken connection between the *sefirot,* returning the Shekinah to her source in the Ein Sof. This function is called *tikkun olam,* repairing the world. The Kabbalah of Isaac Luria achieved wide popularity, especially with Jews who were suffering from the aftereffects of the 1492 expulsion from Spain and, in Eastern Europe, from the Cossack rebellion against the Poles in 1634. The Lurianic Kabbalah validated the sufferings of the Jews and offered them hope. It gave a powerful incentive for faithful religious observance in difficult times. God and Israel would rise together from exile to redemption through the process of *tikkun olam.*

The last great stage of Kabbalah was the movement of Hasidism. Hasidism developed around Rabbi Israel ben Eliezer, the "Baal Shem Tov" (1700–1760), and his circle of disciples. The disciples scattered around Poland and the Ukraine, establishing local Hasidic groups. Each Hasidic leader was addressed as rebbe, not rabbi. The rebbes' authority was based on their charisma, their intimacy with God, rather than on their Talmud scholarship. The early rebbes were mostly miracle workers and faith healers, similar to the religious leaders of charismatic Christianity, which evolved at the same time in nearby southern Germany. The rebbe was called the *tsaddik,* the "righteous one" who could use his knowledge of the *sefirot* to intervene with God. The follower was called a Hasid, a "pious one." The Hasidim came from the relatively uneducated Jewish masses of southern Poland and the Ukraine. They may not have understood the details of the esoteric doctrine of the Kabbalah, but they gained a general understanding through the preaching and teaching of the *tsaddik,* the beloved rebbe. Just as all Americans today have a general understanding of psychology, so Hasidism gave to every Jewish devotee a general understanding of Kabbalah.

The rebbe preached to his congregation on Sabbath afternoon, after morning worship services. He sat at his dinner table for the third Sabbath meal, surrounded by his Hasidim, who crowded into the room. Many had come on pilgrimage from other villages to hear the rebbe speak Torah. The rebbe's talk was full of consolation and encouragement, expressed in the language of popular Kabbalah. Naturally, since it was the Sabbath day, the rebbes based their talks on the *parashat hashavua',* the weekly Torah portion. Many rebbes kept a written record of their talks and published them as Hasidic commentaries on the Torah. Though the talks were given in Yiddish, the rebbes wrote their commentaries in Hebrew, the Jewish language of learning. In this way a new genre of Torah literature was created, interpreting Torah in popularized Kabbalistic terms.

Hasidism took the cosmic tragedy that stood at the heart of Lurianic Kabbalah and transformed it into a psychology. The battle to free the sparks from the shells, in Hasidism, takes place primarily within the individual human psyche. Not just the initiate but even the ordinary Jew may participate in this struggle by fulfilling the mitzvot and serving God with joy in community with the other Hasidim. The psychological aspect of Hasidic Kabbalah is especially pronounced in the work of Rabbi Levi Yitzhak of Berditchev. Had he lived a century later and five hundred miles to the west, perhaps he would have served the role eventually filled by Sigmund Freud.

Among the greatest Hasidic Torah commentaries is the *Kedushat Levi* of Rabbi Levi Yitzhak. Levi Yitzhak (1740–1810) was a Talmud scholar as well as one of the great leaders in the third generation of Hasidism. He filled two roles in Berditchev, serving as both learned rabbi and charismatic rebbe. In the passage from *Kedushat Levi* that we present here, Rabbi Levi Yitzhak uses Lurianic terminology in presenting the mystical concept of the negation of ego, which is called in Kabbalah *bittul ha-yesh*.

The Negation of Ego

> **Torah:** See, I have placed before you today blessing and curse: blessing, if you obey the commandments of YHWH your God which I enjoin upon you today; and curse, if you do not obey the commandments of YHWH your God, but turn away from the path which I enjoin upon you today and follow other gods whom you have not experienced. (Deut 11:26, from the weekly Torah portion *Re'eh*)

> **Commentary:** We may wonder that the Torah offers us "blessing and curse" together rather than offering the blessing separately for

observing God's commandments, and the curse separately for failing to observe God's commandments.

But the truth is that there is a curse contained within the blessing of the commandments. The curse is the curse of egotism, that a person who performs a mitzvah (divine commandment) might think that he is really "something," since he has done a mitzvah, whereas the truth is that he is really nothing, for when one considers the greatness and infinitude of God, one realizes that one can never even begin to serve God, for God is everything and we are nothing.

When a person becomes "something" and thinks that he is a spiritual person and a good person because he is doing mitzvot, he is actually moving away from God and therefore becoming less spiritual, for there is no room for God when a person is full of himself. God is the Creator of all the worlds, and God encompasses and contains all being. How, then, can one say that one has served God? Self-awareness is the curse that accompanies the blessing of the mitzvot.

When one realizes that one is always at the beginning and has not yet even begun to serve God, then one will be filled with passion for God and will serve God with all one's heart and soul. To such a person the Scriptures refer in saying that "their strength shall be renewed" (Isaiah), for they start fresh each day, not thinking that they have achieved anything the day before.

God is Ein Sof, "infinite nothingness," but out of love for us God takes on the aspects of grace and judgment. God expresses grace in the desire to reach out to us and uplift us with God's spirit, and God expresses judgment in willingly limiting the extent of the divine being, turning the infinite into something finite, in order to reach out to us in a manner that we are able to receive, without overwhelming us. God practices *tsimtsum,* intentional self-limitation, in order to establish a pathway between Creator and creation.

Those who wish to serve God likewise demonstrate grace and judgment: grace in reaching up toward God and attempting to serve God, and judgment in recognizing that we are nothing and our efforts are nothing compared to God's greatness.

Lesson Summary: We are by nature something—material beings—but we can rise to the level of communion with God by making ourselves nothing. Only by becoming nothing can we even begin to serve God. God is by nature nothing (infinity is nothingness), but out of God's passion to reach out to us, God becomes something—self-limiting, reaching down into material existence through the self-generated *sefirot*—in order to enter into relationship with us. We find our true existence not in ourselves but in God. God makes this possible for us through God's act of *tsimtsum*, self-limitation.

Note Levi Yitzhak's particular take on *gevurah*, or *din*—divine judgment. He understands judgment as the act of setting boundaries and limits. The virtue or *sefirah* of grace, left unchecked, would flow and merge infinitely into everything else. If God were to act with grace alone, God would fill the universe with divine being, and there would be no room for the existing world. Judgment is in some ways responsible for Israel's predicament, since we are in exile in order to atone for our sins and the sins of the world, but ultimately divine judgment is a reflection of God's love just as much as mercy demonstrates divine love. Judgment, as limit, is necessary for existence itself. The challenge of *tikkun olam*, repairing the world, is not to overcome judgment but to embrace it so that judgment and grace work in harmony.

Chapter Ten

Orthodoxy and Modernity: The Jewish Encounter with Fundamentalism

The Rabbis present a variety of opinions regarding what our forefathers actually received on Mount Sinai. One view (Midrash Rabba 47:1) declares that at Sinai we received the entire Tradition—the Written Law and the entire Oral Law (including Bible, Mishnah, Talmud, Aggada, etc.). Others declare that the B'nai Yisroel received the Ten Commandments only (Mechilta). Another view (Midrash Aseret HaDibroth) is that only the First Commandment was heard by Israel. Another view (Pesikta Rabbati) is that only the first word Anochi was heard. Finally, the great Hasidic master, Rabbi Menahem Mendel of Rymanow (died 1815), declares: "All that Israel heard was the [silent letter] Aleph, the first letter of the word Anochi."

(Rabbi Benzion C. Kaganoff)[40]

Two Forms of Western Religion

The religious people of the Western world may be divided into two categories, fundamentalist and modernist. Whether one is Christian, Muslim, or Jewish, one practices one's faith according to the principles of modernity or according to the antimodernist principles of religious fundamentalism. The fundamentalists of all religions

---

40. Rabbi Benzion C. Kaganoff, "Shavuot: What Did You Get on Mount Sinai?" in *RCA Sermon Anthology 1990–1991/5750–5751*, Rabbi David Stausky, ed. (New York: Rabbinical Council Press, 1991).

in many ways have more in common with one another than with the modernist followers of their own faith. The same could be said of the modernists, that what they share as modernists, regardless of religion, unites them and sets them apart from fundamentalists.

There are numerous social, intellectual, and political distinctions between fundamentalists and modernists, but here we will examine only their views on Holy Scripture. Put simply, fundamentalists believe that their Holy Scriptures are the direct and complete word of God. Religious revelation is the source of all truth. Religious modernists also believe that the Scriptures come from God in some manner, or else they would be secularists, but modernists believe that their Holy Scriptures were written down by human beings in human words. As the Scriptures are mediated by human authors and editors, they become subject to error—specifically, the erroneous, limited, or culturally skewed assumptions of people in the time and place of the composition of the Scriptures. Religious modernists believe that human reason and scientific discovery are sources of divinely revealed truth that can be used to correct or transform the teachings of the Holy Scriptures. The religious modernist takes the view that the Bible, regardless of its divine inspiration, was written by people who lived long ago and we have learned a few things since then.

The difference of opinion between fundamentalists and modernists over the origins of the Bible underlies all of their other differences. The fundamentalist way of living, thinking, and believing makes sense only if their belief about the divine origins of the Scriptures is true. Similarly, modernist religion is only valid if the modernist's assumption about the human composition of the Holy Scriptures is correct. Since the modernist and fundamentalist perspectives on the Holy Scriptures are contradictory, religious modernists and fundamentalists are always in conflict.

Strictly speaking, the term *fundamentalist* applies only within Protestant Christianity. The term arose in America in the 1920s to describe certain conservative Evangelical Protestants. In opposing the historical study of the Bible, these conservative Protestants developed a list of doctrines they labeled the Fundamentals. These doctrines include the divine origin of the Christian Bible (Hebrew Bible and New Testament); the inerrancy of Scripture, meaning that the Bible is factually correct in all of its statements; and biblical literalism, meaning that the Bible is not subject to interpretation. The Bible says just what it seems to be saying, according to the fundamentalists. (A nonfundamentalist might think that the "literal" reading of the fundamentalists is in itself a form of interpretation, but the latter would deny this.)

In the contemporary American media and in popular speech, the term *fundamentalist* is now used to describe any person—Christian, Muslim, or Jew—who believes that his or her Sacred Scriptures constitute the full and only true divine revelation and who lives by the Scriptures in a way that puts him or her into opposition with the forces of modernity. The opposition of fundamentalists to innovation in general was memorialized in the saying, once common among conservative Christians, "If God had meant man to fly, He would have given him wings," said in opposition to the invention of the airplane. The Hatam Sofer, a Hungarian rabbi of the nineteenth century, said, "Everything new is prohibited by the Torah." He validated this conclusion by broadly interpreting a Torah verse that states, "New (grain) is prohibited (to be eaten, until the Passover holiday)." Fundamentalism is a defense not just against the historical interpretation of the Bible but against all the conditions of modernity, which many people find disconcerting and amoral.

Orthodox and Non-Orthodox Jews

In Judaism, the fundamentalists are found among the Orthodox Jews. There are Modern Orthodox Jews who try to live in harmony with the modern world except to the extent that modernity would conflict with halakah, Jewish law. Then there are ultra-Orthodox Jews (called haredi in Israeli Hebrew, meaning "trembling," as in "those who tremble before God"), who try to live as separately as possible from the rest of society. The renowned communities of Hasidic Jews in Brooklyn are of the *haredi* type. They are also informally called "black-hats" after their manner of dress. The ultra-Orthodox dress out of step with the times on purpose in order to distance themselves from contemporary society. They dress in the costume of eighteenth-century Poland, the era before the challenges of modernity began to transform European Jewry. Modern Orthodox Jews dress in contemporary clothes but cover their heads at all times with a *kippah,* a beanie, as a sign of Jewish identity and humility before God. The non-Orthodox movements of American Judaism—Reform, Conservative, Reconstructionist, Renewal, and so on—are modernist in their approach to Torah. As they participate fully in the wider society around them, modernist Jews dress in contemporary clothing. Some of the more traditional-leaning Jewish modernists may wear a discrete *kippah,* often an attractive crocheted head covering or even one with the logo of a favorite sports team.

The Historical Reading of the Torah

Baruch/Benedict Spinoza (1637–1677) was the first significant Western scholar to openly propose that human authorship played a part in the composition of the Bible. Spinoza belonged to a family of Sephardic Jewish *conversos* (forced converts) who reverted to Judaism after slipping out of Catholic Portugal into Protestant Amsterdam. In Holland, Jewish *conversos* from Spain and Portugal who had secretly retained their Jewish identity since the forced conversions of 1492 were permitted to practice Judaism openly. Many *converso* returnees, like Spinoza, had suffered under Christianity but were disappointed by Judaism, which they had imagined would be something like Christianity without any of its human problems. Judaism, like any religion, turned out to have its own all-too-human aspects. Unable to embrace any religion wholeheartedly, Spinoza was a likely candidate to be the first religious modernist.

The German historian Julius Wellhausen (1844–1918) explained in detail how the Torah may have been written by ancient Jews. Wellhausen was an anti-Semite, and no friend to Christianity either. Though he was objectionable in some ways as a human being, he was a great and brilliant scholar. Following the work of earlier historical scholars of the Bible, Wellhausen suggested that the Torah was edited from four earlier source documents. One of these documents is called "J" for Jehovah: this document uses the name YHWH for God. The second document is called "E" for Elohim, the other name for God in the Torah. The third document is "D," the book of Deuteronomy. The fourth and latest document is "P," the priestly source, which includes the story of the seven days of creation, most of the book of Leviticus, and parts of other texts. Each document had its own earlier editors, called redactors. The final redactor was someone in the circle of Ezra the Scribe, from the late Judean monarchy or Babylonian exile period. Wellhausen and his followers taught that the many internal contradictions within the biblical stories result from the fact that the redactor had so much reverence for his source texts that he dared not rewrite them. When he collated the stories from various sources, he did not attempt to harmonize them. This enables us to redivide the Torah into its original sources. For example, the E source of the Noah story has one pair of every animal whereas the J source has seven pairs of the kosher animals. One source says that Noah sent out a raven; another says that the bird was a dove. The redactor placed both versions into the story. Wellhausen's theory of the composition of the Torah is called the Documentary Hypothesis. This theory was accepted by virtually all religious modernists, Christian and Jewish, from the early nineteenth century until nearly the present time. Orthodox-leaning Jews who objected to Wellhausen's Documentary Hypothesis often attributed it to his anti-Semitism rather than to objective historical scholarship, though modernist Jewish historians also supported this theory of the origins of the Torah, based upon the strength of the evidence.

More recently, since the 1980s, Bible scholars have begun to doubt that the Torah can easily be divided into four neat historical source texts. Source analysis has been displaced by literary analysis. Contemporary historians believe that the Torah text had a dynamic history that is no longer easily recoverable. They believe that the final editors of the Torah had a fine sense for words and for literature, that they were not at all blinded by their piety to obvious textual contradictions. Rather, the contemporary scholars believe, the final editors left the contradictions in the text for good reasons of their own. Some historical scholars believe that the writers and editors of the Torah text had reliable sources for the early history of Israel. Others believe that the Torah was a largely fictional production of the late Judean monarchs and the Jerusalem Temple priests in response to the issues and conditions of their own time. This conflict rages between academic scholars, but most Jews, even among the modernists, believe in the essential historicity of the patriarchal narrative, the slavery in

Egypt, the exodus, the divine revelation at Mount Sinai, the wandering in the desert under the leadership of Moses, the conquest of the land from the Canaanites, and the evolution of the Israelite monarchy from the merger of the twelve tribes of Israel. These events constitute the sacred history that remains the basis of Jewish identity to this day. Through a century and a half of modern historical scholarship on the Bible, modernist Jews have generally granted the Torah more credence as a historical record than have their Christian counterparts. Jews, though, even the most Orthodox, have less interest than conservative Christians in defending the historical value of the first eleven chapters of Genesis, which tell the prehistoric tales of creation, the garden of Eden, and Noah's flood.

The Flea That Killed Titus

Christian fundamentalists, who see religion and science as polar opposites in eternal conflict, are known for their rejection of the scientific theory of the evolution of the universe (the big bang theory) and the evolution of human life (Darwinism). They take literally the biblical story that the universe was created in seven days several thousand years ago and that Adam and Eve were the first humans. The conflict between Christian fundamentalism and the findings of science became famous in America in the so-called Scopes monkey trial, in which a Tennessee schoolteacher was tried and convicted for illegally teaching the evolution of humankind in a science class. At the trial Scopes's famous lawyer, Oliver Wendell Holmes, ridiculed the fundamentalist position on creation before the American public, which eagerly followed the case.[41] Many contemporary Christian fundamentalists, having regrouped after the setback of the Scopes trial, now propose the theory of creationism in a renewed attempt to overturn the scientifically accepted theory of evolution. Creationism purports to demonstrate the truth of biblical literalism by using the methods of modern science. But scientists do not take creationism

---

41. The play *Inherit the Wind* dramatizes the Scopes trial. Holmes is the hero of the play, which is strongly anti-Fundamentalist.

seriously; they see it not as true science but as religious doctrine based on principles that are taken on faith.

Jewish fundamentalism is about history rather than science. Orthodox Jews are not biblical literalists. Literalism is a concept alien to the Jewish way of reading the Torah. Jews from the thirteenth century on learned from the great rabbi and philosopher Maimonides that the biblical creation story should be read as an allegory for our scientific understanding of the origins of the universe. In fact, modern-day Jews find a great deal of resonance between the big bang theory and the creation theory of the Kabbalah. Science seems to confirm traditional Jewish teaching on how God went about creating the universe. An Orthodox Jew could be a physicist, an astronomer, or a biologist and not feel disharmony between his work and his beliefs. An ultra-Orthodox Jew has no difficulty believing that the universe is billions of years old or that ours may be one of many universes.

Jewish fundamentalism supports the talmudic view of Jewish history, most particularly concerning the divine origins of the Torah and the divinely guided evolution of the halakah. The Jewish fundamentalist insists on the historical accuracy of the Torah account of the origins of the Jewish people. Orthodox Jews see the divine revelation at Mount Sinai as a historical event, during which Moses wrote down the Torah as we have it to this very day. Orthodox Jews understand history in a way that confirms that the halakah, as developed over the millennia by the Sages and recorded in the Talmud and later Jewish law codes, reflects the eternal and unchanging will of God. No part of the halakah can ever be revoked or changed, in the view of the Orthodox. By contrast, Conservative Jews see the halakah as constantly evolving in the hands of the Jewish folk, and Reform Jews see the halakah as a human invention that can be overruled as necessary to conform Judaism to the demands of modern life. The ultra-Orthodox believe that not only the explicit laws of the halakah but even the social customs of the Jewish people are divinely ordained and so are not subject to change.

The conflict over history between the Orthodox and the Jewish modernists is well illustrated by the now forgotten nineteenth-century conflict over "the flea that killed Titus." Titus was the Roman general who conquered Jerusalem and destroyed the Temple in 70 CE. He later succeeded his father, Vespasian, as emperor of Rome. A legend in the Talmud has Titus boasting that he is mightier than God, since God could not prevent him from destroying God's fortress, the Temple. God replies to Titus: "It was I who destroyed My own Temple, to punish My children for their sins. As for you, the least private soldier in My army could defeat you." To prove it, God sends a flea that climbs up Titus's nose, causing his death.

Jewish modernists began to study writings outside the traditional Jewish curriculum of Torah and Talmud. These non-Jewish books had formerly been prohibited or unavailable to the religious Jew. Jewish modernizers attended European universities, despite the anti-Semitism they encountered there, and read the classics of non-Jewish Western literature. In the Roman historian Suetonius's *History of the Twelve Caesars,* the Jewish modernists learned that Titus lived a long life and died a natural death, but a later Roman emperor, Septimius Severus, did in fact die of a brain infection after a flea crawled into his ear. It was obvious to the modernists that the talmudic authors had created a fictional moral tale based on another historical event. The triumphalists among the modernists believed that, by demonstrating that the Talmud contains mere folklore, they had undermined its authority as a source of divine law. They claimed that the halakah was based on the unfirm foundation of fairy tales. The traditionalists defensively responded that the talmudic record of the historical events must be correct and the pagan historian Suetonius, not guided by the hand of God, must have gotten it wrong. Orthodoxy today has adjusted to the idea that there are legends in the Talmud. Jewish modernists of today have more respect for the Talmud than their earlier counterparts who made war on the Talmud just as the French and American revolutionaries made war on the authority of kings. Many Jewish modernists who take their Judaism seriously now study the Talmud with respect for its insight and wise teachings, even as they keep it in historical perspective. Still, the conflict over halakah and history continues to divide Orthodox Jews from Jewish modernists. Just as fundamentalist Christians have devised their theory of creationism, some Orthodox Jews now use a version of the academic study of history to demonstrate to modernists the truth of the divine origins of Torah and Talmud. One aspect of this attempt is the well-publicized "Bible codes" theory that the text of the Hebrew Bible is full of secret messages that could only have been planted there by God. Dedicated modernists do not take these arguments seriously; like the "scientific" claims of creationism, these historical claims are really missionary arguments. In the nineteenth and early twentieth centuries, fundamentalists were usually on the defensive, but in the early twenty-first century, fundamentalists of Christianity, Judaism, and Islam have gone on the offensive in promoting their version of religious faith.

We will now compare the Orthodox and modernist movements of Judaism by seeing how they variously interpret a text from the Torah. We will compare Orthodox, Conservative, and Reform editions of the Humash, the Torah book that sits in the pews of virtually every American synagogue. The Humash is the most readily available source of Torah teachings for the modern American Jew. Proponents of Orthodoxy and of modernity have used the Humash to teach the "Jews in the pews" the proper interpretation of the Torah according to their own point of view.

The Humash and the Torah Service of the Modern Synagogue

The highlight of the Jewish Sabbath morning worship service is the reading of the Torah. The Torah scroll is removed from the ark, the sacred closet at the front of the synagogue, and paraded around the synagogue for all to kiss and revere. The scroll is opened and a trained reader recites the ancient Hebrew words. In Orthodox and some Conservative synagogues, the entirely weekly Torah portion is recited. In Reform and some Conservative synagogues, only a portion of the weekly parasha is read aloud. After the reading, the scroll is raised, displayed, and dressed with great ceremony. Another reader then recites the haftarah, the reading from the Prophets that accompanies each week's Torah portion. Then the Torah scroll is returned to the ark, again with great ceremony.

The Torah ceremony takes about forty-five minutes to complete. During that time few worshipers actually follow along with the public reading of the Torah. Those who are not scholarly are unable to follow the reading. Those who are scholarly have already studied the weekly portion thoroughly from year to year and know it by heart.

During the reading of the scroll, the worshipers make good use of their time by studying the weekly parasha in the Humash.

The word *Humash* means "five," referring to the five books of the written Torah. The Humash contains the Hebrew text of the Torah, divided into weekly parasha sections. It also contains the weekly haftarah readings from the Prophets and the haftarah readings for the Jewish holidays. (The haftarah, we recall, is recited after the Torah portion in the synagogue service. Each haftarah is connected to the week's parasha either thematically or through a wordplay, or sometimes according to the season of the Jewish calendar.) Some Humash texts also contain the Five Megillot, the short books from the Writings that are read aloud on different Jewish holidays. Thus the Humash contains all the portions of the Hebrew Bible that are recited in the synagogue service in the course of the year.

In an American or English Humash, the Hebrew text is accompanied by an English translation and a commentary in English that may include selected translations from the traditional commentators of the *Mikraot Gedolot* and from the classical midrash. The commentary also interprets the Torah from the contemporary perspective of the scholarly editors. For many decades nearly all American congregations used the Humash first published in 1936 by Soncino Press and created by the Modern Orthodox rabbi Doctor J. H. Hertz, chief rabbi of England in the early twentieth century.[42] In the past two decades, the Reform, Conservative, and Orthodox movements in America have each published their own Humash.

The Union of American Hebrew Congregations, the Reform movement, published its Humash, *The Torah: A Modern Commentary,* in 1981. It is often called the Plaut Humash after its chief editor and commentator, Rabbi Gunther Plaut. The Orthodox publishing house ArtScroll publishes numerous volumes for the English-speaking audience. It published the Stone Humash, named for its primary subscriber, in 1993. The Stone Humash was edited by Rabbi Nosson Scherman, one of the chief editors of ArtScroll books. The Conservative movement's United Synagogue published its own

---

42. The Hertz Humash should not be confused with the Soncino Press Humash, edited by Abraham Cohen, which is used for scholarly reference and has not been placed in synagogue pews.

Humash, entitled *Etz Hayim,* "Tree of Life," in 2001. The modern commentary in *Etz Hayim* was edited by the renowned writer and rabbi Chaim Potok, author of *The Chosen* and other novels. The selections from Jewish tradition in the *Etz Hayim* Humash were edited by Harold Kushner, famed for his book *When Bad Things Happen to Good People.* With this publication each movement of American Judaism has its own Humash, and the Hertz Humash is gradually being retired.

Let us now examine the way the different movements of modern Judaism read the Torah by seeing how their scholars interpret an especially difficult passage in the Torah.

A Challenging Weekly Torah Portion: *Mattot-Massei,* Num 30:2—36:13

> YHWH spoke to Moses, saying, "Avenge the Israelite people on the Midianites, then you shall be gathered to your kin." Moses spoke to the people, saying, "Let men be picked out from among you for a campaign, a thousand from every one of the tribes of Israel."...They took the field against Midian, as YHWH had commanded Moses, and slew every male.... Moses said to them, "You have spared every female, yet they are the very ones who, at the bidding of Balaam, induced the Israelites to trespass against YHWH in the incident at Peor, so that the community of YHWH was struck by a plague! Now therefore, slay every male among the children, and every female who has known a man carnally, but spare every virgin female" (Num 31)....In the steppes of Moab, at the Jordan near Jericho, YHWH spoke to Moses saying, "Speak to the Israelite people and say to them: When you cross the Jordan into the Land of Canaan, you shall dispossess all the inhabitants of the land" (Num 33:50–51a).

Before the modern age, Christians challenged the Jewish way of reading of the Bible on the basis of who possessed the correct interpretation, especially of passages that were understood to predict the coming of the Messiah. Historical analysis of the Bible made this a moot question by demonstrating that all messianic readings of biblical passages originated centuries after the Bible's composition. In the modern age, Christians presented two serious new challenges to Judaism. On the one hand, modernity generated in Christian society a passion to absorb the Jews through social assimilation. On the other hand, modernity generated anti-Semitism, a passionate racial hatred of the Jews, which culminated in the Holocaust. Jews in the modern age are both more welcomed and more threatened by non-Jewish society than in any other period of history. Against the enticements of assimilation, devoted Jews feel a need to affirm the continuing value of the unique message of Judaism. Against anti-Semitic religious scholars, Jews had to respond to the charge that Judaism is an inferior religion. Even if Jewish responses to assimilation and anti-Semitism will not be heard by non-Jews, Jewish leaders must provide Jews with answers that will satisfy themselves.

At the dawn of the Enlightenment in the eighteenth and nineteen centuries, philosophers of religion, following Emanuel Kant, claimed that the value of religion lies primarily in its capacity to make people more ethical. Whereas fundamentalists claim to possess the divinely revealed truth, modernists believe that ultimate truth is yet to be discovered by any religion. The value of religion, in the meantime, is to encourage people to live a good and moral life as they seek that higher truth. In the eyes of the Enlightenment, the best religion is that which generates the best citizens for the modern state. While Orthodox Jews proclaim that the halakah is above any form of human judgment, ethical or otherwise, modernist Jews attempt to re-create Judaism according to contemporary ethical standards—for example, by granting social and religious equality to women.

Ethics are by nature universal, but religious rites are specific to the adherents of a particular faith or sect. The religious modernist seeks to make his or her particular religion into the highest expression of universalism. Early Reform Jews, for example, were fond of a verse from the prophet Isaiah, "My house shall be called a house of prayer for all peoples." They also quoted from Malachi: "Have we not all one Father? Has not one God created us all?" Though originally a reference to priests, Levites, and Israelites, the three castes of ancient Israel, the Reformers applied this verse to humankind in general.

Scholarly opponents of Judaism in the Christian world argued that Christianity was inherently superior to Judaism because Christianity was more ethical, more universalistic, and more spiritual than Judaism. Jews responded by demonstrating that Judaism is ethical, universal, and spiritual. The above passage from the Torah was treated with benign neglect by Jewish commentators through the centuries, as the Jewish nation had evolved from fierce ancient tribes into a relatively powerless international people who prized peace and human compassion. Now, in response to modern forms of Christian anti-Judaism, Jews had to deal with these ethically embarrassing portions of the Torah. How could our holy Torah, the source of our cherished values of peace and generosity, justice and mercy, command the slaughter of the Midianites and the seven indigenous peoples of Canaan? The following selections are response to this challenge.[43]

Commentary of the *Safat Emet:*
The Language of Truth

The *Safat Emet* is a great early-twentieth-century example of a Hasidic Torah commentary, like the *Kedushat Levi*, which we studied in the previous chapter. Rabbi Yehudah Leib Alter was the Hasidic rebbe of Warsaw. As Warsaw had already become a modernized city, he preferred to establish his seat in the village of Gur, outside Warsaw, where his disciples would not be exposed to secular influences. The Gerer Rebbe's Sabbath afternoon talks were so popular that even secular Jews traveled from Warsaw to hear him speak. The Gerer Rebbe welcomed them, along with his Hasidic followers. He saved notes on all his talks and published them as the book *Safat Emet: The Language of Truth*. Although the Gerer Rebbe was aware of the modern world and concerned about its influence, his Judaism is still premodern. His world of Torah discourse is that of traditional Hasidism. The Gerer Rebbe provides us a base for comparison with modernist and fundamentalist interpretations of our Torah text:

---

43. For full information on the Humash editions in the bibliography, see the "Humash" entries.

"This is the land that will fall to you by inheritance" (Num 34:2). *The Midrash says that here God showed to Moses each generation and its teachers.*

Surely the Canaanites had never experienced the category of the "Land of Israel." It was only due to Israel's preparation as they entered the land that the heavenly "Land of Israel" descended upon that earthly land. Thus we have been taught that the earthly Temple is parallel to one above. The same is true of the Land of Israel and of Jerusalem. It was this inward land that God showed to Moses.

The children of Israel are themselves "borders" into which the holiness can flow; it was as they entered into their physical borders that the [upper] Land "fell" into their inheritance. That is why God commanded that they leave none of the Canaanites, for the upper land could not bear them.

The same is true of the individual as well: as we prepare our hearts and souls with Torah, so does God cause holiness to flow into us. Our Sages spoke of this when they said [that a person should conduct himself] "as though a holy being were present in his loins."

Lesson

It is a common belief in mysticism that "as above, so below—as below, so above." The spiritual world in heaven and the material world of earthly existence exactly parallel one another. A spiritual achievement in earthly life thus has the power to transform the upper world and vice versa.

To the Gerer Rebbe, the "Land of Israel" is not a real place but a spiritual category. There exists a spiritual "Land of Israel" in the geography of heaven. When the Jews make themselves worthy vessels to contain this holy land, God causes it to descend into us, like an overlay upon a map.

The Gerer Rebbe is completely lacking in self-consciousness about the moral problem of the conquest of the land of Israel because he reads it entirely as an allegory for a spiritual battle that takes place within the soul of each Jew. The "Canaanites of the Land" are the unworthy aspects of our own soul and our own deeds. When we purify our soul through Torah and mitzvot, we have "expelled the Canaanites from the Land."

In the time of the Gerer Rebbe, the Jews were so utterly powerless and in the hands of their enemies that the moral responsibilities that come with power were not an issue. The Jews had been homeless and without any military force of their own for two millennia. The only struggle that a Jew could engage in and win was the struggle to be a better person. To the Gerer Rebbe, that is the message of the Torah.

Arthur Green, Contemporary Translator and Commentator to the *Safat Emet*

Arthur Green is one of the foremost academic scholars of Jewish mysticism in the world today. He is a professor at Brandeis University, an ordained Conservative rabbi, and a former chancellor of the Reconstructionist Rabbinical Seminary near Philadelphia. His religious position is liberal and modern in thought, with a great respect for the power of traditional religious practice. He has sought to bring the lessons of traditional Judaism to the spiritual seekers of our own time, which is one reason that he prepared his translation of selections from the *Safat Emet*. Green comments on each selection to bring his own modernist reading to the text:

> This text is translated here despite the disturbing nature of its message if translated into contemporary politics. The Canaanites, who had never known the true "Land of Israel," were to be utterly exterminated, for the Holy Land could not bear their impure presence.
>
> When the Safat Emet said these things, it was still inconceivable that Israel in premessianic times would have political power, along with the responsibility that comes with it. The "Canaanites" to him were a purely symbolic entity, a category of defilement symbolized by that ancient and now wholly nonexistent nation. But today, only a bit more than a century later, there are forces within the Jewish people that want to resurrect the "Canaanites," identified with today's non-Jewish inhabitants of the Holy Land, and demonize them as well. This reading of Judaism must be forcefully countered and rejected. We may claim that Jews have a unique relationship with the Land

of Israel, one indeed not quite shared even by Christians or Muslims. But we must do this entirely without transforming others into demonic or less than fully human beings.

We also have the alternative of reading such texts on the individual moralistic level, as the Safat Emet does. But when we do, we should recall that Islam too has a way to internalizing its aggressive side in the form of the "spiritual jihad." We would do well to see this parallel. It was perhaps only our many centuries of alienation from power that allowed us to carry out this spiritual sublimation of violent imperatives to such a high degree. Our return to power politics threatens to undo this process much more quickly.

Lesson

Arthur Green relates the text to contemporary politics. We can appreciate the way the Gerer Rebbe reads the Torah text, but our different circumstances give us a moral obligation to read the text in a different way. The Jew in the modern world has reentered power politics. The Jewish state of Israel has a powerful army. Although the Jews have a moral right to defend themselves against those who would destroy them, they also have a moral obligation to the Palestinians. It would be unacceptable to apply the Torah's ancient commands to them in a literal way. As a modernist, Green interprets the Torah through the filter of contemporary ethics. We must also recognize that though Israel's Muslim enemies have called for a jihad, a religious war, to exterminate the Jews, there exists in Islam as in Judaism a symbolic and psychological understanding of jihad. As the Gerer Rebbe read the command to exterminate the Canaanites as a purely internal struggle for goodness, so also many Muslims understand the term jihad in this way. A liberal-minded and moral approach from Jews and Muslims toward one another leads to hope that political conflicts may be resolved with peace and justice for all.

Hertz Humash, *The Pentateuch and Haftorahs: Hebrew Text, English Translation, and Commentary*

In his commentary to the Torah, Rabbi J. H. Hertz pursued two main goals. First, he presented the work of Jewish historical scholars such as David Hoffman and Umberto Cassuto, who attempted to use the historical method to demonstrate that Moses was the author of the entire Torah, contrary to the Documentary Hypothesis. Second, Hertz attempted to demonstrate that Orthodox Judaism was an admirable religion by modern standards of judgment—ethical, universal, and spiritual.

The attempt by serious historians to demonstrate the Mosaic origins of the Torah text ended in failure. By the mid–twentieth century, all serious biblical historians had accepted the Documentary Hypothesis. Orthodox Jews and Christian Fundamentalists ceased to use historical analysis on the Bible; they now adopted the view that historical study could not lead to valid conclusions when applied to a work of divine origin. One would think that these developments made the Hertz Humash dated and unacceptable to Orthodox and modernists alike, yet the Hertz Humash remained popular. In part, this is because no competing Humash was published, but another reason for the Hertz Humash's enduring popularity was Rabbi Hertz's success in instilling modern Jews with pride in their religion. Writing in the era when hatred against Jews was about to burst into mass murder all over Europe, Hertz defended the honor of Judaism:

The War Against the Midianites

In XXV, 16–18, Moses is bidden to smite the Midianites because they had enticed the Israelites to the licentious and idolatrous worship of Baal-Peor. In the present chapter, he is ordered to carry out the command forthwith; and we are given full details of the campaign.

The war against the Midianites presents peculiar difficulties. We are no longer acquainted with the circumstances that justified the ruthlessness with which it was waged, and therefore we cannot satisfactorily meet the various objections that have been raised in that connection. "Perhaps the recollection of what took place after the Indian Mutiny when Great Britain was in the same temper, may throw light on this question. The soldiers then, bent on punishing the cruelty and lust of the rebels, partly in patriotism, partly in revenge, set mercy altogether aside" (Expositor's Bible). The Midianites affected were only the clans that lived in the neighborhood of Moab. This accounts for the persistence of Midianites in later periods of Israelite history.

3. Execute the LORD's vengeance. The preceding v. refers to Israel's vengeance on Midian; this v. speaks of God's vengeance on Midian. Both mean the same thing. The cause of Israel is the cause of God. "Vengeance" is here used in the broad sense of retributory punishment.

Lesson

Hertz's response to the difficulties posed by the war on the Midianites is intended not so much to clarify the biblical text as to clear contemporary Judaism from the charges brought by anti-Semites. His first point is that the ferocity of the war must surely be justified by circumstances that are no longer known to us. (Note that, as an Orthodox Jew, Hertz takes the historicity of the biblical account for granted.) He compares the war to the response of his own nation's military to the Great Indian Mutiny. That war was conducted with renowned ferocity and violence; both sides committed massacres of civilians. By bringing this comparison, Hertz politely reminds the Christian world that, in light of their own history of conduct in warfare, they cannot be too quick to judge the Jews or the God that Jews worship. Hertz also mitigates the problem by suggesting that the slaughter was conducted only against a local group of Midianites, not against the nation as a whole. In a separate comment on Numbers 31:3, Hertz responds to the charge that the God of the Old Testament is a God of vengeance and not mercy. Hertz interprets the Hebrew *n'kom* to mean not vengeance but "retributory punishment"—in other words, justice.

Hertz shows himself modern in recognizing the ethical problems raised by the Torah text. He shows himself Orthodox in explaining away the problems without casting doubt on the veracity of the Torah account. And he shows himself a defender of Jews and Judaism in reminding his readers that the ethical problem of human ferocity in warfare is universal and so it would be wrong to single out ancient Israel. Those who use biblical analysis to criticize Judaism by suggesting that the Jewish Bible is deficient in grace and mercy should remember that "those who live in glass houses should not throw stones." The day when men will be merciful in the heat of warfare is a day that still lies ahead of us, for Christians and all humankind.

For Hertz, the Holocaust had not yet happened, and the Arab-Jewish conflict over the eventual disposition of British Palestine was not yet in full flame. Hertz's comments gain added poignancy in the light of later events he could not have predicted.

The Torah, A Modern Commentary

The UAHC Humash, also known as the Plaut Humash, was the first non-Orthodox Humash for the English-speaking public. The chief editor, W. Gunther Plaut, is a Reform rabbi, educated in Germany before the Second World War. He is retired from the pulpit of Holy Blossom Temple in Toronto, Canada. Plaut asked his colleague Bernard Bamberger to use his expertise on the ancient Jewish priesthood and sacrifices to write and edit the commentary on Leviticus. Bill Hallo, a professor of ancient Near Eastern history at Yale University, provides a historical introduction to each biblical book.

The UAHC Humash contains extensive commentaries in the form of introductory and concluding essays on each segment of meaning in the Torah as well as verse-by-verse explanations of the simple meaning of the text. Each section also contains a selection from the classical midrash and commentaries, chosen for their relevance to the issues of ethics and spirituality that interest the contemporary Jew.

If there is one glaring weakness in the UAHC Humash, it is that the Humash is not divided into the weekly Torah portions but rather into units of meaning. This makes it difficult to follow during the Torah service in the synagogue. Plaut has apologized for this difficulty. He explains that when he was editing the book, in the 1970s, he thought it would be used only by study groups of learned Jews. He never imagined the "return to tradition" of Reform Jews that has led to a renewed interest in Torah, with the result that the UAHC Humash has been placed in the pews of nearly every Reform temple in North America. It is unlikely that the UAHC Humash will be reedited to reflect better the way it is currently being used, given the expense of typesetting and of replacing books now in use.

The Slaying of the Prisoners

The text reports the killing of all Midianite men by the Israelites, and then, at the express behest of Moses, the further dispatch of all women who might have had a share in the sexual orgies referred to in chapter 25. This report contains historical and moral problems of a high order.

Note first that the war itself is hardly dealt with; the emphasis is on cultic matters—purification and the division of spoils. Note further that, while the enemy is massacred, not one Israelite is reported missing (Num 31:49), which leads to the assumption that this section is not an actual report but a schematic reconstruction of events long past, with the aim of showing how God had protected His people and how, in return, certain things were owed to Him. The non-historical aspects of this account may also be seen in the listing of extraordinarily large numbers of people slain and booty captured. Finally, though "every male" was said to have been killed, such was far from the actual fact. At most only a portion of the Midianites could have been killed, for not only did they not disappear as a nation, but they dominated Israel a relatively short time thereafter (see Josh 6–8). In sum, then, the details of the Midianite war may be said to constitute a form of biblical interpretation of the past [13].

However, this exacerbates the moral question. For if the extermination of the Midianites did not in fact take place, or at least not to the extent detailed in the text, what would move the authors of the Torah to write as though it had taken place? How can the idea of slaughtering so many prisoners be reconciled with the humanitarian ideals of the deep sense of compassion that are the very heart of the Torah?

The matter puzzled the ancients as well. A midrash attempts to relieve God of responsibility and comments that Moses' anger brought him to sin, implying that it was not God but Moses who issued the fatal command concerning the Midianite women, and that God punished him for it.[44] Exempting God from responsibility does not, however, explain why the text, by its silence, appears to condone the procedure.

---

44. The punishment is said to have consisted in God's entrusting the laws of cleansing to Eleazar rather than to Moses (see Num 31:14), which cannot be taken seriously as the intent of the text [12].

The fact is that, as in the matter of slavery and the status of women, the Torah speaks within the context of its time. It accepts certain matters as "normal"—and wars, with their slaughter and cruelties, belong to them. The Torah does, however, require of men who had killed a ritual atonement—a unique provision in any human code [15]—and it introduces certain meliorating rules. (These may be compared to the various Geneva conventions of modern times applying themselves not to war as such but to the treatment of prisoners and civilians whose fate is to be bettered in conflicts still to occur.) To be sure, prophetic vision looked to a time when all wars would be abolished, but such a vision addressed itself to post history or at best to the distant future. The realities have not changed greatly to this day, except that in many ways modern war may have increased the cruelties practiced in ancient, more "primitive" times.

The biblical account, which, as indicated, represents a reconstruction of history, is to be seen as a statement of what should have happened rather than what actually happened. It doubtlessly came from an age when Israel had trouble with the native inhabitants of its conquered territories and when widespread immorality was ascribed to these components of the population. The wilderness history thus became a retroactive judgment by a later age: if the injunction of Moses had been followed there would have been fewer troubles in the centuries to follow. The great leader, it was implied, knew that idolatry and sexual excess often went together, and he had given the prescription for dealing with the problem root and branch. The passages recorded in chapter 31 are concerned primarily with Israel's purity and reflect the belief that as long as idolaters were a significant part of the population the purposes of the Law could never be fully achieved.[45]

---

45. This same belief also underlies the biblical injunction to exterminate the native peoples in Canaan, which command was, of course, never carried out in actual history.

Lesson

The Reform movement of Judaism began in Germany in the 1800s, at the height of the Enlightenment. The early reformers redefined Judaism as "ethical monotheism." The Reformers saw the halakah as only one possible expression of the progressive Jewish spirit, an expression in many ways outdated. Halakah and the written text of the Torah and Talmud all had to submit to the authority of the human ethical conscience, which constitutes God's ultimate revelation. The reformers saw ethical consciousness as progressive; religion must always renew itself according to our growing understanding of what God requires of us.

The ethical consciousness of Reform Judaism makes the ethical problem of our Torah text especially acute. How can Sacred Scripture command an act of killing against which the conscience rebels? Plaut finds a foundation for response in the modern method of reading the Bible historically.

Plaut's first defense of Judaism is that the massacre of the Midianites and the Canaanites never actually happened. Historical analysis reveals that this text provides a fictional re-creation of Israel's early history. Plaut interprets the massacre story in the way that Levinas called "reading in Greek"—seeking to restate the message of the story in our own cultural terms. The tale of the wars on the Midianites and the Canaanites is intended to teach a later generation the evils of idolatry and the need for Israel to remain distinct from the surrounding culture in order to uphold the worship of the one true God. We would not today condone a massacre, but we would still uphold the virtue of remaining true to the distinctive message of Judaism.

Yet, as Plaut acknowledges, to boast of a massacre that never took place makes the moral problem in some ways more acute, as it would imply approval of such conduct. Here Plaut relies on another principle of modern religion, that of progressive revelation. We see in this tale from the Torah not an aspect of God's eternal message but rather the limited perspective of Israel early in its history, before it had learned and absorbed the message of divine compassion. The Jew of today rejects the explicit message of the story. We must consider the message of Torah in the broadest sense of the term, as the Jewish people's response to their continuous encounter with God. We find, even in this ancient story, some hints of our advanced moral understanding, such as the need for atonement after killing another person, even in conditions of warfare.

Plaut, like Hertz, reminds the reader that such ferocious behavior in wartime is unfortunately typical of all nations and peoples. Not only that, but modern societies have advanced more in the technology of committing atrocities than in the moral growth necessary to prevent them. We look ultimately to the peaceful vision of the Jewish prophets. Thus Judaism provides us with a blueprint for ethical action and for improving the world, even as we confront the ethical dilemmas posed by our own history.

The Humash: The Stone Edition

Here we have a commentary from a contemporary, very Orthodox point of view:

> *31. 1–12. The battle against Midian.* Now at hand was the retribution that had been promised against the Midianites (25.17) because of their responsibility for the Jewish sins of immorality and idolatry that resulted in the death of 24,000 Jews in the plague (25:1–9). The Moabites, however, were spared as explained in the notes to 25:17.
>
> All the tribes, including Levi (Rashi to v.4) were equally represented in the fighting force, and they were accompanied by Phinehas (v.6) who had in a sense begun the task by slaying Zimri and Cozbe, and thereby ending the plague that the Midianites had brought upon the Jewish people. His presence with the fighters deflected the inevitable criticism that Israel, too, was at fault for not having resisted the blandishments of the Midianite women, for Phinehas displayed courageous loyalty to God and was thus a source of merit for his brethren. It is noteworthy that God did not command that Phinehas join the army, perhaps because it would have been an implied criticism of Moses, who had not acted against Zimri. But Moses understood that the nation needed the merit of Phinehas and that he was essential to the success of the undertaking (Or HaChaim).
>
> *2. Take vengeance for the Children of Israel,* God spoke of avenging the harm that had been done to Israel, but in the

next verse, when Moses conveyed the commandments to the Jews, he spoke only of avenging the slight to God's honor, for he said, "Had we been idolaters, they would not hate or persecute us. Therefore, the vengeance is for God" (Midrash). Rashi comments that one who wrongs Israel is regarded as if one had wronged God.

Lesson

The Stone Humash does not rise to defend the ethical qualities of Judaism, as do Hertz and Plaut. The editors of the Stone Humash are no doubt aware of the issue. Unlike the Gerer Rebbe, they live of necessity in intimate contact with the modern world despite their Orthodoxy. The lack of response to this issue is no doubt based on principle. Orthodox Jews of today make it a point to live their own way of life, regardless of the opinions of the Gentile world. They take pride in being self-referential and in valuing halakah over what they would regard as the intellectual fads of modernity. It is also generally assumed in the Orthodox world that non-Jewish society is inherently hostile to Jews and Judaism. There is little point, then, in attempting to placate the critics. Not responding to potential Gentile critics of Moses' actions in Numbers 31 demonstrates Jewish pride and self-esteem.

The editors of the Stone Humash make their own ethical statement in their comment on the command to take vengeance. A Jew should not be zealous for his own honor but only for the honor of God. Equally, God is not concerned for God's own honor but acts for the preservation of God's beloved Chosen People. The motive of our actions is not personal vengeance but religious passion.

For the sake of preserving the true path of Torah, our Orthodox commentators permit radical action, even some deeds that a modernist critic might consider to be ethically troubling. In our chapter on Talmud, we note how the rabbinic Sages expressed doubt about the character of Phinehas, the zealot or vigilante of God. In contemporary Orthodoxy, the character of Phinehas is revived as a positive image—not for his violence, which is no issue for the peaceful and gentle Orthodox Jew of today, but for Phinehas's willingness to sacrifice everything for the sake of divine service. Phinehas becomes the model of the Orthodox Jew of today who rejects so many of the creature comforts of the modern lifestyle for the sake of the life of Torah in obedience to the divine halakah.

To the contemporary Orthodox commentator, Numbers 31 is an inspiring tale about resistance to the blandishments of the idolatry of today. We resist today not with the sword but with the same passion for serving God and God alone that inspired Moses and Phinehas.

Etz Hayim: Torah and Commentary

(Midrashic commentary) *Chapter 31:1–3: It seems poignant that Moses' last great task before his death is so out of character—a war of vengeance. However, Moses will choose to end his career not with this battle and the discord that followed (v.14ff.) but with the stirring oration that forms the Book of Deuteronomy.*

In verse 2, God directs Moses to avenge the Israelite people. In verse 3, however, Moses speaks to the people about "the Lord's vengeance." This will not be a war primarily for land or personal gain but to redeem God's name from the dishonor that the Midianites attached to it at Baal-peor. Presumably this is why Phinehas the priest is listed as leading the effort rather than Joshua. "Had we been idol-worshipers, they would not have striven so hard to lead us astray" (Num. Rabba. 22:2).

The reader is likely to be uncomfortable with the notion of a "holy war." Does placing the seal of religious approval on a military undertaking change and sanctify the battle or does it compromise the religion and contaminate it with the stain of bloodshed? When is war "the LORD's vengeance" and when is it human vengeance to which the name of God has been attached?

6. Moses himself does not take part in the campaign. Was this because of his advanced age, or because he had found refuge among the Midianites when he fled Egypt as a young man (Num. Rabba. 22:4)?

8. It would seem that Balaam, instead of returning home, lingered to see if his plan of seducing the Israelites would work. The Midrash comments on his death by sword (Tanh. Balak 8). Isaac had blessed Jacob with the gift of prayer and had told Esau that he would live by the sword (Gen 27). Balaam set out

*to use Jacob's "weapon" against his descendants, trying to harm
them with words. In retaliation, Israel used Esau's weapon, the
sword, against him.*

*(Literal commentary) 2. Avenge...on Hebrew: n'kom...
me-, which means "redress [past wrongs] from." Translating it
as "avenge...on" has no basis in Scripture when the subject is
God. Better: "fight" (and in Deut 32:35, Isa 1:24).*

*3. To wreak the LORD's vengeance on. Better: "to exact the
LORD's retribution on." The Israelites seek redress or compensation from the Midianites for causing the devastating plague of
Baal-peor, but the Lord desires to exact retribution from them
for the sacrilege they committed by seducing the Israelites into
worshiping Baal-peor.*

Lesson

This Humash is the most recent to be published. It summarizes
many of the themes we have seen in the earlier Humash texts, in a
manner deemed appropriate for the devout Conservative Jew—modernist in outlook, traditional in observance, reverential toward the
tradition of the Jewish people, but willing to adapt Jewish practices
to modern conditions.

Our commentators follow Hertz and Plaut in responding to the
possible charge of ethically questionable actions in the war on the
Midianites. Harold Kushner reminds us more than once that the power
of the Jew lies in words, not in weapons. An old midrash teaches that
Jacob, father of the Jews, was granted the power of the tongue. Isaac's
other son, Esau, father of the Roman Empire and its descendants, was
granted the power of the sword. In this case the Jews must act out of
character to defend themselves, but Moses returns to character in the
book of Deuteronomy. Implicit in this commentary is the message
that the state of Israel must defend herself militarily against fierce enemies but her ultimate safety lies in a diplomatic resolution. The
Jewish people have returned, since the Holocaust, to the use of
earthly power. This is good to the extent necessary to defend the
Jewish nation and the Jewish people, but the true strength of Judaism
lies in our Torah teachings.

Kushner raises the troubling issue of holy war from the perspective of the religious modernist. Surely we must fight to preserve

what is truly holy, but we must equally insure that religion does not become an excuse for military aggression. The modernist feels that the name of religion is sullied by the world's history of religious warfare.

This literal commentary, like that of Hertz and Plaut, denies that there is any vengeance in the narrow sense of the term in the war against the Midianites. Here the claim is made, on the basis of the latest linguistic studies of ancient Hebrew, that the translation of *n'kom* as "vengeance" is inaccurate. The word really means "to fight." This is a good example of how literalism can be highly interpretive.

Chapter Eleven

Torah Study Today

Torah Learning in Our Times

In the modern age, Torah learning among Jews is not as wide-spread as it once was. In Israel and in the United States, the two countries where the majority of the world's Jews live today, most Jews attend secular public schools. Jews of today concentrate their studies on subjects such as math, language and literature, science, and social studies. Many modern-day Jews have transformed the traditional Jewish passion for Torah learning into a passion for education in the professions, leading to a proliferation of Jewish doctors, lawyers, teachers, scholars, scientists, and accountants. Perhaps 10 percent of young Jews attend Jewish private schools in America, and about one-fourth of Israeli children attend religious schools, where they receive an intensive education in Torah and Talmud in addition to their secular studies.

The Israeli School System

In Israel there are three separate Jewish school systems. Of the two official state school systems, one is secular, *hiloni,* and the other is traditional-religious, *dati.* The *haredi,* or ultra-Orthodox, Jews have their own schools, which are independent but receive state support through a voucher system.[46] *Haredi* Jews follow the premodern Jewish curriculum with a focus on Talmud study. They teach primarily tra-

---

46. Muslims and Christians in Israel have their own state-supported educational systems.

ditional Jewish subjects. In the religious school system, part of the day is spent on general subjects and part of the day on Torah studies, again with an emphasis on traditional Talmud study. In recent years the *dati* schools have increased the component of Torah with traditional commentaries in the high-school curriculum. They are moving away from the Polish system, in which the Bible was taught only to elementary students and older students learned Talmud exclusively. In the secular Israeli schools, the students study Bible from a historical perspective. They receive little or no education in Talmud and halakah or in traditional commentaries and midrash.

American Schools

American public schools are secular but essentially Protestant in outlook. Unlike Catholic immigrants to America, who established their own private schools, Jewish immigrants to the United States flocked to the public schools. They saw these schools as a vehicle for Americanization and social advancement and so tolerated their Protestant bias. It was unusual in Brooklyn in the early twentieth century for an elementary-school classroom of all Jewish students, with a Jewish teacher, to be singing Christmas carols in class as required by the curriculum. Ultra-Orthodox Jews came to America in large numbers only after the Second World War. The more recent Orthodox immigrants established a system of private Jewish elementary schools and yeshiva high schools and colleges.

Orthodox yeshiva high schools in America come in two basic varieties. Some put the emphasis on integrating modern and traditional Jewish studies. The students at these yeshivot prepare for college while they get a thorough Torah education. The Flatbush Yeshiva in Brooklyn and the Ramaz School in Manhattan, for example, are among the finest college preparatory schools in America. Ultra-Orthodox yeshiva schools put the emphasis on traditional Torah studies, teaching only secular subjects that are necessary for functioning in society and to fulfill the legal requirements of the state. In these more ultra-Orthodox schools, Jewish studies are taught in the morning, when the students' minds are fresh, and secular studies are relegated to the afternoon. The graduates of these yeshivot do not, for the most part, attend secular colleges after graduation.

The Nazis destroyed the traditional bastion of the Jewish yeshiva in Eastern Europe. One never would have imagined, after the devastation of the Second World War, that Orthodox Jews would be so successful in reviving their yeshiva educational system in both Israel and America. The Orthodox justly boast that there are more Jews learning in Lithuanian-style yeshivot today than at the apex of Lithuanian Jewry in the mid–nineteenth century.

There are more than a few American-oriented yeshivot in Jerusalem today. These yeshivot attract Orthodox American Jews who wish to spend some time studying in Israel. Many of these yeshivot have a strong outreach to non-Orthodox Jewish youth who come to Israel to find themselves Jewishly. These *baal teshuvah yeshivot*—yeshivot for penitents or returnees—have outreach personnel who walk the streets of Jerusalem seeking out young adult Jewish tourists. They invite them to come and share a Sabbath. If they are interested, they are welcome to spend a few weeks as a guest of the yeshiva, learning basic Judaism and Talmud for beginners. If they show continuing interest, they are invited to stay and enter into the Orthodox way of life.

In the United States, the Conservative movement of Judaism has an extensive day school program of Solomon Schechter schools, named after the founder of the American Conservative movement. The Reform movement has a small program of private Jewish schools. In these the students receive a standard American education supplemented with Jewish studies. The number and reach of Jewish private schools is expanding in contemporary America. Progressive Jewish high schools include the Heschel School in New York and the Rashi School in Boston. The daughter of this writer is a pioneer student at the American Hebrew Academy, America's first nonyeshiva Jewish boarding school, in Greensboro, North Carolina. Such a project would have been unimaginable only a few years ago.

Supplemental Schools in America

Yeshivot and Jewish day schools provide a good Jewish education, but they touch only a small percentage of American Jewish children. Most American Jews of school age receive their Jewish education from synagogue-sponsored supplemental schools. The students learn about Judaism for two to six hours a week, after school or on Sabbath or Sunday mornings. In these schools the possibilities for Torah education are limited. Much of the available time is spent on bar mitzvah preparation, learning to enunciate the Hebrew of the prayers and the Bible with little emphasis on comprehension. Most American Jews know little more than a few Bible stories and some tales about the rabbinic Sages. They know that the Talmud is an important Jewish book but are not quite sure of its form or contents. American rabbis are often asked by fellow Jews if the Talmud isn't a commentary on the Torah, a question to which "yes" and "no" are both inadequate answers. Despite the problems of inadequate schooling, lack of time, and limited general knowledge, Torah learning is still thriving in some circles of Jews in America and Israel.

Adult Torah Study in America

Torah learning is strong among Orthodox Jews, most of whom have enough learning from their yeshiva education to continue the study of Talmud on their own. Adult Orthodox Jews may participate in study groups in their synagogues on Sabbath afternoons, or on a weekday evening, or during business hours. One hears of lunch hour Talmud study groups that take place in the meeting rooms of Wall Street brokerages and midtown Manhattan law offices. This writer once spent the month of June in Boston. There I attended daily morning worship at the Harvard University Hillel Association, the Jewish student union. A number of Orthodox graduate students in the sciences attended daily prayer. Every afternoon they regathered to learn Talmud. One can imagine how busy these graduate students already were with their doctoral studies, but Torah learning was still their daily priority.

Almost every Reform and Conservative congregation in America has a group of twenty or thirty dedicated members who gather every week for ongoing Torah study. Typically in such groups, the members bring a Bible or Humash. The rabbi or a learned layperson prepares supplementary materials from the Hebrew midrash and commentaries to share with the group. Some of these synagogue groups study the weekly Torah portion, the *parashat hashavua'*. The hour is usually spent on just a few verses. The participants learn the Jewish teachings that have been based on these verses over the centuries, and they apply these teachings to their own life experiences. Many synagogue study groups choose not to be directed by the weekly Torah portion but to study their way methodically through the entire Tanakh over a course of years.

In Reform congregations the weekly Torah study often takes place on Sabbath morning before the worship service. In some congregations the Torah study takes place during the Torah reading of the worship service, a long period of time being reserved for this purpose. In many congregations there is an alternative Sabbath morning worship service for those who want to intensively discuss the Torah portion. In Conservative and Orthodox synagogues, where the worship service takes up the full morning, Torah study may take place on Sabbath afternoon or during the week. Some congregations hold their weekly Torah study on a weekday evening or as a brown-bag lunch group either in the synagogue or in a downtown office.

The weekly synagogue Torah study group in its contemporary format originated in the early 1970s and has been growing ever since. More and more Jews, many with a limited childhood exposure to Jewish learning, are studying Torah on a regular basis these days. This trend bodes well for the future of Jewish learning.

Torah Study Using Modern Technology

The Internet has proved to be a useful tool to bring Torah to the people. Orthodox, Conservative, and Reform Jewish organizations offer a weekly Torah study pages that they send by fax or by e-mail. This writer, like many rabbis, transmits a weekly Torah commentary e-mail that reaches a few hundred households. It contains a lesson based on a short midrash or commentary to a verse in the weekly parasha. Many individuals who might not attend a class devote some serious time each week to learning Torah with the help of an Internet message. The Reform movement's Union of American Hebrew Congregations, for example, faxes and e-mails a weekly Torah commentary entitled *Torat Hayim,* "Life-Giving Torah." The commentary is written by a different Reform rabbi or educator each week under the direction of the UAHC's Department of Adult Jewish Growth.

Some Orthodox Jewish organizations reach out to secular Jews on a one-to-one basis. They provide a volunteer study partner to any Jew who requests this service. The volunteer and the Jewish student participate in *hevruta,* the traditional Jewish way of learning in pairs, over the telephone or by e-mail. The topic may include Torah and Talmud texts, Jewish history, or whatever the *hevruta* partner wants to study with his guide.

In the state of Israel there are numerous Web sites where one can access a weekly Torah lesson or Talmud lecture from a great Torah scholar. Some sites offer recommended questions and guidance for family discussion at the Sabbath dinner table.

Jewish Studies in Colleges and Universities

Before the Second World War, it was nearly impossible to learn about Judaism and Jewish subjects in an American college. Hebrew and biblical studies were placed in departments of Near Eastern studies or departments of religion, which most often were prejudiced against Jews. Topics in post-Christian Judaism were not deemed worthy of serious academic attention. A student who wanted to learn about Judaism while attending college had few options. Yeshiva University in New York offered modern academic studies in an Orthodox environment, and Brandeis University in Waltham, Massachusetts, stood as the only Jewish-sponsored secular university in America. This situation began to change in the 1960s when some colleges and universities began to establish chairs of Jewish studies. Today hundreds of colleges and universities have a faculty of Jewish studies offering a variety of courses. Prestigious universities vie with one another to attract top faculty. Jewish students who take courses on Judaism in college are often interested in reestablishing a personal connection to Torah even as they learn about Judaism on an academic level and earn credits toward college graduation. Popular subjects for college courses include Hebrew and the Bible, Jewish history, Judaism

in the era of Jesus and early Christianity, Kabbalah, Holocaust studies, and Jewish philosophy and literature.

The Hebrew University in Jerusalem was established to be not
just a world-class university but also the intellectual center of the
world for the academic study of Judaism. One can study history, literature, philosophy, for example, at the Hebrew University, all from a
Jewish point of view. Just as one might go to Oxford or Harvard to
gain knowledge of English-speaking culture or Tokyo University to
study the culture and history of Japan, so the Hebrew University is a
center for Jewish studies. Bar Ilan University in Israel has evolved as
the intellectual center for Modern Orthodox Judaism, parallel to
Yeshiva University in America. Bar Ilan University has published a
computer disk with the original Hebrew and Aramaic texts of the
Talmud, major midrash texts, major commentaries, the *Zohar,* and
major halakic works. The ability to do word searches through the vast
library of Jewish Torah literature is of great use to rabbinic scholars
and academic scholars of Judaism.

Bible Study in Israel

Zionism is the national liberation movement of the Jewish
people. The Zionist movement led to the reestablishment of the
Jewish state of Israel in 1948. The Zionist movement originated
mostly among East European Jews in the 1860s. The early Zionists
often came from traditional homes and had a good talmudic education, but in adult life they sought to express their Jewish identity
through the modernist movement of Jewish nationalism.

Many of the early Zionists promoted Bible reading and rejected
Talmud study. They saw the Babylonian Talmud as the product of an
"exile mentality," composed by defeated Jews who needed to adjust
to life under the authority of Gentile governments. The Zionists
hoped to rediscover in the ancient world of the Bible a pattern for
independent and self-ruling Jewish living.

Zionism was a secular movement, but there were also religious
Zionists. Orthodoxy in Europe divided into two camps. The *Mizrahi*
"Oriental" party was pro-Zionist, the *Agudat Israel* "United Israelite"
party was anti-Zionist. The religious Zionists were not anti-Talmud,

but most of the Zionist pioneers were adamant secularists. The famed chief rabbi of Palestine in the early twentieth century, Rav Abraham Isaac Kook, saw these Zionist pioneers as devout Jews who were doing God's work despite their self-professed atheism.

The Zionists engaged in direct reading and study of the Bible without the traditional commentaries, which was unusual for Jews. They read the Bible not in a search for mitzvot to guide their lives but as the history textbook of their people. Many early Zionist thinkers even reversed the moral judgments of the biblical authors, preferring the kings over the prophets. They saw the prophets as the symbol of the antimodernist religious authorities of their own age, and the kings of Israel and Judah as fighters for national independence, like themselves.

It was not unusual in the Jewish villages of Poland and Russia in the early twentieth century for there to be two houses of learning, a *bet midrash* and a library. In the *bet midrash* Jewish men would gather to learn Talmud, law codes, and biblical commentaries in the traditional manner. In the library young Jewish men and women would gather to read the Bible, to study the Hebrew language, and to discuss the latest ideas of the day. The Zionists often acquired these modern ideas from Hebrew-language journals that were created for the modern revival of Jewish culture and spirit.

The halutz was the Zionist "pioneer" who settled in Turkish-ruled Palestine (British-ruled after 1917) to struggle for the reestablishment of the Jewish state. One popular image of the halutz is that he pronounced himself an atheist who had outgrown outmoded religious beliefs, and yet he could quote from the Bible by heart and studied the Bible every night. The halutz built up the land of Israel with a Bible in one hand and a shovel in the other. The Israeli Declaration of Independence refers to the Bible as the source for the values of the Jewish state.

Most secular Israelis today do not share their grandparents' passion for the Bible. Israelis must take a matriculation exam to graduate from high school, but the Bible exam counts only as a minor subject, worth two points, while major subjects are worth five points. Many students in the secular schools learn little more of the Bible than the most popular stories. Every year on Israeli

Independence Day there is a national Bible contest; in recent years only religious students participate.

In the last decade or so, some *hiloni* (secular) Israelis have begun to wonder whether the Bible education that students receive in the secular schools is sufficient to give Israeli children a proper Jewish background. As we have seen, there is a big difference between the text of the Bible and the teachings of Torah in the broadest sense of that word. The insights of rabbinic literature—Talmud, midrash, and commentaries—are necessary to Torah. Attempts to bring *dati* (traditional religious) teachers into *hiloni* schools to introduce the students to rabbinic literature have not been successful because of the culture gap between the two groups. Still, some secular Israeli parents worry that their children are not Jewish enough, that they are not sufficiently steeped in traditional Jewish values, that they do not have the spiritual strength that comes from religious teachings. Like many American parents who turn to religion as a source of values for their children, there are Israeli parents who want their children to know more than just the stories of the Bible. Progressive educators in Israel are working to develop methods of teaching Torah to modern, secular *hiloni* school students. The task of turning a modern state of Jews into a modern Jewish state has only just begun after half a century of Israeli independence.

Torah in a Jewish State

Israelis have certain advantages over Americans when it comes to learning Torah. Their spoken language is Hebrew. A motivated Israeli can open up a volume of the traditional *Mikraot Gedolot,* the expanded Bible, and read the commentaries with only a bit of difficulty over the medieval Hebrew, like a contemporary American reading Shakespeare. It is not too difficult for a Hebrew speaker to learn Aramaic, the language of much of the Talmud. In addition to knowing the language, Israelis are also immersed in a Jewish culture. Americans of no particular religion are Christian by default. They will certainly know when it is Christmas, for example. Israelis live in a Jewish state. The Sabbath day is built into the national culture of Israel. Most of the major newspapers have a columnist who writes on the *parashat hashavua'*, the weekly Torah portion, in the Friday paper. Leading Israeli rabbis and scholars have radio programs on Friday afternoon, the Sabbath eve, in which they teach Torah. The *haredim* run pirate radio stations that play only religious music and Torah lectures.

During the 1960s and 1970s, Torah study in Israel received a major boost from the popular teacher Nehama Leibovitz. Nehama taught everywhere—at army bases, in socialistic-atheistic communal farms (kibbutzim), in schools and community centers. She taught secular Israelis that Torah can be intellectually challenging and worthwhile, and she lured Orthodox Israelis to take a new look at the traditional midrashim and commentators who had been neglected in the East European Torah curriculum. Nehama's teaching method was to quote a challenging commentary and raise open-ended questions that the students had to answer for themselves. In response to popular demand, Nehama mailed out her weekly questions to subscribers all over the country (a Web site would have been useful, but of course there was no Internet then). Nehama Leibovitz received the Israel Prize, Israel's highest civilian honor, for her *gilyonot*—her weekly correspondence course. The World Zionist Organization has published *Studies in...(Genesis,* etc.) based on her work. Unfortunately, Nehama's achievements are unknown to the young generation of Israelis.

If an Israeli wishes to attend a Torah class, there are many options in local synagogues and community centers. Torah classes have proliferated in recent years in Israeli synagogues, as many *dati* Israelis have expanded their horizons from the traditional emphasis on Talmud to rediscover the intellectual challenge and the joy of *parashat hashavua'* study. The Van Leer Institute in Jerusalem has been offering a parasha discourse that attracts a large audience, filling the lecture hall to beyond capacity. Aviva Zornberg has an enthusiastic following for her lectures in English, which combine the insights of Freudian and Jungian psychology with the teachings of the traditional and Hasidic commentators. Zornberg also has an enthusiastic following in America, and she has published books of her studies on Genesis and Exodus.

Modernity has taken its toll, but there is reason to be optimistic about the future of Torah study. Between the Israeli educational system, the yeshiva, the Jewish supplemental school, private Jewish schools, university Judaic studies, and adult education programs in Israel and America, there is a revival of Torah learning among a small but dedicated and growing portion of today's Jews.

Glossary

Aaron: The brother of Moses. First high priest and ancestor of the hereditary Jewish priests who served in the Holy Temple in Jerusalem.

Abbahu: Rabbi who was head of the academy of Caesaria in the fourth century.

Abravanel, Isaac: Leader of Spanish Jewry at the time of their exile in 1492 and author of an important commentary to the Torah.

Aggadah: Lore, legend, story. All aspects of Torah interpretation that are not halakah.

Akiva: Second-century Rabbi. Led a school of Torah interpretation in which every extraneous word refers to a new teaching. Author of a set of notes to the oral Torah that became the basis for the Mishnah. Most-quoted Rabbi in the Talmud.

Amora (pl. Amoraim): Any of the third-to-fifth-century Rabbis quoted in the Gemara.

Aramaic: Language of the Babylonian Empire. Aramaic became the lingua franca of the ancient Near East until the Arab conquest of the seventh century. Language of much of the Talmud.

Ark: Cabinet on the front wall of the synagogue, in which the hand-written scrolls of the Torah are kept.

Ashkenaz: Jewish term for the Rhineland in the Middle Ages. A Jew whose ancestors derive from medieval Christendom is Ashkenazic. Distinct from Sepharad, Sephardic.

Babylon: Greatest city of lower Mesopotamia (modern-day Iraq) in antiquity. Also, the region of lower Mesopotamia. Home to the largest Jewish community outside the land of Israel in antiquity. In late antiquity and the early Middle Ages, home to great Jewish academies. Land in which the Babylonian Talmud was composed.

Bavli (Babylonian Talmud): Greatest compendium of the oral Torah of the Rabbis. Edited in sixth or seventh century. Contains the rabbinic teachings of the rabbis who thrived in the great Babylonian Torah academies. Ultimate reference source for halakah, the rules of living by the Torah.

Beit Hillel: The school of Jewish thought created by Hillel, Pharisee of the early first century. In the Mishnah, intellectual opponents to Beit Shammai. Known for their liberalism and their loose way of interpreting the Torah.

Beit Shammai: The school of Jewish thought created by Shammai, Pharisee of the early first century. In the Mishnah, intellectual opponents to Beit Hillel. Known for their stringency in interpreting the Torah.

Bereshit: The first word in the Torah. Also, the Hebrew name for the book of Genesis.

Bet Midrash: The study house in the Jewish community, where men gathered for informal Torah study.

Bialik, Haim Nahman: Famous Hebrew poet of the early twentieth century, born in Eastern Europe, lived in Tel Aviv. Author of a renowned compendium of aggadah.

Bomberg, Daniel: Italian Christian printer of the sixteenth century who established the standard editions of the two Talmuds and the *Mikraot Gedolot* (Rabbinic Bible).

Codes of Law: Compendia of halakic decisions, organized by subject and without reference to scriptural sources or talmudic debates. Most renowned codes are Maimonides' *Mishneh Torah,* Jacob ben Asher's *Arbah Turim,* and Joseph Caro's *Shulkan Arukh.*

Commentary: From the twelfth century to the present, verse-by-verse or section-by-section explanation of the Scriptures from the point of view of an individual commentator.

Conservative: One of the three major movements of American Judaism. More traditional than Reform, more modernist than Orthodox.

Dati: In Israel, a "traditional" or "religious" Jew. A Jew who strives to live by the traditional halakah. Neither *hiloni* (secular) nor *haredi* (ultra-Orthodox).

Derash: The midrashic interpretation of the Torah. Symbolism, literary interpretation, homily.

Deuteronomy: Fifth of the five books of the Torah. Moses' final speeches to the Israelites, delivered on the Plains of Moab before his death.

Documentary Hypothesis: The modern theory that the Torah was edited from four major source texts, called J, E, D, and P.

Ein Sof: In Kabbalah, the transcendent, ultimate, infinite being of God. The "Godhead." God's unitary being above the level of the *sefirot.*

Elohim: The Deity. One of the two primary names for God in the Torah, along with YHWH.

Enlightenment: The eighteenth-century philosophical movement of science and reason. The philosophers of the Enlightenment placed human reason ahead of divine revelation as the ultimate source of human knowledge.

Exodus: Second of the five books of the Torah. Tells the story of Moses' birth and childhood, his confrontation with Pharaoh, the exodus from Egypt, the revelation at Mount Sinai, a code of laws, the story of the golden calf, the command to construct a tabernacle for the sacrificial service, and the construction of the tabernacle.

Ezra the Scribe: Leader of the Jews, who returned to the country of Judah from exile in Babylon early in the Persian Empire. Ezra is responsible for bringing the Torah of Moses from Babylon to Judah. Ezra initiated the public reading of the Torah, thus "publishing" it in the social idiom of antiquity.

Fundamentalism: A modern religious movement that upholds the doctrine that God is the unerring author of the Holy Scriptures.

Gaon (pl. Gaonim): Literally, "exalted one." A head of one of the two academies in Babylon. From the fifth to the tenth centuries, the gaonim were the leaders of world Jewry.

Gemara: Ongoing rabbinic discussion on the topics raised by the Mishnah, as published in the Talmud.

Genesis: First of the five books of the Torah. The first eleven chapters tell the prehistorical stories of creation, Adam and Eve, Noah, and the tower of Babel. The next thirty-nine chapters tell the stories of the patriarchal era, Abraham and Sarah, Isaac and Rebecca, and Jacob and his wives and children, including the story of Joseph.

Haftarah: Literally, "conclusion." The reading from the books of the Prophets that concludes the scriptural reading, after the reading of the Torah portion, on Sabbaths and holidays.

Halakah: The body of Jewish law. Also, an individual legal ruling. Literally, "the way." Traditionally, halakah prescribes how one is to live as a Jew. Whereas Torah interpretation is broad and accepts contradiction, the halakah attempts to be specific and definitive. Halakah is rooted in the Talmud, the ultimate source on how to live a life of Torah.

Halakic Midrash: Unlike most published books of midrash, which are mainly aggadah, the third-to-fourth-century works *Mekilta, Sifra,* and *Sifre* are primarily halakic, deriving rabbinic laws from their basis in Torah.

Haredi: An ultra-Orthodox Jew in Israel. Not *dati* or *hiloni.*

Hasidism: Charismatic movement of Judaism, founded in the mid-1700s by the Baal Shem Tov. Last great Jewish religious movement to be based on Kabbalah. Hasidim follow a rebbe, a charismatic leader.

Heder: Jewish elementary school. The one-room schoolhouse in which boys learned the Bible. Heder graduates could continue their education with Talmud study in a yeshiva.

Hillel: Great sage of early-first-century Judaism. Probably leader of a school of Pharisaic thought. Later rabbis remembered him as nasi, president of the Sanhedrin, and revered him along with Shammai as "the Fathers of the World," who established the oral Torah.

Hiloni: In modern Israel, a secular Jew. Not *dati* or *haredi.*

Humash: Literally, "five." A book containing the Torah, a translation, and a commentary. The Humash is the Scripture book generally found in the pews of synagogues.

Ibn Ezra, Abraham: Spanish Jew who lived in various European countries, after Rashi the most renowned commentator of the Torah.

Ishmael: Intellectual opponent of Rabbi Akiva. Rabbi Ishmael upheld the "strict constructionist" view of Torah that "the Torah speaks in human language."

Israel: A poetic term for the collective Jewish people. Also, the geographical land of Israel; the modern political state of Israel; the northern kingdom of ancient Israelites, conquered and scattered by the Assyrians in 722 BCE, as distinct from the southern

Israelite kingdom of Judah, which lasted until conquered and exiled by the Babylonians in 586 BCE.

Jerusalem: Capital city of King David, holy city to the Jewish people, home of King Solomon's Temple and of the Second Temple, and capital of the modern state of Israel.

Judah, Judea: The southern kingdom of the biblical Israelites. Also, the name of the reconstituted Jewish country and self-ruling province during the Persian, Greek, and Roman empires. After two Jewish rebellions, the Romans renamed the country Palestine, after the already defunct Philistine nation of biblical antiquity. The land from which the Jews get their name as the people of Judah.

Judah the Prince (Judah the Patriarch, Yehudah HaNasi): Ethnarch, ruler of the Jews in the eastern Roman Empire ca. 200 CE. Edited the Mishnah and sent disciples to establish the Jewish academies in Babylon. In the Mishnah, known simply as "Rabbi."

Kabbalah: Jewish mystical system of thought, developed in the Middle Ages and based upon the ten divine emanations called *sefirot*. The *Zohar* is the central text of the Kabbalah.

Karaites: Literally, "Scripturalists." Jewish sect that arose in the tenth century. Karaites tried to live literally by the written Torah. They rejected the Talmud and the concept of oral Torah.

Leviticus: Third of the five books of the Torah. Contains priestly laws for sacrifices and for maintaining ritual purity. Also contains the "Holiness" law code, including the command "Love your neighbor as yourself," which has often been identified as the essential command of the Torah.

Lithuania: Baltic country, northeast of Poland and northwest of Russia, that was the center of Jewish yeshiva learning in the eighteenth, nineteenth, and early twentieth centuries. Many modern-day yeshivot in Israel and America are based on the Lithuanian model.

Luria, Isaac (the ARI): Great Kabbalist of the city of Safed in Galilee, flourished ca. 1580. Established new Kabbalistic doctrines, including the ideas of *tsimtsum* (divine contraction), *shevirat hakelim* (scattering of the divine sparks), and *tikun olam* (repairing the broken world through mitzvot).

M: Many Hebrew words begin with the letter mem, creating confusion for English speakers—as, for instance, between the terms *midrash* and *Mishnah.* The letter mem is a common prefix in the Hebrew language, denoting various forms of nouns and verbs.

Maccabees: The Hasmonean priestly family and their followers. Judah Maccabee led the Jewish rebellion against the Syrian Greek Empire, 168–165 BCE, rededicating the Jerusalem Temple to the worship of God, as celebrated in the festival of Hannukah. Any book written after the outbreak of the Maccabean rebellion was considered by the Rabbis to be too late for inclusion in the Holy Scriptures.

Maimonides: Medieval rabbi and philosopher. Author of *Guide for the Perplexed,* a work of Jewish Aristotelian philosophy, and the *Mishneh Torah,* a code of Jewish law, among other works. Born in Cordova, Spain, he lived in Egypt, where he was physician to the sultan Saladin.

Meturgeman: In the ancient synagogue, the translator or interpreter who explained the Torah in the Aramaic language while it was recited in Hebrew.

Midrash: The homiletic, lesson-oriented, literary rabbinic way of interpreting Torah verses. The verse-by-verse way of teaching Torah, as distinct from the topical approach of Mishnah. Many books of midrash were published between the third and tenth centuries.

Mikraot Gedolot: The "Rabbinic Bible." The books of the Bible published with the Hebrew text in the top center of the page, surrounded by Aramaic Targumim and multiple commentaries. Versions of the *Mikraot Gedolot* published in recent centuries include the commentaries of Rashi, Abraham Ibn Ezra, and Nahmanides along with various other commentators.

Minhag: Literally, "custom." Along with the mitzvot of the Torah and the halakic decisions of the rabbis, minhag is a factor in determining the proper and divinely ordained Jewish practice.

Mishnah: The book of legal discussions published by Rabbi Judah the Prince ca. 200 CE. The basis for the written record of the oral Torah. Core text of the Talmud, which includes Mishnah and Gemara. Also, an individual entry in the Mishnah.

Mitzvah (pl. Mitzvot): A commandment of God from the Torah. By tradition there are 613 mitzvot. Mitzvot, as the practical expression of God's will, are the basis for all Jewish behavior.

Moses: Greatest prophet of Judaism, leader of the Jewish people during the exodus from Egypt and the forty years of wandering in the Sinai Desert. Went up Mount Sinai to receive the Tablets of the Covenant. In Jewish tradition, Moses wrote the Torah as dictated to him by God. Called in Jewish tradition Moshe Rabbenu, "our Rabbi Moses."

Moses deLeon: Publisher and possible author of the *Zohar* ca. 1280 in Spain.

Nahmanides: Moses ben Nahman, Spanish Jew renowned as a Talmudist for his commentary to the Torah, and for his disputation with Pablo Christiani concerning the message of the midrash. Nahmanides was one of the earliest Kabbalists of renown.

Nebukadnezzer: King of the Chaldeans, the Neo-Babylonian Empire. Under his rulership the Babylonians conquered Judah and Jerusalem, burned down King Solomon's Temple, and exiled the Judeans to Babylon in 586 BCE.

Nehemiah: One of the leaders of the Judean return from Babylonian exile under the Persians. Rebuilt the walls of Jerusalem. The biblical book of Nehemiah describes Ezra the Scribe's first public reading of the Torah.

Numbers: The fourth book of the five books of the Torah. Describes the forty years of Israelite wandering in the Sinai Desert.

Old Testament: Old Christian term for the books of the Hebrew Bible and sometimes also the Apocrypha. In our times the terms *Hebrew Bible* or *Jewish Scriptures* or *Tanakh* are preferred, as the term *Old Testament* is deemed judgmental.

Onkelos: Name given to the most renowned Aramaic translation of the Bible, based on the reputed name of the translator.

Orthodox: In modern Judaism, a Jew who lives according to the halakah. The most traditional-leaning branch of Judaism, as distinct from Conservative and Reform.

Parashat Hashavua': The weekly Torah portion. In ancient Judea the Torah was read over the course of a little over three years. The weekly parasha was fairly short. Modern-day Jews follow the later Babylonian custom in which the Torah is read from beginning to end each year, beginning and ending at the fall holiday of Shemini Atzeret. The ceremony of renewing the annual cycle of reading the Torah is called Simhat Torah. Religious Jews traditionally study the *parashat hashavua'* every week, along with commentaries, translations, and related midrash.

Pardes: In medieval Judaism, an acronym (PaRDeS) for the four levels of reading Torah—*peshat, remez, derash,* and *sod.* These are the levels of literal meaning, allegory, symbolism, and mystery.

Peshat: The plain sense of the Torah text, its literal meaning.

Petichta: A form of midrash in which an opening quote, usually from the Writings section of the Tanakh, is interpreted in a way that leads to the opening quote of the weekly Torah portion, the *parashat hashavua'.*

Pharisees: A sect of Jewish religious leaders in late Second Temple times. Known for their received legal traditions of Torah interpretation and for their doctrine of the resurrection of the dead. The Rabbis who arose after the destruction of the Temple saw the Pharisees as their revered predecessors. Pharisaic tradition is the earliest layer of the recorded oral Torah.

Phinehas: The third high priest, according to the book of Numbers, after Aaron the brother of Moses and Eleazer the son of Aaron. Renowned as the zealot who killed Zimri and Cosbi when the Israelites were mingling inappropriately with the Midianites.

Pirke Avot: Tractate of the Mishnah containing wise sayings by ancient Rabbis. This tractate establishes the "chain of tradition" connecting the oral Torah of the Rabbis back to Moses.

Priesthood: In the caste system of ancient Israel, the nation was led and the religious rites were conducted by hereditary priests. The priests were reputed to be descended in a continuous line back to Zadok, high priest in the time of King David, and before him to Aaron, brother of Moses. The Hebrew for "priest" is *cohen,* pl. *cohenim.* The high priest was the internal ruler of the Jewish nation in the time of the Second Temple.

Prophets: Spokespersons for God in biblical times. Also, writers of sacred books, as inspired by the Spirit of Prophecy, which are included in the second section of the Tanakh. According to

Jewish tradition, prophecy ceased after the construction of the Second Temple.

Rabbi: A wise Sage who was learned in the written and oral Torah and its proper interpretation in the second to seventh centuries. One became a Rabbi by becoming a disciple and learning Torah from the mouth of one's teacher. The words of the Rabbis are collected in the Talmud. After the publication of the Talmud, the term *rabbi* was applied to a scholar who was educated in the Talmud and knew how to derive practical law, halakah, from the Talmudic text. Only in modern times does a rabbi become the pastor of a congregation. Rabbis in the Middle Ages served as leaders, judges, and religious functionaries in self-ruling Jewish communities.

Rabbinites: As distinct from Karaites: Jews in the Middle Ages who accepted the Talmud and the concept of oral Torah. The Rabbinites lived their Judaism according to the laws and traditions of the Rabbis.

Rashi: Rabbi Shlomo Yitzhaki, eleventh-century French rabbi. The greatest Jewish commentator on the Bible and the Talmud.

Reform: The most modernist stream of the three major movements of American Judaism, as distinct from Conservative or Orthodox. Reform Jews consider the halakah to be no longer obligatory in modern times. They adopt a historical view of the evolution of the Torah and the Talmud and of Jewish law and practice.

Remez: The allegorical interpretation of Scripture favored by the philosophers. One of the four levels of Torah interpretation called *pardes*.

Saadia Gaon: Lived 882–942. Head of the yeshiva of Pumbeditha in Babylon, hence the honorific title gaon. Saadia was among the first of the great Jewish philosophers in the Middle Ages and a major intellectual opponent of the nascent Karaite movement.

Saboraim: According to Jewish historical tradition, the anonymous editors of the Babylonian Talmud.

Sadducees: A sect of Jewish leaders in late Second Temple times. They interpreted the laws of the Torah according to their priestly traditions. Their group name probably derives from Zadok, the reputed ancestor of the hereditary priests. The

Sadducees opposed the oral tradition of the Pharisees and the doctrine of resurrection.

Sanhedrin: The ruling council of the Jewish people, with seventy-one members. After the destruction of the Second Temple, a Sanhedrin dominated by Rabbis met in Yavneh, near the seacoast of Judea. The rabbinic Sanhedrin reconvened in Galilee after the Bar Kochba rebellion of 132–135 CE. The Sanhedrin ceased to exist in the fourth century. According to traditional Jewish law, no decision made by a Sanhedrin (as recorded in the Mishnah) can ever be revoked or changed except by a greater Sanhedrin.

Scholasticism: Medieval Christian intellectual movement active in the great universities of Europe. Influenced the direction and thought patterns of Jewish commentaries on the Torah.

Scripture: A term for the Bible or Tanakh, literally, "that which is written." Comparable to the ancient Hebrew term *mikra.*

***Sefirah* (pl. *Sefirot*):** In the Jewish mystical system of Kabbalah, one of the ten divine emanations.

Sepharad: Jewish term for Medieval Spain. Sephardic Jews trace their ancestry to Spain, often to the Spanish expulsion of 1492, after which Sephardic Jews spread to North Africa, the Turkish Empire, Holland, and Italy, with small communities also in England and southern France. Sephardic Jews have their own nuances of Jewish law and practice. At its height in medieval Spain, the Sephardic community created great works of philosophy, codes of law, and Torah commentaries.

Septuagint: The ancient Greek translation of the Bible, the earliest published Bible translation. Used as the Holy Scriptures of the Greek-speaking Jewish community in Alexandria, Egypt.

Shammai: Intellectual opponent of Hillel. Known for his stringent interpretation of the law and for his forbidding personality but considered the intellectual equal of Hillel.

Shul: A Yiddish term for a synagogue, from the same Germanic root as the English word *school.* Suggestive of the function of the synagogue as a place for Torah learning.

Sinai: A mountain on the desert peninsula between Egypt and the land of Israel. According to the Torah, the Israelites gathered at the foot of this mountain to hear the Ten Commandments.

Moses went up on the mountain for forty days and nights, bringing down the Tablets of the Covenant, which, according to later Jewish tradition, contained the entire five books of the Torah.

Sod: The secret, mystical, esoteric level of meaning in the Torah, according to the four levels called *pardes*.

Spinoza: Lived 1637–1677. Dutch Jewish philosopher who was in many ways the first modern philosopher. First significant thinker to state openly that there was a human element in the composition of the Holy Scriptures.

Sugya: A unit of meaning in the Talmud, in the literary form of a discussion between rabbinic Sages over the topics in the Mishnah.

Talmud: The ultimate record of the oral Torah. The teachings and legal opinions of the Rabbis. The Jerusalem Talmud was completed in the fourth century, the Babylonian Talmud in the sixth or seventh century. Each Talmud consists of the Mishnah and rabbinic opinions, called Gemara, raised by the subject matter of the Mishnah. The Talmud is considered in traditional Judaism to be part and parcel of the divine revelation of Torah, the completion of a process of oral transmission that began with God speaking to Moses at Mount Sinai.

Tanakh: The Hebrew Bible. An acronym *(TaNaKh)* for the three major sections of the Bible: Torah, Nevi'im (Prophets), and Ketuvim (Writings).

Tanna (pl. Tannaim): A Rabbi who is quoted or named in the Mishnah. The Tannaim thrived from the first century BCE to the second century CE.

Temple: The sacred center of ancient Judaism, in Jerusalem, the sole location where sacrifices could be offered up to God. The First Temple was built by King Solomon ca. 950 BCE and destroyed by the Babylonians in 586 BCE. The Second Temple was constructed by the returned exiles ca. 516 BCE and periodically reconstructed on a grander scale, culminating in the grand Temple building project of King Herod. This Temple building was barely completed when it was razed by the Romans in 70 CE. Jews traditionally prayed for the construction of a third and final Temple in the future days of the Messiah, but many modern Jews no longer desire or pray for another Temple. The

Muslim Mosque of Omar, also called the Dome of the Rock, stands on the site where the ancient Temples once stood.

Tikun Olam: In Kabbalah, repairing the broken state of the world through the performance of mitzvot. Many modern-day Jews see *tikun olam* as a process of working for social justice, inspired by the biblical vision of a perfected society.

Torah: The first five books of the Bible: Genesis, Exodus, Leviticus, Numbers, Deuteronomy. More broadly, Torah is the totality of sacred texts that contain or explain the divine revelation—Bible, Talmud, and the *Zohar* and various works of midrash and commentary. More broadly still, Torah refers to any book, writing, or conversation that unfolds a teaching based on divine revelation.

Torah Lishmah: Literally, "Torah for its own sake." *Torah lishmah* is Torah learning for the sake of learning and its spiritual benefits to the soul, without regard to practical application.

Tosafot: The disciples and descendants of Rashi who composed their own commentary on the Talmud. In the standard edition of the Talmud, the Mishnah and Gemara are printed in a central column, with Rashi on the inside of the page and Tosafot on the outside of the page.

Tosefta: A work parallel to the Mishnah, containing many Tannaitic teachings that are not included in the Mishnah or appear in somewhat different form in the Mishnah. Not as authoritative as the Mishnah itself for determining Jewish law.

Tractate: One of the sixty-three subsections of the Mishnah and Talmud. A subdivision of the six major books, or "orders," of the Mishnah and Talmud.

Wellhausen, Julius: Lived 1844–1918. German historical scholar who publicized the Documentary Hypothesis for the composition and editing of the Torah.

Writings: The third section of the Hebrew Bible. This section of the Bible was formally closed early in the second century, bringing the Tanakh to its final form in the Jewish religion. The Rabbis saw the Writings as composed in the Holy Spirit, on a lesser level of revelation than the Torah and the Prophets.

Yavneh: Village near the seacoast west of Jerusalem, where the rabbinic Sanhedrin convened in 70 CE after the Roman destruction of Jerusalem. In Yavneh the rabbinic oral Torah began to be the normative Jewish way of understanding and living by the Holy Scriptures.

Yerushalmi (Jerusalem Talmud): The Talmud of the land of Israel, edited in the fourth century. Contains the Gemara of the rabbinic scholars of the land of Israel, particularly those who thrived in the great academies of Galilee between the end of the Bar Kochba revolt (165 CE) and the dissolution of the patriarchate and the Sanhedrin in the fourth century.

Yeshiva (pl. Yeshivot): An academy of higher Jewish learning in which Talmud study is at the center of the curriculum. Equivalent to a high school or a college in the traditional Jewish educational system.

Yetzer Tov, Yetzer Ra': The two motivating forces in the human psyche, according to the rabbinic psychology. The "good impulse" and the "evil impulse."

YHWH: The four-letter name of God—Yud, Heh, Vav, Heh. God's unpronounceable personal name. One of the two common terms for God in the Torah, along with Elohim. Also called "the ineffable Name." Because of its sacred power, Jews do not attempt to pronounce this name. English-speaking Christians may refer to this name as Yahweh or Jehovah.

Yihud: In Kabbalah, a religiously motivated act that causes a "unification" between God and the created world.

Zionism: The national liberation movement of the Jewish people. The Jewish nationalist movement, formally organized at the First World Zionist Congress in 1897, which led to the creation of the modern state of Israel in 1948.

Zohar: The central text of Kabbalah, the Jewish mystical system. Published ca. 1280 by Moses deLeon in Castile, Spain. Teaches the doctrine of the ten divine emanations, called *sefirot*.

Bibliography

Bialik, Hayim N., and Yehoshua H. Ravnitsky. *The Book of Legends, Sefer Ha-Aggadah: Legends from the Talmud and Midrash.* Translated by William Braude. New York: Schocken Books, 1992.

Bible: *HarperCollins Study Bible.* New York: HarperCollins, 1993. New RSV, contains Hebrew Scriptures, Apocrypha, and New Testament.

Bible: *The Soncino Books of the Bible.* Edited by Rev. Dr. A. Cohen. 14 vols. London: Soncino Press, 1947.

Bible: *Tanakh: The Holy Scriptures.* Philadelphia: Jewish Publication Society, 1988. The new JPS translation. The "official" Jewish translation of the Bible into English.

Cohen, Abraham, and Jacob Neusner. *Everyman's Talmud: The Major Teachings of the Rabbinic Sages.* New York: Schocken Books, 1995.

Cohen, Norman J. *The Way into Torah.* Woodstock, VT: Jewish Lights, 2000.

Cohen, Shaye J. D. *From the Maccabees to the Mishnah.* Philadelphia: Westminster Press, 1987.

Culi, Rabbi Yaakov. *The Torah Anthology: MeAm Lo'ez.* Translated by Rabbi Aryeh Kaplan. 9 vols. New York: Maznaim, 1977.

Ein Yaakov: Rabbi Jacob Ibn Habib. *En Jacob Agada of the Babylonian Talmud.* Revised and translated by Rabbi S. H. Glick. 5 vols. New York, 1916.

Finkelstein, Louis. *Akiba.* Cleveland: Meridian, 1936.

Gersonides, Levi ben Gerson. *The Wars of the Lord.* Translated by Seymour Feldman. 3 vols. Philadelphia: Jewish Publication Society, 1984–1999. Commentary to the Torah.

Ginzberg, Louis. *The Legends of the Jews*. 7 vols. Philadelphia: Jewish Publication Society, 1968.

Greenberg, Aharon Yaakov. *Torah Gems*. Translated by Rabbi Dr. Shmuel Himelstein, Y. Orenstein, Yavneh Publishing House Ltd., 3 vols., Tel Aviv, Israel: Hemed Books, 1992.

Herford, R. Travers. *The Ethics of the Talmud: Sayings of the Fathers*. New York: Schocken Books, 1962.

Holtz, Barry W., ed. *Back to the Sources*. New York: Summit Books, 1984.

Humash: *Etz Hayim: Torah and Commentary*. Edited by David L. Lieber et al. Philadelphia: Jewish Publication Society, 2001. Produced for the Rabbinical Assembly and the United Synagogue of Conservative Judaism.

Humash: *The Humash: The Stone Edition*. Edited by Rabbi Nosson Scherman et al. ArtScroll Series. New York: Mesorah Publications, 1993.

Humash: The *JPS Torah Commentary*. 5 vols. Philadelphia: Jewish Publication Society, 1989–1996.

Humash: *The Pentateuch and Haftorahs: Hebrew Text, English Translation, and Commentary*. Edited by Dr. J. H. Hertz. 2nd ed. London: Soncino Press, 1960.

Humash: *The Torah, A Modern Commentary*. Edited by W. Gunther Plaut, Bernard Bamberger, and William W. Hallo. New York: Union of American Hebrew Congregations [Reform movement of Judaism in America], 1981.

Kushner, Lawrence, and Kerry M. Olitzky. *Sparks beneath the Surface: A Spiritual Commentary on the Torah*. Northvale, NJ: Jason Aronson, 1995.

Leibowitz, Nehama. *Studies in the Book of Genesis*. Translated and adapted by Aryeh Newman. Jerusalem: World Zionist Organization, 1974. Also later *Studies in Shemot, Vayikra, Bamidbar, and Devarim*.

Levinas, Emmanuel. *Nine Talmudic Readings*. Translated by Annette Aronowicz. Bloomington: Indiana University Press, 1990.

Mekilta de-Rabbi Ishmael. Translated by Jacob Z. Lauterbach. 3 vols. Philadelphia: Jewish Publication Society, 1933. Repr., 1961.

Midrash: *The Classic Midrash.* Translated and edited by Reuven Hammer. Mahwah, NJ: Paulist Press, 1995.

Midrash Rabbah. Translated and edited by Rabbi Dr. H. Freedman and Maurice Simon. 10 vols. London: Soncino Press, 1983.

Mielziner, Moses. *Introduction to the Talmud.* New York: Bloch, 1968.

Mishnah. Translated by Herbert Danby. London: Oxford University Press, 1933.

Mishnah: *Mishnayot.* Translated and edited by Philip Blackman. 2nd ed. 7 vols. New York: Judaica Press, 1964. With pointed Hebrew text, English translation, commentary, and notes.

Montefiore, C. G., and H. Loewe, eds. and trans. *A Rabbinic Anthology.* New York: Schocken Books, 1974.

Neusner, Jacob. *From Politics to Piety: The Emergence of Pharisaic Judaism.* New York: Ktav, 1979.

———. *There We Sat Down: Talmudic Judaism in the Making.* New York: Abingdon Press, 1972.

Old Testament Pseudepigrapha. Edited by James Charlesworth. 2 vols. New York: Doubleday, 1983.

Pesikta de-Rab Kahana: R. Kahana's Compilation of Discourses for Sabbaths and Festival Days. Translated by William G. Braude and Israel J. Kapstein. Philadelphia: Jewish Publication Society, 1975.

Ramban (Nahmanides). *Commentary on the Torah.* Translated by Charles B. Chavel. 5 vols. New York: Shilo, 1971.

Rashi. *Pentateuch with Rashi's Commentary,* Translated and edited by Dr. A. M. Silbermann. 5 vols. Jerusalem: privately published, 1929.

Safat Emet: Rabbi Yehudah Aryeh Leib Alter of Gur (the Gerer Rebbe). *The Language of Truth.* Translated with modern commentary by Rabbi Arthur Green. Philadelphia: Jewish Publication Society, 1998.

Sanders, E. P. *Judaism: Practice and Belief, 63 BCE–66 CE*. Philadelphia: Trinity Press International, 1992.

Schiffman, Lawrence. *From Text to Tradition: A History of Second Temple Rabbinic Judaism*. Hoboken NJ: Ktav, 1991.

Steinsaltz, Adin. *The Essential Talmud*. New York: Basic Books, 1984.

Talmud: *The Babylonian Talmud*. Edited by I. Epstein. 35 vols. London: Soncino Press, 1935–1952.

Talmud: *The Talmud: Selected Writings*. Translated by Ben Zion Bokser. Mahwah, NJ: Paulist Press, 1989.

Talmud: *Talmud: The Steinsaltz Edition*. 21 vols. to date. New York: Random House, c. 1989–.

Talmud: *Talmud Bavli: Schottenstein Edition*. 72 vols. to date. New York: Mesorah Publications, 1997–.

Tanna debe El,iyyahu: The Lore of the School of Elijah. Translated by William G. Braude and Israel J. Kapstein. Philadelphia: Jewish Publication Society, 1981.

Zohar: The Book of Enlightenment. Translated by Daniel C. Matt. Mahwah, NJ: Paulist Press, 1983.

Zornberg, Aviva. *The Beginnings of Desire: Reflections on Genesis*. Philadelphia: Jewish Publication Society, 1995.

————. *The Particulars of Rapture: Reflections on Exodus*. New York: Doubleday, 2001.

General Index

Frequently recurring names, terms, and words are included in the Index only when they are central to the theme of the passage (e.g., Moses, Torah, God, Judaism, Christianity, etc.).

Index of Biblical and
Rabbinic Quotations